SUFFER THE LITTLE CHILDREN

Clutching their eight-week-old sister in their arms, three-year-old Frances and six-year-old Loretta Reilly were abandoned by their mother outside the gates of the Poor Sisters of Nazareth convent in Belfast. It was 1956. Little did the children know these walls were to imprison them for the next thirteen years. In the charge of the sisters, Frances lived with daily brutal and bloody beatings, treated as a slave to be abused, raped and molested. She fought a decade-long court case against the Poor Sisters of Nazareth order to bring to account the nuns who so viciously stole her childhood. She is a survivor.

SUFFER THE LITTLE CHILDREN

Suffer The Little Children

by

Frances Reilly

Magna Large Print Books
Long Preston, North Yorkshire,
BD23 4ND, England.

British Library Cataloguing in Publication Data.

Reilly, Frances
    Suffer the little children.

    A catalogue record of this book is
    available from the British Library

    ISBN   978-0-7505-3192-4

First published in Great Britain in 2008 by Orion Books,
an imprint of the Orion Publishing Group Ltd.

Published in Large Print 2010 by arrangement with
Orion Publishing Group

Magna Large Print is an imprint of Library Magna Books Ltd.

Printed and bound in Great Britain by
T.J. (International) Ltd., Cornwall, PL28 8RW

3/0129282579

To Josephine,
for your friendship.
This book is for us both.

ACKNOWLEDGEMENTS

To my sons Darren and Christopher – thank you for all your encouragement and support during the process of writing this book. It meant a lot to me.

To my granddaughter Ellisa – thank you sweetheart for all your support and for sending all the good luck cards and text messages. I love you x

To my grandson Kieran – thank you my wee darling for having loads of faith in me and for all your support and kisses. Love ye lots x

To Kevin Young, my ex-husband and very good friend – I can't really thank you enough for all your encouragement and support with the court case and this book. Your hard work and advice at every stage of the book have been invaluable.

To Ann-Marie Hanna and Deirdre O'Donoghue – thanks for your support with this book and for having the strength to come forward as witnesses. I hope this book does not bring back too many bad memories.

Special thanks also to my agent Robert

Smith for your complete belief in me and in the book, and for your determination and passion to see it published. Thanks also for your continued advice and friendship.

To Rebecca Cripps – thanks for all your help with the editing of my book.

Many thanks to Amanda Harris and all the other dedicated people at Orion who helped with the publication of this book. Special thanks to my counsellor Merril Mathews, for caring so much. Talking with you helped me to put everything into perspective; helping me move on with my life. Your warm, caring personality makes you a very special person.

To the two policemen at the Child Rape Unit in Belfast (you know who you are), thank you for your gentle understanding and for the respectful way you treated me.

Finally, thanks to my legal team in Belfast. With special thanks to my solicitor, Ceiran McAteer, for his mild manner, gentle understanding and for coming to my rescue. And to Emily, his secretary, for her hard work, continued support and for always being there at the end of the phone.

Frances Reilly
May 2008

CONTENTS

Author's Note

AUTHOR'S NOTE

This is the true story of my childhood in care. My sister Loretta was six and I was two when our nightmare began, so the first chapter of the book is based on what she later told me; the rest I remember only too well.

PROLOGUE

'Look at this, Frances,' my ex-husband, Kevin, said, pointing to an article in the newspaper.

My eyes swam as I read the first paragraph. A group of women in Scotland were taking an order of nuns to court for abusing them during their childhood.

'The Poor Sisters of Nazareth,' I gasped. I felt dizzy and found it hard to breathe.

The Scottish women were taking action against the same order of nuns who had abused me for most of my childhood; some of the women were around my age.

Vivid, unwanted memories flooded into my mind. It didn't feel like it had all happened more than thirty years ago; suddenly, it was all so fresh that it seemed like only months ago. Filled with panic, I found myself unable to read on, so Kevin read the article to me. As I listened to these women's stories they all rang true to me, and I could feel their pain. I wasn't surprised or shocked, as some readers might have been, and I really hoped that these women would be listened to and believed.

I'd left the convent a very damaged person,

carrying with me a lot of emotional problems. I was often severely depressed and on many occasions contemplated suicide. There didn't seem to be anyone outside the convent who understood what I was feeling. Because of the troubles in Northern Ireland, I didn't come into contact with anyone who wasn't a Catholic, and whenever I tried to speak out about the abuse I wasn't believed. People didn't want to hear a bad word said about the Catholic religious orders. No one back then would have gone up against them.

I learnt quite quickly to keep my mouth shut and to suppress my feelings. I tried to push all the bad memories out of my mind, to pretend that they hadn't happened and to behave as normally as I could. This made it easier for me to be accepted in the Catholic housing estates where I was living at the time. I didn't report the abuse to the police because I was sure they wouldn't believe me, or wouldn't want to know.

Once I accepted that people didn't want to believe or hear what I was saying, I had to find a way to survive. Over time I developed two survival mechanisms. First, I tried to hide the most painful memories by putting on a front. Every day I was living a lie. On the outside I was outgoing and cheerful, but inside I never stopped hurting. Also, I erected barriers to stop people, except my children, from getting close and hurting me.

While my children needed me, these mechanisms worked well enough, although I struggled, especially with relationships. Sometimes it all became too much: the mask would slip, and I would sink into a deep depression. As my children became less dependent, my defences started to fail, and by the time they'd left home, they had collapsed completely. The memories I'd tried to bury returned to haunt me, and the barriers I'd erected began to collapse. My life started to fall apart. Flashbacks to the convent became much more regular. I started to get frequent panic attacks and developed severe agoraphobia. I'd always suffered from periods of depression, but these became more pronounced.

My cleaning compulsion developed into obsessive compulsive disorder; I exhausted myself by repeatedly cleaning and tidying, doing work that didn't need doing; I imagined that germs were everywhere and that I had to protect myself and my family against them. I would panic if I ran out of bleach and nobody was about to go to the shops for me. If a family member moved one of my video cases so that it wasn't in line with the others, it would be enough to upset me for the whole day. I would cry if a baked-bean can wasn't neatly stacked on the correct shelf and facing outwards, and I shopped not for food but to restore order to my cupboards. I stopped eating properly and became anorexic. I was a mess. I became suicidal and knew that something had to change.

In January 1999, five months after reading the article about the Scottish women's court case, I found the courage to go to a solicitor to try to seek justice. But after bottling my feelings up for so many years, I found it hard to choke out even the most basic description of what had happened to me. Instead, I just sat in his office and sobbed uncontrollably. I couldn't find the words. Finally, after several visits, I managed to explain to him what had happened to me as a child. My fight for justice had begun.

CHAPTER 1

The Arrival

Omagh, Northern Ireland, December 1956

'Shhhh!' said Loretta. 'Can ye hear something?'

My brothers and I fell silent. There were voices coming from the living room downstairs. Mammy was talking to someone – a man – but Loretta didn't recognise his voice.

Christmas was coming, and Loretta had been telling us about the cards and presents she was going to make at school the next day. Now she was up and out of the camp bed we shared and tiptoeing across the room to the landing at the top of the stairs, where she could hear the voices more clearly.

'Sure, I'll pick yous up early in the morning, Agnes. Have the wee ones ready; it'll be a long journey for them to Belfast,' the man said.

Loretta skipped back into the room and slipped into bed beside me. 'We're going to Belfast tomorrow!' she said excitedly.

None of us had ever been out of our small town of Omagh, some seventy miles from Belfast, so this was big news.

'Sure, I knew yous must have been going somewhere, because me and Michael are going to our Aunt Mary for the day,' Sean whispered.

He and Michael shared another camp bed in the same room. Sinéad, the baby, was in a cot next to us.

'Why aren't yous coming with us?' Loretta asked, surprised.

'I don't know, sure,' Sean replied.

'Well, I hope our teacher lets me make Christmas presents another day,' she said.

Suddenly, baby Sinéad started to cry.

'Quick, settle down and go to sleep before Mammy catches us!'

It was still dark when our mammy woke us the next morning. Loretta helped me get washed and dressed in my favourite red trouser suit. She enjoyed helping me; it made her feel grownup. Meanwhile Mammy saw to Sinéad, who was eight weeks old and very demanding.

Loretta took me to the kitchen for breakfast, where Michael and Sean were just finishing up. They put their plates in the sink and grabbed their coats from the hallway.

'See ye later on, sure,' Michael shouted as he and Sean ran out through the back door.

'Loretta! Watch the baby a wee while,' Mammy said, laying Sinéad down on an armchair.

We listened to her footsteps as she dashed frantically from one room to another, dropping things along the way. By now I'd caught my sister's excitement about the trip, even though the boys weren't coming with us. At least we'd have a lot to tell them when we got back, Loretta said.

A car horn beeped outside. Mammy ran downstairs and waved through the kitchen window to a man standing next to a black car. Picking Sinéad up from the chair, she told Loretta to bring me outside.

The atmosphere was tense on the journey to Belfast. Our mammy was usually loud and chatty, but she hardly said a word. Loretta began to worry. Suddenly, everything about the trip felt wrong. Too young to pick up on the tension, I, on the other hand, was enjoying the ride. It was a long drive, and as we approached Belfast patches of fog began to obscure the way ahead, which slowed the driver down. Eventually, we came to a stop.

It was hard to tell if we'd reached the end of the journey. Peering through the car window, all we could make out was a high brick wall rising up through the fog. Loretta got out of the car, glad of the chance to stretch her legs. Mammy and the driver began an intense whispered conversation, which they abruptly broke off when Loretta reappeared.

Mammy got out of the car. 'Hold on there to your wee sister,' she said to Loretta, walking alongside the high wall.

Loretta grabbed me by the hand. Looking up, she noticed that there was broken glass sticking out of the top of the wall, with coils of barbed wire above that.

'Maybe it's a prison,' she said as we rushed to keep up with Mammy.

We caught up with her just as she stopped at a big wooden gate built into the wall. It didn't occur to Loretta that we'd be seeing what was on the other side, but something felt wrong all the same. She tightened her grip on my hand, and I yelped with pain. Mammy handed Sinéad to Loretta, who had to let go of me as she struggled to keep hold of the tiny infant in her arms.

'Now, Frances,' Mammy said, looking down at me, 'stay close to Loretta. I'll be back for ye soon. Loretta, give this to who-ever answers the bell.' She handed Loretta a letter and pulled on a cord hanging from the wall next to the gate. Then she dashed back to the revving car, which immediately drove off.

We watched in horror as the car dis-appeared into the distance, its exhaust fumes merging with the fog. I started to cry, shouting and screaming for my mammy to come back. Loretta stood next to me, shocked into silence, holding on tight to Sinéad. She couldn't cry. She desperately wanted to, but the tears wouldn't come. Instead, a cold, disabling numbness crept through her body. The rear lights of the car winked before they faded into the mist.

The gate in the wall opened with a heavy creak, and a woman said, 'I'm Sister Lucius. Can I help you?'

We dragged our eyes away from the road. There was a nun at the gate wearing flowing robes. All that was visible under her habit and veil was her round Irish face, her cheeks red from the cold. Loretta handed over Mammy's letter in silence.

'I'll be taking ye now to see the Reverend Mother. Follow me,' the nun said. She locked the gate and led us through a deserted walled garden, walking briskly ahead of us with her arms tucked up inside her habit. An enormous redbrick building loomed up before us, and soon we came to a pair of doors with latticed panes, which opened on to a high-ceilinged lobby area just inside the building. Sister Lucius told Loretta to hand Sinéad over to her. Loretta desperately wanted to keep hold of her baby sister, but, powerless to argue, she did as she was told.

Tall marble statues of St Anthony and the Virgin Mary loomed over us as we passed through the silent, flower-filled lobby, which soon narrowed into a dim, gloomy corridor that seemed to stretch for miles. The air inside the corridor was thick with the smell of overcooked food. The dark, green-brown walls looked as though they were sickening for something. There was no one around. It was deathly quiet. As we edged our way along the cold stone floor, past locked wooden doors with big metal handles, Loretta still wasn't convinced that we weren't inside a prison. What was behind those doors? Where was everyone?

Finally, Sister Lucius came to a halt outside a huge door. She knocked loudly. 'Enter!' came the summons from the other side, in a tone of voice that would have sent a shiver down anyone's spine, let alone a child's. Loretta trembled at the sound of it. In we went. Sister Lucius closed the door behind us.

We found ourselves in a room that resembled a small library. Leather-bound hardbacks lined the shelves, and small piles of books lay neatly stacked on wooden tables. Along one wall stood rows of filing cabinets and a long carved desk. Behind the desk, hunched over a book, sat a nun of obvious importance. After several minutes she raised her head and gave us a cold, appraising look. She had a penetrating stare, like a storybook witch's. Judging by her expression, it seemed clear that she thought we were contaminated in some way.

Sister Lucius placed Mammy's letter on the desk. The nun picked it up and began to read. I started crying again. Loretta stood next to me, feeling helpless and confused. The nun put the letter into a filing cabinet and turned towards us.

'Come closer. I'm the Mother Superior,' she said. 'Your mother has expressed her wish for you to stay here with us and devote your lives to God.' She paused, staring at us coldly. 'We have a lot of rules for you to follow, and I suggest you learn them quickly. Anyone breaking the rules will be dealt with severely. First, before mixing with the other girls, you will need a bath. You will go with Sister Lucius now. I will see you all again later. And from now on you will address me as Reverend Mother.'

We followed Sister Lucius out of the room. As we walked along the corridors, she explained that we were in a convent that was also an orphanage for unwanted children and children whose parents had died and had no one else to look after them. The orphanage was called 'Nazareth House Convent', and the order of nuns was the 'Poor Sisters of Nazareth'. Loretta didn't yet know how apt her first impression of the convent had been. It was indeed a prison: a prison for children – young girls and babies – whose only crime was being born. The broken glass along the top of the walls was to keep us in, not the world out.

We turned off the corridor into a massive bathroom. The floor was tiled, and the walls were painted in the same sickly colours as the corridor. There were two rows of sinks, a long row of toilets and a row of large white baths with feet.

'Hold your wee sister for me while I get some help,' Sister Lucius said, handing baby Sinéad back to Loretta.

She left the bathroom, returning a few minutes later with another nun. They turned on the bath taps, put on plastic aprons and rolled up their sleeves. Sister Lucius picked up a large can from the floor and poured some dark brown liquid into the bath. Loretta couldn't read the writing on the side saying, 'Jeyes Fluid', but it didn't smell too nice. Sister Lucius washed Sinéad in one of the large sinks, while the other nun bathed Loretta and me. The brown liquid felt like it was burning us, but it didn't seem to matter to the nun how much we cried or tried to get out of the bath – she just kept scrubbing and pushing us back down into the murky water. By the time she'd finished and we were allowed to get out, our skin was rubbed raw and we were crying uncontrollably.

The Reverend Mother came into the bathroom. In her hands were what looked like potato sacks, some long grey socks, white vests and navy-blue knickers.

'Put these on,' she said. Using just one finger and thumb, she picked up the clean clothes we'd been wearing and dropped them into a green plastic bag.

Seeing this, I broke free from the nun who was rubbing me down with a rough towel and ran towards the Reverend Mother crying, 'I want my suit! Give me back my suit!'

Sister Lucius pulled me back, while Loretta explained tearfully that the little red trouser suit had been a present from our father, who was away in India with the army. The Reverend Mother looked very angry.

'We don't have personal possessions in the Lord's house!' she snapped, her voice getting louder with each word. 'Everyone's the same here, and you will learn to live with it.'

As the nun spoke, a paralysing chill gripped Loretta's body, and for the first time in her life she felt really afraid. I must have felt it too because I immediately stopped crying and gave up the idea of getting my suit back. We obediently put on our convent-issue clothes, while Sister Lucius dressed Sinéad in a plain nursery gown, and then we followed the Reverend Mother to another room. With no idea of what might happen next, there was nothing to do but sit and wait. Time passed slowly. Every now and then I'd ask Loretta when our mammy was coming back to get us. Each time I asked she replied, 'Soon,' in an attempt to comfort me. 'We won't be here long,' she told me. 'Mammy will come and get us as soon as she can, so ye'll have to be very brave.'

Of course, she had no idea when our mother would come for us. She told me later that she was hoping that she'd turn up right now and say that this was all some sort of mistake, but deep down she knew it wasn't going to happen.

After what seemed like well over an hour, we heard voices on the other side of the door. Sitting quietly, we strained to hear what was being said. The nuns were talking in whispers, and it was difficult to make anything out, but Loretta heard one of them say, 'They won't like being separated.' The door opened and two nuns entered the room. One snatched Sinéad out of Loretta's arms and abruptly left the room; the other nun told us to follow her. We walked along more corridors and up several flights of stairs. No one spoke, not the nuns or the girls we passed on the way. The silence seemed unnatural, and a wave of intense homesickness swept over us.

We arrived at a dormitory, which reminded Loretta of an old picture she'd seen of an army hospital ward. The ceiling was high and the windows tall. Holy pictures of Jesus and various saints hung on the walls, which were painted the same sickly green as the corridors. Hard horsehair-filled mattresses lay on the floor, coated in DDT powder. Iron beds were lined up military style in two rows along the longest walls, with bedding folded neatly at the foot of each. Slotted between the beds were small wooden lockers. The nun led Loretta to a bed at the end of the dormitory.

'This is your bed. You will stay here until the bell goes,' she said. Scooping me up, she began to make her way out of the dormitory.

Panicking, I screamed and reached out to Loretta with desperate arms, kicking against the nun with every last drop of energy. 'Loretta! Mammy! Noooo!' I shrieked, hysterical now. Loretta ran to the dormitory door and watched, distraught, as I was carried away, struggling fiercely. She could still hear my piercing screams long after I'd disappeared from view down the corridor.

She walked back to her bed and tried to make sense of what was happening. She couldn't understand why our mammy had left us at the gate. Plucked out of her home, separated from her family and torn away from Sinéad and me, she'd lost everyone she loved and had no idea why. Unable to think clearly, she sat on the edge of the high bed and began to sob quietly to herself. What were we doing here? Where had the nuns taken Sinéad and me? And when was Mammy coming back to get us?

29

CHAPTER 2

Juniors

Four years passed. Our mother didn't return. The nuns' brainwashing had worked and we were now obedient convent girls. There was no point trying to fight it. The only way to survive was to try to stay out of trouble.

Loretta's reward for behaving well was to visit Sinéad and me in the infants' section once a week. We looked forward to her visits and made the most of every minute she was with us. She'd sing to us and tell us stories about Mammy coming back, about getting a big house and being happy together. So, for a few minutes a week, Sinéad and I got to imagine what it might be like to be normal.

Loretta also told us about our big sister, Marie, who lived on the opposite side of the road behind another high wall, at the Good Shepherd Convent. She explained that Marie had gone to the Good Shepherd before I was born, which was why I had no memory of her. She was several years older than Loretta. Every Christmas we got a card from her, and once in a while someone would sneak in a message from her, but I had no idea what she looked like or what sort of person she was.

My memories of life in the infants' section are sketchy at best, and only a few clear images remain. We slept in long rows of cots with metal bars in a cavernous room with a single dim light. One night I woke up in the middle of a nightmare, sweating and terrified. Rattling the bars of my cot, I called and screamed for someone to come, but no one did. Another time I remember being repeatedly pushed back down onto a freezing-cold chamber pot and told to stay there until I went to the toilet, even though I didn't want to. Other memories come back in flashes: the strange taste of hot milk served in plastic cups, the clink of a metal mug against my teeth, endless meals of stale bread soaked in milk.

I was six now, which meant that I was moving to the juniors. Loretta was in the seniors, but I'd be able to see a lot more of her, as we'd be in the same part of the building. She tried to prepare me for the move by telling me what would be expected from me as a junior. I listened carefully, not wanting to get anything wrong. For me, the move was both exciting and frightening. One of my best friends, Mary, had already gone to the juniors, and I was looking forward to seeing her again. With any luck,

31

we'd be in the same dormitory. But I was worried about leaving Sinéad. I knew I'd miss her and my little friend Josephine. Josephine and I had a really special friendship. She was devoted to me and followed me around everywhere, like a little duckling.

Sister Thomas came to get me. I was terrified of her straight away.

'You will be in my dormitory,' she said, 'and I will be watching you every minute of the day.'

Her harsh tone sent chills through me. Her eyes were filled with malice. We walked through the convent in silence.

Sister Thomas was in charge of St Joseph's Dormitory, which was the worst dormitory you could get because Sister Thomas was the worst nun in the convent, according to Loretta. She was young in comparison with the other nuns and not unattractive, but the coldness and cruelty of her personality gave a severe edge to her features. She had very heavy, prominent eyebrows and never smiled unless there was a priest present, or someone from outside the convent. There was spite in her hazel eyes and her default expression was one of disgust or loathing.

We stopped off at a clothes storeroom on the way to the dormitory. All the girls wore donated clothes, and in the juniors and seniors we had to wear a checked gingham apron, too. The storeroom nun gave me a blue-and-white apron and showed me how to wear it over my clothes, buttoned at the back. Then she handed over a pair of heavy black lace-up shoes and a pair of socks that were supposed to last an entire year. I was responsible for washing them myself, she told me. She also gave me a dull navy ribbon with which to tie my hair back.

In the juniors and seniors each girl had a number, which was called out when we were allocated work. We were sometimes called by surname, but our Christian names were very rarely used.

'You're number four, Reilly,' she said. 'You will sew a number four onto all your clothes.'

Soon we moved on to the dormitory, which was quiet and empty. Sister Thomas explained curtly that the others were at chapel for prayers. She showed me to my bed.

'I'll send someone for you when it's dinnertime. Wait by your bed until then.'

To my relief, she left the dormitory. I looked around me. The room seemed huge, particularly so because I was very small for my age. The beds and lockers were much bigger than I was used to in the infants. Climbing up onto my bed, I sat with my legs dangling over the side, gazing at the empty beds and wondering who'd be in them and what they'd be like. Then I tried to imagine how the dormitory would feel at night. Scary, I thought.

I'd been alone for around twenty minutes when I heard footsteps, the sound of someone skipping or running. I leapt off my bed as Loretta and another girl came in. I was thrilled to see my sister and even happier when she told me that I'd be sleeping in the bed next to hers. At the same time I had another pang for Sinéad, the sister I knew best.

Loretta and her friend had come to take me down to the refectory for dinner. We had to rush to be on time, so any further chatter would have to wait till later, Loretta said. But on our way, even though talking in the corridors was strictly forbidden, she introduced me to everyone we met.

'This is my little sister,' she said, obviously keen to show me off.

Joining a line of girls walking in single file, we entered a large room filled with row upon row of wooden tables and chairs. Each girl walked to a chair and stood behind it. Loretta found me a chair and placed it next to hers. A few minutes later the Reverend Mother came in, and we put our hands together for prayer. After grace, each table of girls lined up at a wooden hatch set into the far wall.

'Come on, we have to get in line for dinner,' Loretta said.

She shoved me in between two younger girls. They didn't seem to mind and were clearly in no hurry to receive the food they were about to be given. I understood why when my turn came to pass my plate over to the nun behind the hatch. An absolutely disgusting smell hit me. Loretta whispered that it was a combination of boiled cabbage and dead animals, and it had made her feel quite sick the first few times she'd smelt it. The nun took my plate and ladled on some potatoes and cabbage from two huge saucepans. Water dripped from the ladle as she slopped its contents onto the plate. This was followed by a spoonful of something that I didn't recognise. I took the plate and followed Loretta to the table, where the girls were now talking in whispers. The Reverend Mother had gone, but two nuns were walking around, patrolling the tables.

'I can't eat this,' I said, staring down at my plate of slop and gristle. The food in the infants had been bad, but not this bad; anyway, I was so nervous and scared that I was sure I wouldn't be able to hold anything down.

'Ye have to eat it all, or ye'll get it back every meal until ye do. Hang on, and I'll eat it for ye this time. But ye'll have to get used to it because it doesn't get any better than this.'

Loretta snatched my plate and ate the food quickly, before the nuns could see. I appreciated what my sister had done for me but knew I'd have to eat it myself next time. Still, I wasn't going to worry about that for the moment. I heard a bell and turned to see where the sound was coming from. One

35

of the nuns was walking up and down ringing a hand bell and chanting.

'Pudding! Tapioca, I think,' Loretta said, and she pushed me into another line.

A nun dropped a dollop of tapioca into my bowl. Loretta told me that it always reminded her of the frog's spawn Daddy had shown her once. She'd been served it on her first day at the convent and hadn't been able to imagine putting it in her mouth and swallowing it. Another girl had eaten it for her when the nuns weren't looking.

By the time dinner was over, everybody knew who I was. Loretta's friends kept smiling at me, and I felt a bit self-conscious. I'd seen Mary in the refectory but hadn't got a chance to talk to her yet. Another bell rang, and we stood up, said grace and lined up again in silence.

'Where are we going now?' I whispered.

'Benediction. Ye'll have to be quiet or we'll get into trouble.'

We walked in single file from the refectory to the chapel, where a nun sternly watched as each girl genuflected in front of the altar. One girl's knees didn't meet the floor, and as she stood up, the nun grabbed her by the ear and forced her down until her knees hit the floor. I was careful not to make the same mistake.

After Benediction we went into the convent grounds. Loretta explained that we had to stay outside for an hour's recreation. It was freezing, and the cold winter air stung my skin. The girls split up into small groups. Some of them had races to keep themselves warm. Others skipped or played games they'd made up. Loretta and I walked around in circles, while she went over what was expected of me in the juniors. There were so many rules to remember. It seemed that the day was made up mostly of praying and cleaning or lining up to a bell. There were two hours a day for recreation: one hour had to be spent outside, but during winter the other hour could be spent in the hall.

'When the nuns call your number,' she told me, 'ye have to answer, "Yes, Sister." We can call each other by name, but we're just a number to them.'

We sat down on the outside steps, hugging our knees to keep ourselves warm, and she told me more about her first day at the convent. It had all seemed so strange compared to home – the silence, the bells, the lines of girls and the disgusting food. For the first time I began to get a sense of how devastated she'd been, how desperately she worried about Sinéad and me. We talked and shivered until the bell went for us to line up again.

I followed Loretta around all day as she helped me get used to the routine. Every time the bell went, she'd guide me into the right line. We spent the afternoon working in the laundry, where Sister Mary was on duty. Sister Mary didn't seem as rigid as the other nuns I'd met that day and let Loretta and me work together, but she still expected the work to be done properly. We worked on one of the long rolling machines. Loretta fed the sheets in one end, and I took them out of the other, folding them exactly as Sister Mary had shown me. It was hard going and tired me out, but at least the steam from the rollers kept us warm. Time passed quickly, and soon the bell went again. This time it was back to the chapel for Rosary which seemed to go on forever. I wasn't used to long, formal services. We'd done a lot of praying in the infants but never in the chapel with the older girls.

Then it was back to the refectory. Tea was white boiled fish and a slice of stale bread with a small amount of butter. I managed to eat it myself this time. It didn't have much taste, but I was hungry after all the work I'd done.

I thought it was really good having my big sister to show me around and look out for me, but I was really missing Sinéad, who wouldn't be coming to the juniors for another two years. Loretta must have sensed how I was feeling.

'Don't worry,' she said, 'you'll see Sinéad once a week, with me.'

But I didn't like the thought of seeing my little sister for just a few minutes a week. I knew that I would have to accept it, but I worried that Sinéad had no family around her. I decided that the only way I could help her now was to pray for her, so I closed my eyes and asked God to take special care of her.

I finally managed to catch up with Mary at recreation time. We were so pleased to see each other that we talked constantly until the bell went for Irish dancing in the hall. With its sickly green walls and bare floorboards, the hall was as dismal as the rest of the convent, but I loved Irish dancing, and the nuns said I'd be good at it if I put my mind to it. Everyone had to pick a partner, and I was glad when Mary chose me. One of the nuns put on a crackly record, and Mary and I danced well together.

I noticed some of the other girls being dragged around the floor by nuns. 'Lift your feet up, girl!' one of the nuns shouted. She slapped the girl across the face and head.

I looked on, horrified, as the girl's face crumpled with pain and embarrassment. But everyone else carried on dancing as if nothing unusual had happened, which it hadn't. Suddenly, the girl screamed, and I turned around to see the nun pulling her out of the room by the hair. The hall's heavy wooden doors banged shut. There were a few more muffled screams and then everything went quiet, except for the sound of the Irish dance music.

I felt really sorry for the girl but was relieved that the nun hadn't picked on me. My time in the infants hadn't been pleasant. I'd been pushed, pulled, rapped on the knuckles and shouted at more times than I could remember, but it wasn't as bad as this. I was suddenly aware of just how harsh the juniors was going to be, and I decided to try to be good at everything so that the nuns would have no reason to hit me.

After dancing we went back to the dormitory to get ready for bed. First we washed, then we lined up to show Sister Thomas our clean necks, hands and faces.

'Thank you, Sister. Number four, Sister,' I said when it came to my turn. I was glad it was bedtime. It had been a long day compared to our days in the infants. I lay in bed and thought again about Sinéad, about how much I loved and missed her. I prayed long and hard for her until I was sure that God would look after her.

'Lights out and no talking!' Sister Thomas's voice bellowed across the dormitory. 'I'm watching you, Reilly,' she added.

I froze with fear. Why me? I hadn't done anything wrong, had I? Like everyone else, I had to lie on my back with my hands across my chest to keep the Devil out, and I tried to lie as still as possible so that she wouldn't pick on me. The dormitory lights went out, the heavy door banged shut, and the sound of her footsteps faded as she moved away along the corridor.

'Are you all right, Frances?' Loretta whispered from the next bed, but I was too scared to answer in case Sister Thomas came back. She got out of bed and came over. 'Are you all right?' she whispered again, putting a comforting hand on my shoulder.

'I'm OK,' I whispered, not wanting to worry her.

All night long I lay awake with fear, the way I imagine a prison inmate might feel after being moved to a tougher jail with a much stricter regime. In my despair, tears rolled down my cheeks onto my pillow, and it was dawn before I finally drifted off to sleep, only to be woken almost immediately, or so it seemed, by the sound of the bell for morning prayers.

I dragged myself out of my large bed and knelt on the floor to pray. Sister Thomas's voice rang harsh and cold through the dormitory as she started morning prayers. I could hardly keep myself awake and chanted the prayers robot fashion, aware of her eyes boring into me. By the time prayers were over, there was only one thought in my mind. How was I going to make it through the day without getting on the wrong side of Sister Thomas and the other nuns?

CHAPTER 3

Josephine

'Sister Thomas is coming!' hissed Bernadette.

'What mood is she in?' I asked, knowing that if she was in a bad mood, then I was going to get it. In the months that followed my move to the juniors, she'd made it clear, on a daily basis, that she hated me. Still, nothing could have prepared me for what happened next.

'We have a pagan in the convent!' she screamed as she swept into the dormitory waving a stick. 'Where is she?'

I cowered next to my bed, hoping desperately that she didn't mean me.

'Reilly!' she shrieked, pointing the stick in my direction. 'You are a heathen, a child of the Devil! Nobody is to come anywhere near you!'

My knees gave way. I began to tremble from head to toe. What did 'heathen' mean? What had I done wrong?

'Please, Sister—' I started to say.

'Silence!' she yelled, running towards me, her face crimson with fury. 'The Devil's in you, Reilly! We'll beat him out of you now!'

She leapt at me, bringing the stick down on my head. The next thing I knew, she was chasing me down a corridor shouting, 'Demon child! Devil spawn!'

She drove me into a room in the nuns' section of the convent, where she began to beat me even more viciously. Not long afterwards Sister Francis and Sister Kevin came into the room and began to join in, shouting, screaming and raining blows on me. I lay hunched on the floor, while Sister Thomas slapped me across the face and the others whacked me all over my body. Soon after that, I passed out.

I woke up on the floor, alone. My head throbbed with pain, I was covered in red marks and every bone in my body ached. There was a noise outside the door. A young nun came in holding a tray. Giving me a nervous look, she set the tray down on a small wooden table. I raised my head and tried to get up.

'Don't come near me!' she said fearfully. 'You pagan! I'll be back for your tray shortly.' She scurried out of the room.

My head swam. What did she mean? What did any of it mean?

Nothing was explained to me. It was only later that I pieced it all together. In order to take Holy Communion, you had to be baptised into the Catholic Church. And if you hadn't been baptised, you were going straight to Hell. So, with my First Communion coming up, the nuns had applied to my mother's church in Omagh for my baptism lines, a certificate to confirm that I'd been christened. Unfortunately for me, although Loretta and Sinéad's baptism lines were sent on to the convent, mine weren't. Either the priest had mislaid them or my mother hadn't had me baptised – and the nuns had obviously decided to believe the worst.

I was locked in that room for three days. It was a large, empty waiting room containing a long, polished wooden table with old-fashioned dining-room chairs arranged along the walls. At night I pulled two chairs together and slept curled up across them, shivering without a blanket or cover. The only people I saw were the nuns who delivered my food and Sisters Thomas, Francis and Kevin, who returned several times to 'beat the Devil out' of me. By the time I was dragged up to the chapel for my baptism, I'd begun to believe that I was evil. There was no reason not, to, after all. The nuns were married to God, so they had to be right. I'd been born bad and I was full of sin, so it was my fault that this was happening.

In the chapel I was told to stand on a chair and lean over the font. I was tiny for my age and could hardly reach up that far. Mrs

Montgomery, a part-time teacher at the convent, stood up as my godmother. The priest chanted and crossed himself, and the nuns prayed along with him.

Suddenly, water was pouring down the side of my face and onto my clothes. The priest pushed me forward, knocking my head against the font, and continued pouring water over me. The top of my dress was soaking wet. Now they were trying to drown the Devil out of me.

It was less of a baptism than an exorcism, and I simply didn't have a clue what was going on. Two weeks later I received my First Communion dressed like a little bride, wearing a plain white convent-issue dress, a white veil, white socks and plimsolls covered in shoe whitener.

Sister Thomas had her excuse now, not that she needed one, because she'd had it in for me since the day we'd met. Everyone else in the dorm knew it. They heard her telling me I had the Devil in me and that I was going straight to Hell. They watched her order me out of bed to pray for no reason, and they saw her slap me and punch me and beat me with a stick. What they didn't see – the beatings she inflicted when no one else was around – they could imagine when they saw the cuts and bruises on my arms and legs. She didn't care who saw the wounds she inflicted, unless there was an inspection coming up, when she was more careful about where she hit me. Some days she'd walk past my bed, ringing the morning bell, and give me a look that said, 'I am going to make your life miserable today, Reilly.'

But while I was the main object of her fury, she also had pets, a group of girls whom she treated less severely than the rest of us, even going so far as to give them pieces of fruit and other treats. I think they could sense that it would please her if they were mean to me, so they picked on me all the time. Some of the other girls followed their lead, and I found myself with only a few friends. Luckily, I wasn't someone who liked to hang around in groups, but obviously I found it hard being picked on.

Mary had left the convent – she'd only been in for a short-term stay and had now gone back to her family. So I was really happy when my little friend Josephine moved up to juniors. I taught her all the rules, just as Loretta had done for me. She became my closest friend, and we spent most of recreation time together, talking about what we'd do when we got out of the convent. Such dreams were important to enduring our present desperate situation, and we really let our imaginations run riot.

Of course, we had our little arguments from time to time. Sometimes it irritated me the way she followed me around like a duck, trying to get my attention. I'd snap at her when she touched me under the chin to make me look up, and I teased her for ending every sentence with 'you know'. But most of the time we were inseparable. I lived for recreation time and the chance to chat to Josephine. Talking was restricted for so much of the time in the convent that it was a relief to be able to babble away to my friend.

The winter of 1962 was the coldest in Ireland for many years. One bitter Christmas morning, on our way to chapel, Sister Austin took Josephine out from the line of girls.

'There's a family who would like to adopt you,' she said, 'but first you'll spend the weekend with them to see if they like you. Now, come with me and get ready.'

My heart sank when I heard Josephine's news. Of course, I was pleased for my friend that she was getting out of this awful place, but already I felt the pain of losing her.

Without her, the weekend seemed to go very slowly. Envious of her for being on the outside, I kept wondering what she was doing and tried to imagine what life was like beyond the walls. But it was almost impossible, so I decided to wait until she returned on Sunday night. Hopefully, there would be time for quite a few chats before she left for good – that was, if the people she was visiting liked her. Selfishly, I hoped that they didn't, because then she wouldn't leave the convent, but I hated myself for having such uncharitable thoughts and worried that I'd burn in the fires of Hell for them.

Sunday finally came, but by six o'clock Josephine still hadn't come back. Nobody seemed to know what was keeping her. I grew more and more impatient as the evening wore on. Then, Sister Austin was called to the phone, and when she got back to the dormitory she looked as though she'd seen a ghost.

'What's the matter, Sister?' one of the girls asked.

But for once the nun appeared to be blind and deaf to us. Zombie-like, she walked to the end of the dormitory and into the room where she slept, known among the nuns as a 'cell'. Leaving the door half open, she knelt by her bed and started to pray.

After that, things got even stranger. The nuns on duty kept being called away, returning pale and tight-lipped, if they returned at all, and we didn't recognise the nuns on patrol in the refectory. We weren't told off for talking in line, and no one checked to see if we'd washed properly before we went to bed. Something big had obviously happened, but none of us could find out what it was. By lights out we were sure it must be something bad.

I lay in bed wondering what it all meant. Mostly I worried about how it might affect my sisters and me. Usually, someone would have found out something by now, even just by listening outside a door to the nuns talking among themselves. But the nuns were saying nothing – to us or to each other.

At least Josephine's safe, I thought. The people who'd taken her out for the weekend must have liked her so much that they'd decided to keep her while the adoption went through. It wasn't the way things were usually done, but I couldn't think of another explanation. Although I hoped that she was having a good time and liked her new family, I was sad to think that I wouldn't get a chance to say goodbye properly. How lucky she is to be free, I thought, as I drifted off to sleep.

The nuns remained preoccupied for several days, and still none of us managed to find out why. Josephine hadn't returned, and I'd started spending my recreation time with a girl called Chrissie. Neither of us fitted in with the gangs that hung out during recreation, and as we got to know each other we discovered we had quite a bit in common. We were both small, we enjoyed Irish dancing, and we preferred the company of one or two best friends to hanging around in a group. I missed Josephine a lot, though, and talked about her all the time. Chrissie didn't mind; she just hoped that one day we could become as close as Josephine and I had been.

Every recreation time was spent the same way, quietly talking and walking through the recreation ground. Then one day our routine was broken. As Chrissie and I walked along, arm in arm, our attention was drawn to two policemen who were striding through the grounds towards the main convent buildings. Everyone looked on in amazement until they vanished from sight around the side of the buildings. Silence descended over the recreation ground. None of us had ever seen policemen in the convent before.

We appreciated anything that broke the monotony of convent routine, and the arrival of the policemen had certainly done that. It gave us all something new and exciting to think about. Everyone was busily dreaming up theories about what might have happened, or might be about to happen, and we were even more intrigued when the bell for the end of recreation time failed to sound.

Inevitably, curiosity got the better of some of the girls, who began to move in small groups towards the main convent building and peer in through the windows. By now the only nun left in the grounds was old Sister Clare, whose eyesight was so bad that she couldn't make out what any of us were up to. Still, Chrissie and I stayed where we were. Sister Clare might be as blind as a bat, but the other nuns could appear at any time.

The next day, during morning prayers, Sister Thomas asked everyone to pray for Josephine, who would not be with us again. I was pleased for Josephine. Obviously, everything must be going well with her new family. At the same time it was really painful to think that I wouldn't ever see her again. Tears ran down my cheeks as I joined in the rest of prayers. I prayed for her really hard that morning, asking God to please make Josephine happy with her new family.

On the way to morning Mass whispered messages started to travel down the line of girls.

Someone tapped me on the shoulder and hissed, 'Josephine's dead. She drowned in the River Lagan.'

'That's not true. She's been adopted,' I said, not moving my head for fear of being caught talking.

I wondered who could have started such a terrible rumour. For a few moments I considered whether it could be true, but the slicing pain I felt at the thought that she was dead was just too much to bear. No, it was ridiculous. Josephine was safe with her new family. She simply had to be OK. I felt angry towards whoever had started the rumour. It wasn't the first time a story like this had gone round the convent, but none of the others had been true, so why should anyone believe this one? As we moved inside the chapel, the whispering stopped.

The priest moved to the front of the altar and began to speak. 'We are offering the Mass up this morning for Josephine Mc-Cann. Josephine is no longer with us. We hope she is in Heaven with God. Your prayers this morning will help her. I'm sure God has his reasons for taking Josephine so young.'

The priest went on talking. I could see his lips moving and even hear some of his words, but none of them made any sense. I couldn't take in the fact that my best friend, my only real true friend, was dead. It wasn't till Mass had nearly finished that it began to sink in. Josephine's dead, not happy in her new life, but dead. I felt the life draining from my own body – and the next thing I knew I was outside the chapel and a nun was telling me to put my head between my legs because I'd fainted. I didn't recognise the nun. She must be new, I thought, or one of the nuns that didn't have much to do with the girls. I started to come around a bit. Then, as it hit me for a second time that Josephine was dead, I began to feel sick and tremble. The nun asked if I was all right, and I broke into loud sobs.

'Josephine's dead! She's my best friend, and I'm never going to see her again!'

I started to panic for her. I'd never really thought properly about what it meant to be dead. An image of Hell, of unbearable heat and flames, filled my head. But Josephine was really nice; surely she wouldn't be in a place like that. So, instead, I tried to picture her in Heaven, in a white dress, like an angel. It was much nicer to think of her up in Heaven, smiling down on me and everybody else.

The next few days were horrific. I felt numb, as if a part of me had died with Josephine. Only now, with Josephine gone, did I fully realise just how close we'd become. The things that had irritated me about her were now the things I missed most about her. I would have given anything to have her back. I'd always been quiet, but now I withdrew into myself completely, responsive only to the mention of her name.

Stories of how she'd died started to filter into the convent. Apparently, she'd gone missing early one evening, and the family she was staying with said that they'd thought she'd gone to get some sweets. Once they realised she was missing, the police, some with sniffer dogs, along with loads of volunteers, went out searching for her. Eventually, several days later, she was found on some wasteland by a police dog, her tiny hand sticking up through the ice of a small frozen pond.

I couldn't understand it. None of it made sense. Josephine had been in the convent most of her life; she was only six, very timid and used to doing exactly as she was told. I was sure that there was no way that she'd have gone out on her own, especially after dark. Where would she have got the money to buy sweets? And why had it taken the family so long to notice she was missing? If they cared for her, they should have realised straight away that she was gone.

One of the rumours going around the convent was that the family had gone out for the evening and left Josephine on her own. But even if that were true, I still couldn't imagine her running away. She would just have been too frightened. I talked to Loretta about it, and she agreed with me – it just didn't add up.

Later Loretta told me that one of the day-girls had read in the paper that Josephine had been found on some waste ground near the M1, about two and a half miles from where she'd been staying. As Loretta pointed out, it must have taken her hours to stray that far. How was it that no one had noticed her? But if she hadn't run away, how had she ended up in the pond?

By the time of the funeral I had strong suspicions about the people that had been looking after her and felt sure they must have done something to her. She was too timid to go out on her own, so either she must have been so terrified that she'd felt she had no choice but to flee or they'd done something to her and then dumped her body. And what of the nuns? How could they have let this happen? Surely they should have made certain that the people who took Josephine in could be trusted to look after her properly? But now the nuns were saying that perhaps Josephine had been trying to make her way back to the convent. As if. No one in their right mind would have wanted to return to that place.

My last memory of Josephine is of the Mass held for her in the convent chapel. It was a terrifying experience. Whenever someone from the convent died, the nuns held a service for them. The body, usually that of an elderly nun, would lie in an open coffin in front of the altar. During the service, everyone in the convent had to approach the coffin and touch the body. We all hated having to do it, and today, instead of a dead nun, it was Josephine's body that lay in the small white open coffin at the altar. To make things worse, the family that had taken her out were sitting in chairs at the front of the chapel, and I would have to walk past them, as if nothing had happened. I noticed they'd shown up in their best Sunday coats and hats, but not one of them shed a tear.

On one side of the chapel, the benches

were packed with nuns praying. We trudged in single file down the aisle towards the coffin, where a nun was posted to make sure that each girl touched the body. I screamed when my turn came, overwhelmed with fear. There was no way I could touch my dead friend's cold body. But the nun grabbed hold of me and pulled me, fighting and screaming, towards the coffin, forcing me to touch her. As I bent over, I saw that she was dressed in the white dress and shawl that she would have been wearing in a few weeks' time at her First Communion. She looked peaceful, like a miniature angel.

How could God let this happen? I asked myself. No one should die so young and with so little love in their short, sad life.

CHAPTER 4

The Saturday Routine

Monday to Friday was awful, but Saturdays were appalling. Everyone hated Saturdays. For starters, there was double the amount of work of any other day of the week because the following day, the Sabbath, was devoted to prayer. Also, Sunday was visiting day, so by Saturday bedtime the convent had to be spotless.

Perhaps if the Reillys had had visitors to look forward to on Sundays, Saturdays might not have seemed so bad, but no one ever came to see us. I often wished that one day we'd get a visit. It wouldn't matter who it was, just so long as they cared enough to come. But so far it had never happened.

I'd been in juniors for over a year now, so I was used to the Saturday routine. The day started just like all the others, with the bell for morning prayers. After prayers we washed and dressed, then returned to our beds for the humiliating ritual of mattress and sheet inspection. If your sheets or mattress were stained, even the slightest bit, you knew you were in for a humiliation or possibly a beating. Worse still, anyone who wet their bed had to stand with the soiled sheet over their head – for as long as Sister Thomas wanted her to – and then take it down to the laundry where Sister Mary would hit her with a walking stick. Fortunately, I wasn't one to wet the bed. But I remember that a girl messed her bed once. She had it rubbed in her face, literally.

After mattress and sheet inspection came morning Mass, followed by breakfast. After breakfast we lined up and waited for a nun to call out our number and allocate jobs for the day, which normally involved cleaning, although you could also be sent to work in the laundry or kitchen. Whatever the job, it had to be done perfectly. If you were responsible for polishing the stairs and one of the nuns later found a speck of dust on the staircase, then you wouldn't be going to bed until you'd done it all over again. So on Saturdays the atmosphere was always tense.

I was sure I was given the worst jobs and hated waiting for my number to be called. Saturdays always seemed to be spent washing and polishing floors, and at the end of the day my knees and back ached terribly. Not again, I'd think, when the nun called my number and sent me away to scrub down an entire corridor.

We spent the mornings cleaning and then returned to the chapel for Benediction. After chapel it was back to the refectory for lunch and the inevitable prayers before lunch and prayers after lunch. As if we didn't do enough praying in chapel.

After lunch we lined up for hair inspection, when the nuns checked each girl thoroughly for nits. If any were found, then the girl's head was shaved at once. My long, black hair was one of the only things that set me apart from the other girls, and I dreaded the thought of having it shaved off. So on Friday nights, whenever possible, Loretta and I would carefully check each other's hair. The next day, waiting in line to be checked, I always prayed hard that we'd both be clear.

We changed our navy knickers once a week after knicker inspection, when we had to stand in a semi-circle with our knickers off and hold up the gusset for Sister Thomas to scrutinise. If there were even the slightest stain on the gusset of your knickers, she would slap you and scream that you were a filthy, dirty animal. 'Yes, Sister. Thank you, Sister,' you had to say when you finally received a clean pair. Things could get even more humiliating for the girls who happened to be on their period. Sometimes a girl would be standing in that semi-circle for so long that blood would begin to drip down her legs. Sister Thomas always pointed it out, before hitting the girl and shouting that she was unclean. The whole experience was totally degrading for all of us.

As much as I hated the extra inspections and cleaning, the worst part of the Saturday routine was bath time. It wasn't that I didn't want to be clean; in normal circumstances – in a normal home – I would have loved the luxury and privacy of a hot bath. But nothing about bath time in the convent could be considered remotely normal.

Bath time occurred last thing on Saturday evening. Although modesty was generally very important in the convent, different rules seemed to apply at bath time – and during knicker inspection. There was absolutely no privacy. I was shy and found it extremely embarrassing.

The exact arrangements for bath time varied according to the nun in charge. Generally we shared baths, with three or four girls in a bath at a time, and we washed ourselves down using large rectangular bars of rough carbolic soap. By the time the first set of girls had finished, the water would be cold and murky, but there was no change of water. As the first lot of girls got out, the next lot got straight in.

All the time a nun looked on, reminding us that 'cleanliness was next to godliness' and that 'people who were not clean would not get to Heaven'. It seemed to me that hardly a day passed when I didn't hear someone say those words. Yet, I couldn't understand why, if cleanliness was really so important, the nuns made us bathe together and didn't change the water. Perhaps, I thought, they don't really want us to get to Heaven. All of this was enough to make me hate bath times, but what made the whole experience even more dreadful was Jeyes Fluid.

Jeyes Fluid was used for every kind of cleaning job, from washing drains to scrubbing floors. It's an evil, thick, dark-brown liquid that smells positively vile. To this day, whenever I smell it, I feel sick immediately, and it was the same back then. For some nuns, soap and water were not enough to ensure the girls' cleanliness and so they would add Jeyes Fluid to the bath. As well as smelling awful, the cleaning agents it contained stung your skin, especially your private parts and any cuts. And if you winced in pain, you were scolded and reminded again that 'cleanliness was next to godliness'. To me, it didn't make sense that Jeyes Fluid had to be used to clean everything, including us. I'd never heard it mentioned in the Bible that children should be bathed in the horrible stuff. Later on I became convinced that it was just another way in which the nuns could take their frustrations out on us. They did it because they could; there was no one there to speak out on our behalf.

Though the weekend routine varied little,

one particular Saturday was to stand out in my mind. My job, as usual, was to scrub and polish floors, but this time I was sent to work in an unfamiliar part of the convent, in an area used solely by the nuns. Before I left, Sister Francis told me that when she came to inspect my work later, she wanted to be able to see her face in every surface.

I set to work, scrubbing as hard as I could, humming a tune to keep myself going. Soon my hands were wrinkled, my arms ached, and my knees were cold and sore.

Every now and then a sound resembling a muffled moan emanated from behind one of the doors in the corridor. I tried to ignore it. This part of the convent was very quiet, and there didn't seem to be anyone else about. I hummed a bit louder and tried to focus on my work.

Then, as I was scrubbing directly outside one of the doors, I heard another moan. I stopped humming and listened out for a few moments but heard nothing. I felt uncomfortable not knowing what or who was making the noise, so I hummed a little louder.

'Who's there?' croaked a voice from the other side of the door.

I got to my feet. 'It's Frances Reilly,' I said, sounding confident but feeling nervous. I didn't want to open the door or go inside the room.

I heard another moan and the words 'Let me see you.' I wiped my hands on my work apron and opened the door, which was old and heavy and creaked as it moved. Inside the room, I saw a frail old nun lying in her bed. I closed the door behind me.

'Come closer, child, where I can see you.'

I approached the bed, not sure if I was doing the right thing. I desperately hoped that no one would find me here and accuse me of not working. The nun pointed a bony finger at the jug of water on her bedside locker. There was a glass next to the jug, and I wasted no time filling it and holding it up to her lips. The effort of taking a few feeble sips seemed to exhaust her. When she'd had enough, she lowered her head onto her pillow.

'So you're Frances Reilly,' she murmured.

'Yes, Sister,' I replied, slowly edging towards the door to make my escape. I was no longer afraid of her, just worried about getting into trouble for being away from my work. I'd almost made it to the door when she spoke again.

'If you go to that top drawer, child, you will find some boiled sweets there. Take a couple for yourself.'

I could hardly believe it. I hadn't had a sweet since I'd arrived at the convent. Before she could change her mind, I quickly went to the drawer, opened it and found a brown paper bag containing brightly coloured boiled sweets. My mouth began to water. No longer thinking about work or getting into trouble, I took out four sweets and clenched my fingers around them.

'Thank you, Sister.'

'Now get on with what you were doing. And will you call in to see me when you've finished?'

'Yes, Sister. Thank you, Sister.'

Back in the corridor, I unfurled my fingers and gazed at the jewels in my hand. This is my lucky day! I thought to myself, picking out the orange one, which appeared brighter than the others. I took one last look at its beautiful orange colour before popping it into my mouth. A wonderful flavour hit my taste buds. I rolled the sweet around my mouth and sucked it to release its gorgeous fruity flavour. What bliss, what luxury! With a shock, I realised I was smiling. Suddenly, I felt very happy.

Knowing that I would have to get back to my work soon, I began to think about where I could hide the remaining sweets – a red one, a yellow one and a green one. It felt like I was in possession of an amazing treasure that was mine alone and mustn't be seen by anyone. I had no intention of sharing these sweets, not even with my sisters or best friend.

We weren't allowed to have pockets, and

for a moment or two I couldn't think where to hide them. Then I had an idea. I tucked them firmly into the bottom of my sleeve and folded the sleeve around them until it reached my elbow. After checking carefully to see if there were any lumps or bumps that could get me caught out, I rolled up the other sleeve in line with the first.

I was in a much better mood now. My work didn't seem to be so much of a chore, and I found I was happily singing to myself. I worked faster than usual because I wanted to get back to see the old nun, partly in the hope that I might get a few more sweets but also because I'd liked her. I couldn't help thinking how much nicer she'd seemed than the nuns who were normally on duty and wondered if she'd ever been as bad as the nuns that I'd known and come to hate so much. Some nuns were better than others, but even for the nicer ones, moments of kindness were rare. Maybe she was only being kind now because she was old and very sick and wanted to make her peace with God. Whatever her reasons, I decided it didn't really matter. I was just glad that she was nice now and planned to sneak back to see her whenever I could.

When my work was finished, I went back to see if she needed a drink or anything else before the bell went. I knocked on her door, but she didn't answer. I knocked again. Not wanting to wake her if she was asleep, I crept into the room and across to the bed.

'Sister, it's me, Frances Reilly. I've finished my work and I've got to go. Can I get you a drink of water?'

The old nun said nothing. I moved closer to the bed.

'Sister, I have to go now,' I said, in a last attempt to say goodbye. I looked into her face, and a chill ran through me. Her mouth and eyes were still open, but there was no movement there at all, and her old wrinkled skin looked sallow and lifeless.

'Oh my God, she's dead!' I said aloud, feeling really scared. I was in a room where I had no right to be, with a dead nun. If any of the other nuns discovered me, I would be in for a beating. Perhaps they might even think that I was to blame for her death. Although I was very concerned about her, I was also frightened for myself and knew that I had to get out of the room as quickly as possible.

'Goodbye, Sister. Thank you, Sister,' I said, in the belief that she was now looking down at me from Heaven. As I hurried away to collect my cleaning stuff from the corridor, a sudden thought struck me: what if she wasn't actually dead and needed help? I racked my brains for a solution. Perhaps there was something I could do for her without getting into trouble.

As I stood there, in turmoil, a young nun swept past me into the old nun's room. I hung around, feeling awful that I hadn't done anything. Then the young nun rushed out of the room and dashed off up the corridor, passing me almost at a run. This had to mean that the old nun was definitely dead, which saddened me. It also freaked me out to think that I'd been speaking to her less than half an hour before and was the last person to see her alive.

At Benediction I prayed for the nun who had shown me some kindness. I was starting to feel like I'd lost a friend, which was strange, considering we'd met only briefly.

I was so wrapped up in my thoughts that I forgot about the other sweets until recreation time. I decided that I'd try the glassy red one next. I could almost imagine what it would taste like. Sister Kevin was on duty, and I wasted no time in asking permission to go to the toilet.

'Yes, go on then, but be quick about it, Reilly,' she said, misreading the look of desperation on my face.

'Thank you, Sister,' I said, dashing off excitedly. I told myself that the old nun would have wanted me to enjoy the sweets.

Inside the toilet cubicle, I leant against the door to stop anyone from pushing it open. Then, very carefully, I unfolded my sleeve and tipped the three remaining sweets into my hand. I took a good look at them again before unwrapping the red one and placing it in my mouth. It tasted different to the orange sweet but every bit as wonderful. This time, though, I didn't have time to suck it and savour it, so I bit down hard until it broke into pieces with a loud crunch. For a second, I froze, hoping that no one had heard, but there didn't appear to be anyone about, so I carried on crunching, which made the flavour stronger, although the sweet didn't last as long.

I guessed that I had time to eat another sweet before returning to recreation. I picked the green one because it seemed to me that the yellow one was the next best, and I wanted to save that till last, when I was in bed. It would give me something to look forward to. So I wrapped the yellow one back up into my sleeve and put the green one in my mouth.

I heard someone go into the toilet next to me and held my breath, worried that if I even exhaled loudly, the person in the next cubicle would know what I was up to and take my last sweet away from me. I stood there motionless until I heard her leave. The green sweet was lovely but with a weaker flavour than the other two. I bit into it, and it shattered into small sharp pieces in my mouth, which reminded me of broken glass. After swallowing the last piece and making sure that the remaining sweet was safely in my sleeve, I made my way back to the others at recreation.

I began to wish that the day were over so that I could enjoy the final sweet under my bed covers. The hours seemed to drag, but eventually, it was bedtime, and I couldn't wait a moment longer. Straight after lights out I sneaked under the covers, removed the sweet from its temporary hiding place under my pillow and slipped it into my mouth. Peace at last, I thought, snuggling into a comfortable position and enjoying the lemony flavour. Some of the girls were whispering to one another, but I couldn't be bothered to listen to what they were saying. My mind was filled with thoughts of the strange day I'd had. It felt as if the old nun were watching me now, enjoying my last sweet under the covers, and I drifted off to sleep with it still in my mouth.

CHAPTER 5

The Lord's Work

Loretta and I ached to be free of the cold, damp, ugly, cruel world we inhabited, a world controlled by monsters in black and white habits. We had nothing to look forward to, no parties or presents or toys and no pretty clothes, just a plain, brown, oversized convent dress each. Birthdays were not acknowledged, let alone celebrated, and Christmas was a purely religious event. We were never allowed to feel normal, to look pretty or to be happy, and there was no colour in our lives. It seemed to us that everything nice was a sin and that Sister Thomas had been sent personally by God to make sure we had no time to sin, by filling every moment of our lives with what she called 'the Lord's work'.

Most of the girls in the convent attended lessons regularly, but for us and a few others, there were few lessons – apart from Bible studies – and we were never taught to read and write. We went to class every afternoon for the calling of the register, but then someone would usually arrive at the classroom door and say that Sister Thomas had asked for us. It was all down to the whim of the nun in charge, and Sister Thomas said that the Reillys were scum and only fit for cleaning, so she pulled us out of class almost every day. With no parents to report back to, we were easy targets. There wasn't a library, and we had no access to books. While the other girls were in class, we laboured in the convent, scrubbing and polishing corridors and floors, washing down walls or working in the laundry or kitchen. There were no mops or vacuum cleaners so we spent hours at a time on our hands and knees, on cold stone floors that seemed to stretch for miles. The 'Lord's work' had to be done every day, and the nuns were on constant patrol to see that it was completed to the highest standard.

One cold, frosty morning we got up to our normal routine. After two Masses and a meagre breakfast we answered to our numbers and were given our duties for the day. I prayed to get anything but scrubbing floors. After weeks of kneeling my knees were killing me and looked more like the knees of an old woman than an eight-year-old child. Loretta and I were called together.

'Here, Reverend Mother,' we said in unison. At least we'd be working together.

'Corridor duty.'

My head drooped. There was to be no respite today. But at least I'd be with Loretta. Every moment spent with her was precious. We were each given a heavy metal bucket full of water and Jeyes Fluid, a large wooden scrubbing brush, a cloth and a bar of carbolic soap. We took up our position in the corridor and began scrubbing. As usual, the horrible musty smell of the Jeyes Fluid made me feel sick.

I tried to ignore the pain in my knees, but after a while I could hardly move my legs.

Loretta noticed me struggling along the corridor with my bucket. 'You stop for a while, and I'll go faster,' she whispered.

'Thanks,' I said, sitting down with my back resting against the corridor wall. I didn't think I'd be able to stand up again. I tried to bring life back into my knees by rubbing them hard with the palms of my hands.

'Are you all right?' asked Loretta, who was scrubbing as quickly as she could.

'I'll be all OK in a minute.'

I tried to stand up, but as I got to my feet and felt the blood starting to circulate, I was paralysed by the sensation of burning red-hot pins and needles in my legs. Struggling, worried about what would happen if I was caught skiving, I forced myself to walk up and down the corridor. The feeling was slowly returning to my legs when Sister Thomas came round the corner.

By the time she reached us, her face was

flushed red with anger. She grabbed my head and lifted me into the air by my hair. The pain was agonising. A few seconds later she released her grip, and I fell like a sack of potatoes onto the floor. She bent down to slap me viciously around the face and head.

'It's my fault, Sister!' Loretta said. 'Her legs are sore so I told her to stop working for a while.'

Sister Thomas stopped hitting me. 'To my office, both of you.'

We knew what we were in for and somehow that made it worse. I hobbled along, my heart beating faster the closer we got to her office. Sister Thomas had hidden depths of anger, wells of it, and seemed to enjoy inflicting pain. There was nothing we could do now but hope for a miracle from God. But we knew there'd be no miracle, because we'd prayed for one so many times before and nothing had happened.

Death must be better than this, I thought. The waiting was awful; Sister Thomas knew it was awful and so she deliberately drew it out. The harder things were on her victim, the more pleasurable it was for her. Sometimes she sent girls away for days before finally beating them, but today she was too angry to be so cruelly patient. I began to sob in expectation of what was to come. Loretta stood perfectly still, her expression grim.

Over years of abuse Loretta had learnt to

appear indifferent to even the most savage punishment. It was something she'd perfected painfully. She simply wouldn't give the nuns the satisfaction of ever seeing her cry. It was a small act of defiance but an important one. However, it came at considerable cost to herself because the ferocity and duration of her beatings increased in response to her apparent indifference. I looked up to her and wished I could be as strong as she was, but that day was a long way off.

Sister Thomas walked to the cupboard and took out one of the canes. She began pacing back and forth, tapping the cane against the palm of her hand, as if deciding which of us she'd hit first. My sobs grew louder, and she looked at me coldly, then raised the cane high above her head and brought it down by her side with a swish.

'You'll be first!' she shouted at me. 'Put your hand out and don't move it until I've finished, or you'll get double.'

I held out my hand and shut my eyes. I heard the whoosh of the cane and a stabbing, throbbing pain shot through to the very tips of my fingers. Instinctively, I pulled my hand back and tucked it under my arm, before realising my mistake.

'Put out your hand!' Sister Thomas screamed, her face flushed and frenzied.

'Sister, it wasn't her fault!' Loretta shouted. 'I told her to have a break and that I'd do her work. Her legs are so sore she can't kneel on them.'

'I will have no more excuses for not doing the Lord's work!'

She raised her arm again and started beating me all over my body, harder and harder, until eventually the cane snapped in half. I lay huddled up on the floor of the office, my arms curled protectively around my head. Almost immediately, she dragged me up again by my hair.

'Stand on your feet, girl!' she shrieked.

The moment I stood up a hard slap on the face sent me flying across the office. Bouncing off the wall, I fell to the floor, momentarily stunned.

I heard Loretta scream, 'Leave her alone, just leave her alone!' followed by the sound of scuffling. I wiped away my tears with my sleeve to see what was happening. As I began to focus, I saw Loretta pushing and shoving Sister Thomas, who was trying desperately to slap or grab hold of her.

'Oh God, if you can hear me, please help us!' I prayed aloud. 'You're the only one who can help. Please hear my prayer. Please hear my prayer.'

Sister Thomas grabbed Loretta by the shoulders and started shaking her. 'You Reillys are children of the Devil!' she yelled. 'It's no surprise your mother hasn't come for you. Nobody wants you, so we have to put up with you. You'll all burn in the fires of Hell because there is no way you'll get into the Kingdom of Heaven. Is this how you repay the nuns for taking you in? Well, we'll soon knock the disobedience out of you.'

She stopped shaking Loretta and began pacing the floor again. Loretta and I exchanged glances. The deep sadness I felt at that moment was mirrored in my brave sister's eyes. Up until then it had never occurred to us that our mother didn't love us or want us. For so long Loretta had fed me the dream that she must be having a really hard time and was still trying to sort things out for our return that I couldn't imagine any other explanation for her absence. Since I couldn't remember anything about her, I'd built up a picture of a flustered, overworked matronly type in an apron, but now Sister Thomas had said the unthinkable. Maybe she was right when she said we weren't wanted, that our mother would never come back for us. If so, the only thing that had been keeping us going for all these years had been nothing but an illusion.

Sister Thomas broke the silence. 'Get yourselves ready for chapel. I'm already late, so I'll have to deal with you later. And believe me, I won't forget! I'll reflect on what your punishments will be after prayers.'

As we left the office, Loretta put her arm around me. 'Are you OK?' she said.

76

I didn't reply. I was far from OK. In fact, I was in a tremendous amount of pain; my knees creaked as I walked, and the rest of my body felt like it had been used as a punch-bag. We made our way along empty corri-dors and up a long flight of stairs leading to the chapel door. Pausing, we listened to the sound of girls praying. We didn't want to go in, partly because we'd be stared at for being late but mostly because there was no accept-able excuse for not being in line for chapel as far as the Reverend Mother was concerned. If she was in a good mood, she just might listen to our explanation, but if she wasn't, we'd be getting another punishment.

'It's all my fault,' I sobbed.

'No, it's not. You can't help it if you're in agony. Anyway, I've got an idea,' Loretta said. 'We'll go down the stairs and around the corner, and when everyone comes out we'll try to get in line with them, without the nuns seeing us. I think it will work. Come on, it's too late to go in now, anyway.'

She helped me back down the stairs, and we stood next to a wall where we wouldn't be noticed. Just then the big chapel door opened, and we heard footsteps on the stairs.

'Quiet now, here they come,' Loretta whispered, pushing me close to the wall.

Our hearts were racing. Sister Anthony came into view, followed by a long line of girls. So far, we hadn't been spotted. Then came Sister Thomas, followed by another line of girls. She'd entered the chapel by a door near the altar that only the nuns were allowed to use. Just then Loretta saw a few of her friends. Pushing me forward, she fell in step behind me, and we disappeared into the line.

'Where have you been?' Bridget murmured.

'I'll tell you later.'

We carried on walking until we came to the refectory. So far nobody had noticed that we hadn't been in chapel, but we still couldn't relax. Sister Thomas's next punishment hung over us like a thick black cloud.

By the end of dinner Loretta had told Bridget everything. Bridget couldn't believe that she'd attacked Sister Thomas. She was really worried for her.

'I wouldn't want to be ye, Loretta, when she gets her hands on ye.'

Loretta came to find me. 'Come on, Frances, the bell's gonna go in a minute.'

I tried to stand, but my legs had seized up. 'I can't move! My knees are locked.'

Loretta leant over and tried to straighten my legs out, and Sister Justin came over to see what was going on. Sister Justin was an overweight nun in her late fifties, and although she was very strict, she was in no way as bad as Sister Thomas. She looked at me through her thick-rimmed glasses.

'Are you going to sit there all day? The bell will be going off soon.'

'We know, Sister,' Loretta said. 'We're trying, but she can't move her legs.'

'Why? What's wrong with your legs?'

'I don't know, Sister. They've been sore all day, and now I can't move them.'

'You'll have to see Dr Hanna. Loretta, get someone to help you carry her to the dormitory and get her into bed. If anyone asks what you're doing, say I told you. I will have the doctor here as soon as he can get away from his surgery.'

'Thank you, Sister. I'll take Bridget with me.'

'Hurry along, then.'

We waited until everyone else had lined up and left, then Loretta and Bridget clasped hands to make a cradle for me to sit on. I was very small and light so it wasn't too much of a problem getting me up to the dormitory. In no time at all they were helping me into bed.

They sat on the end of the bed and chatted, while I listened in. We knew from experience that it would be quite some time before the doctor arrived. He'd only come after his surgery and regular rounds were complete, so it was likely to be early evening before we saw him. It was a running joke among us that he was often accompanied by the strong smell of Irish whisky.

'Well, Frances, it looks like Sister Thomas

is going to have to leave ye alone for a while now. But she'll have it in for me, though, for sure,' Loretta said.

'But once the doctors says what's wrong with my knees, she'll know we were telling the truth. She can't punish us then.'

'Ye know it won't matter if we're telling the truth or not. She gets some sort of kick out of hitting us. Why did she ever want to become a nun?'

It was a good question, and one that we had often pondered.

'No, Frances,' Loretta went on, 'I'm still going to have to face her, especially after going for her. I bet she drags it out, though, just to make me suffer some more, the old witch. God forgive me, I'd love to see someone lay into her with one of those sticks. She needs a dose of her own medicine. Perhaps one day I'll get her back for all of us.'

'Oh God, Loretta!' Bridget exclaimed. 'How can you even think of doing something like that?'

I sensed that Bridget was unsure how much more Loretta could take before either breaking down or exploding. Because Loretta was always putting on a brave face, she sometimes seemed like a ticking bomb of unexpressed pain and anger, and what made her most furious of all was seeing me being harmed.

'Can you imagine what the nuns would do

to you?' Bridget continued. 'What the rest of your life here would be like? It would just be awful. The only winners in here are the nuns. They get away with everything and still have a place reserved in Heaven because they're nuns. For God's sake, it's not fair, but that's the way it is and we can't do anything about it.'

'We can when we're grown up,' I said. 'One day I'll write a book about this place and tell the world what the "good sisters" are really like.'

'But ye don't even know how to write, sure,' Bridget laughed.

'Quiet, someone's coming,' Loretta whispered.

She and Bridget jumped to their feet, not wanting to get into trouble for sitting on the bed. We could hear movement outside the dormitory door, and Loretta and Bridget busied themselves tidying up my bed, tucking and smoothing. The door opened and in walked Sister Aloisius on a routine cleaning check.

'What are you girls doing in here?' she demanded.

Bridget explained about the doctor's visit.

'Well, it looks to me like you're all done here,' said Sister Aloisius said. 'Now be on your way. I'm sure you've work to do.'

'Yes, Sister.' They hurried away.

Sister Aloisius wandered around the

dormitory running her fingers along every available surface where dust could gather, including the windowsills, skirting boards and bedside cabinets. She completed her inspection with a methodical examination of the floor underneath each girl's bed before coming over for a chat.

Sister Aloisius liked me, and I preferred her to the other nuns. I'd always found her to be quite fair, but unfortunately, we only ever met when she was on dinner or recreation duty. She didn't seem to pick on girls just for the sake of it, although she could be as strict as any other nun if she was crossed. I often wished that she were in charge of my dormitory instead of Sister Thomas. It would certainly make life a lot more bearable. But there was little point in wishing for something that was never going to happen. I told her about the pain in my legs, and she suggested that we pray together.

When she'd gone, I lay on my bed for hours before anyone came. It was a relief not to be standing or kneeling. Every part of my body seemed to ache from the battering I'd received that morning. My hands were in the worst condition. It was getting dark, so I couldn't see the wounds clearly, but I could make out long red welts across my palms and fingers. The fingers of my right hand were particularly painful, especially when I tried to move them. I found similar wounds on my back, my legs and particularly on my arms, which I'd used to protect my head. The back of my head throbbed, and I had a huge bump just behind my left ear. I knew that by morning the bruising would be much worse and that I would be in pain for days. But at least the beating was over, for now.

More troubling was the thought of what Sister Thomas would do to Loretta. I was so proud of my sister for trying to protect me but knew she was in for it now. I was convinced it was all my fault. If I hadn't stopped working, then none of this would have happened. Demoralised and over-whelmed by feelings of worthlessness, I decided that it would have been better for the rest of my family, especially Loretta, if I'd never been born.

Reeking of alcohol and swaying, Dr Hanna finally arrived and prescribed tights. Not rest or lighter work duties, but tights – to keep my legs insulated as I slaved away on my knees. I suppose he was just being practical, but at the time I could have done with a bit more support from the so-called medical profession. I slept fitfully that night and dreamt about Mammy. 'Don't worry, I'll be back for you, Frances,' she said in the dream. 'I'll be back just as soon as I can.'

CHAPTER 6

The Visitor

By now Loretta and I had lost all real hope of our mother ever coming back for us. We talked and dreamt about it, but neither of us really expected it to happen. We both knew that life for us was our miserable existence in Nazareth House, which really was more like a prison than a children's home. The 'good sisters' ran their prison with an iron grip, with the full moral backing of the Roman Catholic Church and, presumably, of the community at large. We accepted the regular beatings and other punishments – including losing the 'privilege' of seeing our younger sister – as a normal part of our everyday life in the convent. What other choice did we have?

Now we were worried, however, because we hadn't seen Sinéad for a long time. Often, when we were due to see her, one or both of us would be summoned by Sister Thomas, who would accuse us of doing something that we hadn't done. We'd get beaten until we owned up and then get beaten some more for the offence, and, of course, we wouldn't be allowed to see Sinéad. Obviously, we could have just owned up straight away, but there was always the hope that this time she might believe us. Besides, we'd been brainwashed into believing that lying was a mortal sin and that anyone who lied would burn in the fires of Hell forever.

We were desperate to know how Sinéad was, and she was always on my mind. I comforted myself by thinking that at least she didn't have Sister Thomas on her back night and day.

One day I was scrubbing the kitchen floor when Sister Francis stormed in.

'Reilly! Leave your work and come with me,' she shouted.

What have I done now? I thought, sure that Sister Thomas had sent for me again. My fears seemed to be confirmed when I was shoved into an empty room with Loretta. But then, almost straight away, Sister Lucius came in holding an armful of clothes.

'Here, put these on,' she said. 'You've got a visitor.'

A visitor? Loretta and I exchanged glances, but we both knew better than to ask who it was. My heart leapt into my mouth. Could it be that Mammy had finally come back for us?

I could tell Loretta was thinking the same thing. Maybe our mammy had finally sorted things out and was going to take us away from this awful life. Maybe we'd walk into the visiting room and run into her arms, and then she'd tell us how much she'd missed us and that she was taking us home to our brothers. Please, God, I prayed, please let it be our mammy.

'You're to be on your best behaviour, do you understand?' Sister Lucius went on, her voice sharp. 'You must tell the visitor how good the sisters have been to you.'

A few minutes later, dressed in clothes we'd never seen before, we were standing outside a big wooden door with Sinéad by our side. Sister Lucius knocked, pushed it open, ushered us inside and shut it behind us.

Across the room, by the empty fireplace, sat a handsome, fair-haired man in his mid-thirties. His skin was tanned, his hair sun-bleached, and he was wearing British army uniform. Next to his chair, I noticed a walking stick. Seeing us, he made an attempt to stand up but immediately winced with pain and sat back down again. He held out his arms.

'My wee girls,' he said in a soft Irish accent. 'Come over here and give yer daddy a kiss.'

Loretta and I looked at him in amazement. Could this really be our daddy? He was a shadowy, half-forgotten figure in our minds, the last person we'd expected to see. And wasn't he overseas?

We didn't know it then, but he'd been away

serving in India for many years and was soon to leave the army on medical grounds, after developing gangrene in his legs. He'd sent money home regularly to our mother without knowing that she'd put us into the convent. And then, just before his return, she'd sent him a letter telling him what she'd done and where he could find us. He'd come straight to the convent the moment he arrived back in Ireland.

He couldn't seem to get over how big we'd grown. Delving into his pocket, he took out a large bag of sweets.

'Share these with your sisters,' he said, handing the bag to Loretta, who hid it inside her clothes and unwrapped some sweets for us.

'Eat them quickly and don't make a mess,' she said.

Sinéad and I enjoyed the sweets, while Loretta and our father talked. Since we'd been warned to be on our best behaviour, she didn't dare say anything about how badly we were being treated. Instead, she listened attentively to all that he said.

'Now, Loretta,' he said gently. 'I have something to tell you, and I need you to be strong for your sisters. I'm going into hospital today, but I don't want you to worry. I had an accident some time ago, and it damaged part of my legs. The doctors have got to take the damaged bit away so that the rest of it can get better. But it will mean that when I come out of hospital, part of my legs will be missing and I'll be in a wheelchair.'

Loretta looked horrified. He took her hand.

'I know it's a shock for you, but I've known for a long time now, and I've come to accept it,' he went on. 'As soon as I'm fit again, I'll be back for you. Even though I'll be in a wheelchair, I hope to take you all out of here to live with me, but I shall need you to help with your sisters. We've a lot of catching up to do.'

Loretta couldn't believe what she was hearing. 'Of course I'll help, Daddy. I'm a really good worker,' she said. Suddenly, she wasn't so worried about his operation. He sounded very positive about our future together and that made her feel much stronger.

By now Sinéad had chocolate all over her face and hands. Loretta excused herself and took her away to clean her up.

My daddy picked me up and put me on his knee. I liked the smell of his clothes and his aftershave. They were much nicer than the convent smells I was used to. He told me a story about his time in India. I thought he had a kind, gentle voice, and when he spoke, I felt warm inside. It was a wonderful feeling and not something I was at all used to.

I felt that I must be the happiest person in the world. Having a visitor – our first-ever visitor – felt incredibly special, and I could have sat there all day listening to his stories. Most of the other girls saw their families regularly, but no one had come to see us in all these years. It had been impossible not to feel jealous of the others, but now it was our turn, and it felt fantastic, unbelievable. It felt so good to have him there and to feel, at last, like part of a real family. Here was our daddy telling us how much he loved and missed us.

Loretta arrived back with Sinéad, all washed and clean. We sat for a little while longer and talked about the things we'd do when we got a home together. Then Sister Austin came for us. She told us to say good-bye and go straight to the chapel for the Rosary.

One by one, Daddy kissed and hugged us.

'Hang in there. I'll be back as soon as I can to take you home,' he said affectionately.

Sister Austin helped him to his feet and handed him his stick.

'I'll see you out,' she said, walking him to the door.

We smiled and waved goodbye.

'Look after my daughters till I return for them please, Sister,' he said as he limped away.

Sister Austin nodded at him and smiled.

Bursting with happiness, Loretta and I got to the chapel just as the Rosary was starting.

It felt so good to have seen our father and know that we were getting out of the convent. We prayed to God for his recovery to be quick and to give him the strength to cope after the operation. It was going to be hard for him to raise his daughters from a wheel-chair, and Loretta knew that he would be counting on her help, especially with Sinéad, but it was a challenge she was looking forward to. I knew I'd do whatever it took to be of help to him, too. After all, nothing could be as hard as convent life. With so many thoughts racing through our minds, it was impossible to concentrate on the service.

At last there was a light at the end of the tunnel. We could hardly wait to tell our friends. It was such a great feeling to have someone who really cared about us. Maybe now Sister Thomas would leave us alone, but even if she didn't, it didn't matter. We could put up with anything for the short time we had left. The Rosary finally ended and we lined up to go out for recreation. It wasn't too cold – at least, not as cold as it had been for the previous few months. I caught up with my friend, Chrissie, and told her what had happened.

'We got sweets, and I sat on my daddy's knee, and he is going to take us out of here as soon as he's better. But he's got to go to hospital first for an operation...'

I was talking so fast that Chrissie couldn't

get a word in. 'Slow down, Frances!'

'Oh, I'm sorry, Chrissie,' I said, noticing that tears had started to roll down her face. 'It's just been the best day of my life.'

'I'm really pleased for you, Frances, but I don't know what I'm going to do when you've gone. You're my best friend, and it's going to be awful in here without you.' She brushed away her tears with her sleeve as she spoke.

I felt awful. 'I'll come to visit you, Chrissie, I promise. I'm sure my daddy won't mind bringing me on visiting days. You'll still be my best friend. I'll never forget you, I swear.'

Chrissie smiled. 'I won't forget you either, Frances. It's going to be awful without you, but I'm happy that at least one of us will be out of this dump. Promise you'll visit as often as you can.'

'I promise, Chrissie. Please don't be sad.'

Over the next few days everyone noticed a big difference in the Reillys. We went about our duties with a smile. In chapel we prayed very hard for our father's recovery. But best of all, since his visit, Sister Thomas hadn't blamed us for anything. For the first time ever all three of us were happy.

'Come along girls,' bellowed the Mother Superior as she rang the bell for morning prayers. She had a voice like a foghorn, and it would have been impossible to sleep through it. But even worse was the insistent, penetrating ring of the hand bell. I hated waking to that sound at five o'clock every morning.

We all loathed getting out of bed and onto our knees at that time, especially when it was cold. I didn't mind so much today, though. I would be out of here soon and waking up to the sound of birds singing, or to a shout from my sisters or father. And perhaps he would send for us today or at least by the end of the week. Either way, it didn't really matter. As soon as he'd recovered, we would be out. I jumped out of bed and knelt on the cold wooden floor.

The radiators had packed up again, and we shivered as we waited for morning prayers to begin. I wondered why the Mother Superior was taking them instead of Sister Thomas.

'In the name of the Father and of the Son and of the Holy Ghost, amen.' Morning prayers had started. 'I would like to offer up our prayers this morning for the Reillys' father, who died last night in hospital,' the Mother Superior said, very matter-of-factly. 'May he rest in peace.' Then she continued with normal morning prayers.

No. It couldn't be true. Surely there must be some mistake? How could my daddy possibly be dead? My head dropped forward, my shoulders slumped, and I began to shake uncontrollably. Tears welled up in my eyes, and a horrible sick feeling filled my stomach. I tried to carry on with the ritual of morning prayers, but a lump filled my throat and stopped the words coming out. I tried to focus on what prayers were being said, but the droning sound of the others praying was beginning to drive me mad.

I wished they would all go away and leave me alone with my grief, but I knew the nuns wouldn't allow me that luxury. My sisters and I would be expected to carry on with the normal routine of the convent. The prayers and chanting seemed to go on and on. I wanted to scream out, 'Shut up!' but didn't dare. I knew better than that. Years of brainwashing by the nuns had taught me not to express my true feelings. If I could have got up and run out of the dormitory right then, I would have. But my legs wouldn't move, which was just as well because the nuns, especially Sister Thomas who had no reason now to hold back, would certainly have punished me. So I just knelt there while the prayers dragged on, shaking with anger and sorrow.

My father was dead and with him had died all hope: hope of love, hope of freedom and hope of a normal family life. I wondered why God had allowed it to happen. First I'd lost Josephine, and now my daddy was gone. What had I done that He should keep making me suffer? The nuns often preached about how God loved all children and how He watched over them, but it was hard to believe. If He was watching, how could He let us endure so much?

The Bible is full of miracles and stories of the power of God – God, who created everything and made us in His own image. So why wasn't He doing something to help my sisters and me? Why didn't He stop the nuns? Why didn't He make the pain go away? The more I thought about it, the less I felt like praying. There just didn't seem much point any more.

Unaware that prayers had finished, unaware of everything, I went on kneeling by my bed, still shaking, while the others started getting washed and dressed.

I felt a gentle hand on my shoulder and heard Loretta saying, 'Come on, Frances, prayers have finished.'

Turning around to look at her, I saw she had also been crying. I'd never seen Loretta cry before. I didn't think she'd cry over anything; she'd always been so brave. Even though I couldn't bear to see her sadness, somehow it made me feel closer to her. I realised that she was in just as much pain as I was and that we were sharing the same grief, so I didn't feel so alone. We went together to get washed and dressed and had just finished making our beds as the bell sounded for morning Mass.

Lining up with the rest of the girls, we proceeded in a daze along the familiar dreary corridors. In chapel everyone's eyes seemed to be on us. Father Hughes entered the chapel by the sacristy door and everyone stood up. He faced the congregation.

'You probably know by now that the Reillys' father passed away last night. We will offer the Mass for his soul and hope that it will help him get into Heaven.'

Tears streamed down our faces onto our clothes. Once again 1 found it hard to join in with the prayers or hymns. I wasn't sure if I even believed in God any more. He'd condemned us to a life of misery in the convent by taking from us the one person who loved us and was going to get us out. Sister Thomas looked across the chapel at us, her eyes boring into us. Loretta stared straight back at her defiantly, blazing hatred, but I couldn't bring myself to look at her. With our father gone, there was no one now to protect us, and I knew that it wouldn't be long till she found some excuse to pick on us again. It would probably be even worse this time, since she'd been compelled to be 'nice' to us for the last few days and would want to show us she was in charge again at the first available opportunity.

On our way to breakfast, Sister Austin took us out of the line for a talk.

'I have arranged for you to see Sinéad after breakfast. If you go outside to the recreation ground, Sinéad will be brought to you. I'm sorry about your father. He was a very nice person, and I'm sure he's in Heaven.' There was genuine sorrow in her voice.

'Thank you, Sister,' said Loretta.

I was still crying and couldn't say anything, but we both appreciated her kind words. By the time we arrived at the refectory, breakfast had started. Our food was already on the table, and every pair of eyes was on us as we moved to our seats. We joined our hands, bowed our heads and quietly said grace, chanting the words without even thinking about them, mostly out of habit, but also because Sister Mary Louise was watching us. We certainly didn't feel like thanking God for anything, especially the food in front of us. I felt sick at the sight of that disgusting porridge. Loretta started eating and I thought I'd better eat as well if I wanted to be allowed to see Sinéad. Also, the porridge would be back on the table for me at lunchtime if I didn't eat it now. Just as I raised the spoon to my mouth, Chrissie tapped me on the arm.

'I'll eat it for you. Pass it over when they're not looking.'

'Thanks, Chrissie,' I said, relieved to have at least one less thing to worry about. We scanned the room, and as soon as it was safe, we quickly swapped bowls and Chrissie ate my soggy square of porridge.

Talking wasn't allowed in the refectory, so

no one had the chance to say anything about Daddy. I was glad of that; anything anyone said about him now would only make me feel worse. The tears I was trying so hard to hold back could easily start again, and I didn't want anyone, least of all the nuns, to see me cry. Still, I could see that many of the girls wanted to say how sorry they were for me. I tried to stop thinking about Daddy by focusing instead on the meeting with Sinéad, but as much as I tried, I couldn't get the pain to go away.

After breakfast Loretta and I went to the recreation ground and waited for Sinéad at the railings, which separated the infants from the rest of the convent grounds. Sinéad looked pleased to see us, and we would have hugged her if we could, but the iron railings prevented any close contact. We felt we needed to be strong for her, so we fought to hold back the tears. But as she stood on the other side of the railings, her blonde hair blowing in the breeze and a smile on her face, it struck me that in fact she didn't seem at all upset. Maybe the nuns hadn't told her about our father's death. Gently, I asked her if she knew that Daddy was dead. Looking up at me, she started to laugh.

Her laughter infuriated me. Suddenly, I was overwhelmed with rage. I began shouting and screaming at her. 'Stop laughing! Our daddy's dead. Don't you realise we've lost everything?'

I was hurting so much that it didn't occur to me that someone aged five would have little, if any, understanding of the concept of death. The idea of having a father, or of escaping from the convent, probably didn't mean much to her, either. But I was so angry that I couldn't think straight. Worried that I'd draw the attention of the nuns, Loretta tried to calm me down, but I was completely oblivious to her pleadings. Unable to contain my fury and hurt, I began venting them on Sinéad. I thrust my hands through the railings and grabbed her by the hair. Wrapping my hands around her head, I pulled as hard as I could.

All three of us were screaming and crying now. A group of nuns ran over, shouting at me to stop, but I couldn't hear them. I was out of control and unaware of my surroundings. They tried to pull me away but couldn't loosen my grip on Sinéad. Blind with rage, I went on pulling her head until it was fully through the iron railings and she was stuck. Still shouting at her, I kept a stubborn grip on her hair.

Eventually, I became aware of Loretta and the nuns. My small fingers were prised apart, and I stood there, pale and in a state of shock, clutching large clumps of Sinéad's blonde hair. I didn't feel at all sorry yet for what I'd done. I loved my sister dearly but couldn't forgive her for laughing.

The nuns now turned their attention to Sinéad and went to assist the nun who was trying to pull her head back through the railings. They didn't have much luck, and Sinéad started to panic, even though Loretta was trying to comfort her and calm her down. One of the nuns went off to get the Mother Superior. Loretta and I were ordered back inside to await our punishment. The visit with Sinéad was clearly over.

Not long afterwards we heard fire engines outside. Although there had been no fire alarm, some of the other girls were worried there was a real fire, but then an ambulance arrived, and soon the news about Sinéad had spread throughout the convent.

Locked away in another part of the convent awaiting my punishment, I had to rely on the other girls for information about what was happening. Finally, the news came through that Sinéad had been released and was OK. As I calmed down and the reality of what I had done sunk in, I felt awful. I loved my little sister and wondered how I could have done such a thing. Loretta and Sinéad were the only family I had, and I knew it would be ages now before the nuns let either Loretta or me see Sinéad again. We might even have to wait till she moved up to juniors. Also, there was a strong feeling between us that we should stick together, which I'd betrayed. I was desperately worried that Sinéad would never talk to me again.

CHAPTER 7

My Dead Dad's Feet

Every year, around Christmas, we put on a concert for the inspectors and parents. It was usually a combination of singing and Irish dancing, although one year we put on a production of *The Gondoliers*. We got to dress up in different clothes and wound our hair around bits of torn sheet at night to make ringlets, but it was all taken very seriously, so it wasn't any fun. Since I had no visitors – and there was nobody in the audience who mattered to me – there was nothing to get excited about.

I was too shy to sing in front of the nuns because I was so frightened of them. Worried that I'd be told I was no good, I hardly made a sound at chapel or in the concert rehearsals. I'd be slapped on the legs and told, 'Sing!' but that only made it more difficult. In the end, it was generally assumed that I couldn't sing, so I was told to mime, along with the other non-singers. We had to shine for the inspectors or be quiet.

This year the rehearsals were going well. The Irish dancing and the choir were almost perfect – the nuns, as usual, would settle for nothing less. One night Sister Constantine asked me to stay behind and sweep the hall. She was one of the nicer nuns. There was a soft spot in her, although she, too, had her moments. I picked up a broom and began sweeping the stage. Everyone else had gone to the dormitories, so I was alone. Looking down from the stage at all the chairs that needed to be stacked before I swept the hall, I knew it was going to be a while before I'd be finished, but I didn't mind. It gave me a bit of time to be alone with my thoughts, which was rare in the convent.

There was a song going through my head, the song that Kathleen O'Neil hadn't been able to get right at the rehearsal. Kathleen, a senior, was the only girl singing solo at the concert. Although she'd practised the song many times, she was still having problems with it. I knew it well – it was a ballad – and because I was on my own, I sang it as I swept. I found it easy to reach all the notes and couldn't understand why it was a problem for Kathleen. I sang it again, much louder this time, making full use of the hall's acoustics and the fact that I was alone. I put my heart and soul into it, and the stage was done by the time I'd reached the last few bars. Suddenly, the sound of clapping startled me. Sister Constantine stepped into view.

'There will be no more excuses from you for not singing in future. You have a beautiful gift, and I'm sure Our Lord gave it to you so you could use it.'

I froze at the realisation that I wouldn't be able to get out of singing in front of people now, even though the idea petrified me. Sister Constantine helped me stack the chairs and sweep the hall and asked me to sing some more as we worked. On the way back to the dormitory I felt pleased with myself for getting the songs right but wondered if they would sound so good in front of an audience. I soon found out. Sister Constantine wouldn't let it go and so I joined the choir. Later I went on to be head choirgirl in the chapel. I even sang the solo at the concert the following year.

There was no one in the dormitory when I got there, but I could hear some girls in the washroom. Two nuns and a group of girls were having a discussion by one of the toilet doors. Immediately, I sensed that something odd was going on. One of the nuns was shouting at the door, 'Come out this instant! You will open this door right now!'

I spotted Chrissie among the girls and made my way over to her. 'What's happening?' I whispered.

Chrissie explained that whoever was locked in the toilet wouldn't answer or come out. The nuns couldn't figure out who it was, as no one seemed to be missing, and they were going to break down the door soon if the person didn't open it.

I was as puzzled as everyone else and stepped towards the door to give it a push. Suddenly, it flew open, before I'd even touched it. Startled, I jumped back and looked to see who was there, but the cubicle was empty. It was mystifying. The door had definitely been locked, or else jammed shut, so how could it suddenly fly open? One of the nuns stepped inside the cubicle and locked, unlocked and opened it several times with no difficulty. She turned around and gave me the strangest of looks, then ordered all of the girls to kneel down and pray.

Several weeks passed and nothing unusual happened; so far it had been a rather un-eventful day. I hadn't been feeling very well but was managing to struggle through. It was now early evening, and Irish dancing had begun. I danced the four-hand reel and was finishing the eight-hand reel when I suddenly felt sick.

'You've gone really white,' said my part-ner, Margaret. 'Are you OK?'

'What are you two girls whispering about?' Sister Kevin snapped. She walked over with her stick pointed accusingly at us.

'I'm sorry, Sister, but I don't think

Frances is feeling well, and I just told her she looked really pale.'

'Can't you speak for yourself, Reilly?'

'Yes, Sister,' was all I could say. I clamped my hand to my mouth in an attempt to hold back the vomit that was rising up my throat.

'Outside! Quickly, girl!' she shouted. I made it to the outside drain and threw up. Sister Kevin was behind me. 'Now get a bucket of water and Jeyes Fluid and clean out the drain,' she barked. 'Then get yourself off to your dormitory. You're no good to me like this.'

I struggled back to the drain with a large metal bucket full to the brim with hot water and Jeyes Fluid. The smell of the fluid and the sight and smell of the vomit made me nauseous again, but I managed not to retch as I carefully washed out the drain. When I was sure that all traces of vomit were gone, I returned the bucket and slowly made my way to the dormitory.

It was a relief to lie down to rest for a while. I still felt ill, but nowhere near as bad as I had a few minutes earlier. Closing my eyes, I concentrated hard on trying to switch myself off from my surroundings, but after about twenty minutes I had to get up and go to the toilet, which was annoying, as it wasn't very often that I managed to find time to relax.

The strangest thing happened as I sat on

the toilet. Looking down at the floor, a pair of boots appeared in front of me. I couldn't believe what I was seeing. The boots were black and well worn with heavy green cloth wrapped around the tops but no legs or body connected to them. I shut my eyes tightly and covered them with my hands, assuming that I must be hallucinating. Tentatively, I parted my hands until I could just see the floor. To my relief, there was nothing there. But then, almost immediately, the boots reappeared. They looked so real that I felt sure I could reach down and touch them. I was completely spooked, so I closed my eyes, quickly pulled up my knickers and fumbled about for the door handle. Yanking the door open, I jumped out of the cubicle, dashed through the bathroom and dormitory and flew down the stairs. I had no idea where I was running to when I bumped right into the Mother Superior.

She seemed really annoyed at first, but seeing that I was shaking violently – and that what little colour there normally was in my face had drained away – she realised I was terrified.

Quickly regaining her composure, she tried to calm me down and find out why I was running scared, but I was still in a state of shock and unable to speak. I tried to explain, but the words wouldn't come out, so she guided me to her office.

I walked along beside her, unsure if I was in trouble or not. Once in the office I was told to sit. She sat down in her own chair, behind the desk, and once more told me to calm down and explain myself. I was afraid that I might not be believed, but soon the truth came spilling out. She quizzed me about the boots and the green cloth, and I was amazed to find that she was taking me seriously.

'You have a special gift from God to be able to see these things. I'm sure those feet were your father's. You know he was in the army, and the boots you describe sound just like the sort of boots he would have worn. The green cloth could have been his army gaiters. I think your father is asking you to pray for him. His soul may not be in Heaven yet. It may be in Purgatory, and only prayers will get him to Heaven. Now we must pray. Let's get back to your dormitory.'

I was relieved that she'd believed me. By the time we got back to the dormitory, the other girls had returned from Irish dancing. The Reverend Mother told us all to kneel down by our beds while she said some prayers with us. I noticed that some of the other girls didn't look too pleased to be praying again; they probably thought they already spent more than enough time on their knees. The Reverend Mother went on to explain what had happened to me in the toilet and that our prayers were to be offered up for the Reillys' father, to get him into Heaven. Some of the seniors threw me disgusted looks. I felt awful at being the cause of their extra prayers and worried that some of them might try to get back at me.

As we prayed, I wondered if my father would appear to me again, and if he did, would I see more of him than just his boots? I hoped I'd see him again and was determined to try to talk to him the next time. Now I knew it was him, I was sure I wouldn't be at all afraid. Perhaps he might even have a message for me. The Reverend Mother kept us praying for quite some time before she was happy that we had done all we could for Mr Reilly.

After she had left the room, I heard some of the girls saying that I was a freak, which was hurtful. It was clear that they were annoyed with me for getting them extra prayers, but after what had happened with the toilet door, this made me even more of an outsider. I was often called a freak after that. Still, Chrissie, my best friend, was fascinated, and as soon as we were alone, I told her all about it. She thought I was really special to have seen something like that and said that the other girls were probably jealous of my powers, or frightened of them. I was so glad to have a friend like Chrissie.

CHAPTER 8

Christmas

Carol practice was coming to an end, and Sister Francis, who was conducting us, seemed pleased with our efforts. We had no idea what her arm-waving gestures meant or why she bothered with them, since they made absolutely no difference to the way we sang and made her look ridiculous. Still, our harmonies sounded good.

We were singing 'Silent Night' when Sister Kevin and Sister Thomas entered the hall. They stood quietly by the door, their heads bowed reverently as they listened. Eventually, the bell sounded for dinner and we moved into lines.

'Not you, Reilly!' Sister Thomas called out. 'You come with me.'

What now? I tried to think of something I'd said or done that could have got me into trouble, but nothing came to mind. If I could only think what it might be, then perhaps I could come up with an explanation. As I waited for the others to leave the hall, I became really worried and could feel my body trembling. Some of the girls gave me

109

discomfiting looks, as if to say, 'What did you do?'

As the last girl left, Loretta and Sinéad walked in. I breathed a sigh of relief. I wasn't in trouble. Then, suddenly, it dawned on me what this was all about. We hadn't seen our mammy since the day she'd left us outside the convent, but every year, just before Christmas, a tea chest filled to the top with presents would arrive from England. I used to imagine that it took her a whole year of scrimping and saving to fill it up.

The time had come around again to go through the yearly ritual of seeing what she'd sent us, without being allowed to keep any of it. There was always three of every-thing – three dolls, three selection boxes and three sets of clothes. Each item would be taken out and shown to us, and once we'd had a good look at everything, the nuns would confiscate it, telling us it was going to 'a more deserving cause'. I never quite understood why they bothered to show us the gifts in the first place, but even though we wouldn't be getting any of it, I did like to know what Mammy had sent.

We followed the nuns to a storeroom where there was a large tea chest covered in stamps, with an address written in hand-writing that I'd come to recognise. It seemed odd to me that even though I didn't know what our mammy looked like, I knew her handwriting straight away.

The tea chest was our only evidence that she existed, that she still thought about us and perhaps, one day, would come for us. A strange feeling came over me as I stared at it. I wanted to get as close to it as possible because our mammy's hands had touched it and everything inside it. I experienced a rush of sadness. Why had she never come back for us, not even for a visit?

Inside the chest was a letter. Sister Thomas opened it. All letters that came to the convent had to be read first by a nun, who would decide if they should then be handed on to the girls. It was the same rule for letters going out. If the nuns didn't approve of them, they wouldn't be posted.

Sister Francis lifted a large box out of the chest. 'This one has your name on it, Loretta Reilly,' she said, placing it on the floor.

My mouth dropped open. Standing inside the box was the most beautiful doll that I had ever seen. Dressed like a bride, it was as big as Sinéad, with curly blonde hair that looked like real hair and could be brushed into different hairstyles. The face was Delft porcelain. The eyes looked so real that they seemed to be staring straight at me.

Sister Kevin pulled out two much smaller boxes, about a third of the size of Loretta's, and handed one to Sinéad and the other to me. Inside my box was a small black doll with little gold earrings and short black hair. I looked across to see what Sinéad had got – a doll the same size as mine but with a pink dress and long yellow hair. Our dolls were nice, and I tried to look pleased, but I was deeply disappointed that they didn't compare to Loretta's. I looked back at the beautiful bride doll, with its gorgeous satin dress and shoes to match, and I couldn't help but think that our mammy must love Loretta the most.

It was the same with all the gifts. Loretta got the biggest and the best, while Sinéad's and mine were smaller. There were boxes of chocolates, selection boxes, dolls' clothes, puzzles and games, a mixture of other toys and lots of clothes. Everything was really lovely, but all I could focus on was the big doll. Sinéad didn't seem to be looking at anything else, either, and I assumed she was feeling the same as I was.

I put my arm around her and said, 'Your doll's lovely, too.'

She said nothing but seemed to be on the verge of tears.

Sister Thomas told us that Mammy had written to say that she would try to come to see us but 'was finding it hard at present'.

That's what she always writes, I thought. Usually, I believed her words, but this time I didn't want to get my hopes up only to have them dashed again.

'Now, put your dolls down on this table and get yourselves back to the other girls for dinner,' Sister Kevin said. 'These presents will go to children more deserving of them.'

'They've got no right to take our stuff,' Loretta muttered angrily as we walked away.

'It's not fair. Nothing's fair,' I sobbed, wiping away my tears.

Sinéad didn't speak. She just walked along with her head down.

'Come on now, we have to be strong. We'll get out of here one day, I promise ye, and I hope it won't be too long till it happens,' Loretta said, trying to cheer us up. For the moment it seemed to do the trick. We wiped our eyes and put on a brave face before joining the others in the refectory.

One glance at my plate of stew made me feel sick, and I began to wish I'd missed dinner. As usual there was no sign of meat on the plate. I shunted the fat and gristle around with my fork, dreading the moment I'd have to put it in my mouth.

'Ye'd think, by now, that we'd be used to eating this slop,' I said.

'Ye never get used to it,' Mary said, from across the table.

'I bet ye the nuns wouldn't eat it,' added Rita.

'I'll never eat one bit of fat ever again when I get out of this place,' I vowed.

Normally, I ate what was in front of me

without complaint. After all, what was the point in moaning? It wouldn't change anything. But today I couldn't stop thinking about Loretta's beautiful bridal doll and was consumed by the awful suspicion that our mammy didn't care as much about Sinéad and me as she did about Loretta. I also found myself thinking about my older sister, Marie, whom I'd never met.

A few days earlier someone had smuggled in a Christmas card from Marie, which Loretta had hidden. It seemed strange to be getting a card from a sister that I didn't know, and I'd been thinking about her a lot over the last few days. What did she look like? Did she think about us often? Did the nuns at her convent hate her as much as the Reillys were hated here? And why had our mammy put us in separate convents, instead of keeping us all together?

Right now I was wondering if Marie also got presents at Christmas, and whether she'd received a bridal doll like Loretta's. I felt myself starting to get jealous of Marie. I'd always believed that our mammy loved us all the same, but now I wasn't sure.

I'd made endless excuses to the other girls for why she never came to visit. She was too sick, I'd say, or she lived so far away that she couldn't afford the fare. I'd repeated these excuses so often that I'd begun believing them myself, but now I wondered what was true. If our mammy really loved us, she would visit us, wouldn't she?

Picking up on my despair, Mary said, 'I'll eat that for ye, Frances, and ye can do me a favour one day when I need help. Put it on my plate when we're not being watched.'

I felt my face light up. 'Are ye sure, Mary?' We weren't close, so I was shocked that she would want to eat my disgusting food for me.

'Yeh, I'm sure. Now hurry up before I change my mind.'

Glancing furtively behind me, I scraped my dinner onto her plate and watched in amazement as she cut up the fat and gristle and swallowed each piece, without chewing it, until the plate was empty.

CHAPTER 9

The Farm

'Come with me, Reilly,' Sister Thomas's spiteful voice sent a shiver through me.

What had I done wrong this time? 'Yes, Sister.' I jumped to my feet and threw my scrubbing brush into a bucket.

She walked briskly ahead along the corridor, and I had to run to keep up. Girls weren't supposed to run, so I was lucky she didn't notice. On the other hand, I'd be in trouble if I didn't match her pace. My knees were aching, and my hands were frozen, wrinkled and wet. I wiped them on my skirt as I hurried along.

Soon we arrived at a large, unfamiliar room, where groups of nuns stood at big wooden trestle tables sorting through all manner of items donated to the convent. Most of it was children's clothing, but there were also boxes of toys, bedding and all sorts of other knick-knacks. On one table, I spotted some really pretty dresses; on another, a beautiful coat, and I thought how wonderful it would be to change out of my drab convent clothes and to dress like an ordinary child for once. Sister Thomas must have read my thoughts.

'You won't be getting anything like that to wear, Reilly, so take your eyes off them.'

She told a small, thin nun that a good Catholic family from outside Belfast was taking me out, and I needed some sensible clothes, plus a small suitcase, 'but nothing too fancy, mind, she's one of the Reillys'. The thin nun gave Sister Thomas a significant look and wandered off to a huge cupboard where she began picking out skirts and jumpers. Sister Thomas told me to strip down to my underwear. Soon the other nun was back with an armful of clothes.

'Try these on,' she said.

Sister Thomas selected the items she felt were appropriate for a Reilly, The thin nun returned with a small, tattered but functional brown suitcase, which she handed to Sister Thomas, and a coat, which she gave to me. The coat was double-breasted, beige, with a brown collar and six large brown buttons. It felt heavy and itched against my bare arms and legs, but I didn't mind a bit. Not only was it much better quality than anything I normally wore, but it was also a symbol of the world outside the convent.

'That will do fine,' Sister Thomas said to the thin nun. She packed the clothes into the suitcase, along with a hairbrush, comb and toothbrush, closed the case and handed it to me. 'Take this to the dormitory and wait there for me.'

On my way to the dormitory I passed a group of girls working on their knees. Each girl had a bucket by her side and a large wooden scrubbing brush in her hand. The familiar smell of Jeyes Fluid filled my nostrils. The girls stared up at me as I walked by with my suitcase and coat, as if to say, 'Where are you going?' But no one dared speak. I felt very strange. It was clear that I was going somewhere, but I had no idea where.

I wondered whether Loretta or Sinéad were coming with me. Although we were often kept apart inside the convent, it was comforting to know that they were close at hand, and I'd got used to Sinéad being with me again since she'd moved up to the juniors. To be separated by many miles, and perhaps for several days, was a frightening prospect, but I tried to push the idea out of my mind.

The dormitory was empty, I put the suitcase on the floor and placed the coat neatly at the bottom of my bed, then sat on the edge of the bed and waited, feeling quite bewildered. A few minutes later Mary came in to get something from her locker.

'Are you getting out?' she asked.

'Yes. I think it's for the weekend, but I don't know for sure.'

'Well, good luck. I wish it was me.' She

seemed even more fed up than usual, which didn't surprise me – we all had our own dream of what it would be like to get out, and seeing someone else going, no matter how pleased you might be for them, made you feel even more trapped.

Mary left, and I sat alone waiting for Sister Thomas, worrying about what might happen next. After about half an hour I heard the approach of heavy footsteps. I jumped up, tidied the bedding and was waiting smartly by the bed when she entered the room.

'You're staying on a farm for the weekend with a family called the Murphys. You will be on your best behaviour, Reilly! You will say nothing bad about the good sisters who have taken you in off the street and cared for you. Do you understand?'

'Yes, Sister.'

I tried to picture where I was going, what would I see and whom I'd meet. I was apprehensive but also very excited. I found it hard to imagine what the countryside looked like, although I'd formed a rough idea from talking to the other girls, most of whom came from rural backgrounds.

'Remember, God watches you all the time, and we will be getting reports from the Murphys.'

She didn't seem happy that I was going on a trip and continued with her list of instructions. Mostly it comprised things I was not to talk about and how to answer questions. I listened carefully. I didn't want to get anything wrong, as I was terrified about what Sister Thomas would do if the Murphys said anything bad about me. They were obviously friends of the convent, so I was going to have to pretend that the nuns were great.

Just as I was beginning to feel that the list of dos and don'ts would last forever, she said, 'Get ready now, they will be here soon.' She placed the suitcase on my bed and opened it. Fumbling about inside it, she pulled out a set of clothing. 'Put these on. Quickly, Reilly! I'll be back for you when they arrive. And don't forget all I've told you. God is watching you, Reilly,'

I breathed a sigh of relief as she left – at least now I knew what was happening. As I got dressed, I went over everything she'd said. The list of instructions was long, and I couldn't remember everything, but the general idea was clear enough. I was to make out that the Poor Sisters of Nazareth were angels and that all the girls, especially the Reillys, were so grateful and lucky to have been taken in and looked after by them. If it weren't for the nuns, where would we be?

Sister Thomas needn't have worried. In spite of how much I hated the nuns, especially her, I'd been in the convent long enough to know the rules and understand that it was pointless trying to go against them. No one would believe me if I said anything bad against the Poor Sisters. And if I dared to criticise them, I knew I'd be severely beaten.

Suddenly feeling sick, I sat on the edge of the bed wondering why I wasn't happy and excited to be getting out of the convent for the first time. But putting on the strange clothes had made me feel like a different person – the yellow dress and white cardigan felt good but alien to me. For as long as I could remember I'd worn nothing but regulation convent clothing, so wearing something different was going to take some getting used to. In fact, I was so preoccupied with my new outfit that I didn't notice Loretta come into the dormitory. Standing right in front of me, she held out her hands to give me a hug.

'I heard you were getting out for the weekend. Take care of yourself now, and bring me something back if you can.'

We hugged, and suddenly, I felt a whole lot better.

'If I don't see Sinéad, tell her that I'll try to bring something back for her, too – and that I'll see her as soon as I can after the weekend,' I said.

'I will. Now you go on and enjoy yourself. I'd better be gone. I'm not supposed to be here. 'Bye, Frances.' Loretta dashed off.

I was used to our brief meetings – she'd become skilled at sneaking away to find

Sinéad or me. If caught, she would be in big trouble, but the risk was worth it. Explaining to the nuns that she was just saying goodbye would have been a waste of time, though. What did they care? No sooner had she left the dormitory than Sister Thomas returned.

'They're here for you. Now remember, Reilly, don't embarrass the convent. Follow me!'

I picked up the suitcase and coat and followed her down several flights of stairs towards the entrance hall. As we approached the main door, I saw the Reverend Mother talking to a middle-aged man. The man was holding a cap in one hand and a pipe in the other.

I waited quietly next to Sister Thomas, a few feet away from the Reverend Mother and the man. I looked briefly at him but was afraid of being caught staring, so instead raised my eyes to the big statue of Our Lady, who seemed to be gazing directly at me with her sad stone eyes. Soon I sneaked another glance at the man. He wore heavy brown trousers, plain brown shoes and a worn tweed jacket. His hands were huge. I wondered if all farmers had big hands. His hair was short and silvery grey; he was big and tall but well built rather than fat.

'Ah, here she is at last. This is Frances Reilly. If you have any problems with her, just bring her straight back.'

The Reverend Mother spoke as if they'd been waiting around for me all day. The man leant over and picked up my suitcase. The Reverend Mother swept off down the corridor.

'Now, Frances,' Sister Thomas said in a markedly different tone to normal. 'Put your coat on, and I'll see you to the gate.'

I was so shocked by her change in manner that I couldn't help but stare at her. We were never called by our first names, and it was really strange to hear her talking that way, as if she cared. The man took me by the hand, and we followed Sister Thomas along a gravel path to the main gate, where they said their goodbyes and God blesses. We stepped outside, and the gate closed behind us.

I listened to the sound of the gate being locked from the inside. It felt very strange to be locked out of the walls, rather than inside them. Also, this was the first time I'd been on the road into Belfast since the day, six years before, when I'd last seen my mother. As I watched the cars go by, I couldn't help but think back to that day with an over-whelming sense of loss. I missed my mother and two brothers and wondered if I'd ever see them again. I glanced across the road to the Good Shepherd Convent, home to Marie, the older sister I'd never met. Just as I was beginning to wonder about her, the stranger holding my hand said, 'I'm Tom

Murphy, and you're Frances, is that right?'

'Yes,' I said, trying to get used to being called by my first name.

Mr Murphy explained that we were going on a bus and then a train to Moira, where he lived on a small farm with his brother, Barry, his brother's wife, Siobhan, and their children. He said he was Uncle Tom to everyone who knew him and that he'd love it if I called him that, too. I liked the idea of having someone to call uncle, as I hadn't had anyone apart from my sisters to think of as family until then.

It felt nice to hold his hand, and I started to feel part of something other than the convent, but then my heart sank as I realised that Loretta and Sinéad weren't going to like this – they weren't going to be part of this uncle. Suddenly, I felt awful and wished that my sisters were with me. I told Uncle Tom about them, hoping that he could get them out, too, but although he showed some interest in what I was saying, he made it clear that there was only room for me.

'Just one convent girl, to help out the Poor Sisters, who are so kind,' he said, like it was going to get him into Heaven.

We came to a bus stop and didn't have to wait long for the bus to arrive. Tom guided me to the seats at the back of the bus, and I watched, fascinated, as the conductor walked down the aisle collecting fares and issuing tickets. When he got to us, Tom asked for one and one-half to the station. The conductor rolled out the tickets.

'Is this your wee girl? Isn't she well behaved,' he said, smiling down at me. I smiled back.

'She's one of those orphans from the convent. I've got her out for the weekend,' Tom said.

The other passengers turned and looked at Tom like he was some kind of martyr. A women shouted out, 'God bless ye, mister.'

I was embarrassed, but Tom appeared to love the attention and he nodded at them, saying, 'Thank you, thank you.'

I lowered my head to hide my face. When I raised it again, people were smiling at me with pity in their eyes. I didn't much feel like smiling back, so I sat with my gaze riveted to the floor.

The bus stopped several times before I lifted my head again. Various people had got on and off, and no one was staring any more. Feeling better, I looked out of the window and tried to enjoy the journey, and it wasn't long before we arrived at the train station. I was transfixed by the sight of so many people rushing around and thought how great it must be to be able to do what you wanted and go where you pleased. I envied those people their freedom and wondered if I would ever become one of them.

Tom guided me off the bus and into the station. He seemed to know his way about and told me that we'd have to hurry to the platform because the train was about to go. I held on to him tightly as we rushed through the crowds. On the platform, a guard was hurrying people into the train and closing doors behind them. Tom lifted me up and into a seat.

Opposite us sat a middle-aged woman with shopping bags and a young girl. Before long Tom was explaining that he'd just picked up an orphan from Nazareth House for the weekend. The woman seemed really interested and told Tom how wonderful she thought he was for taking me in. She went to her purse, took out a few coins and told him to buy me some sweets. Looking around the carriage, I again saw that look of pity in people's eyes. My face grew hot and red, and I wanted to disappear. It was clear that Tom wasn't going to miss an opportunity to introduce me as his little weekend orphan girl. I hated that word, 'orphan', and would have been a lot happier if he hadn't kept describing me that way, I could have pretended that I was a normal child out with my uncle for the weekend, instead of feeling like an animal at the zoo. I tried to block out the staring faces by turning my attention to the view.

The train had left Belfast and was now travelling through the countryside. I'd been too young when I entered the convent to have any clear memories of life outside its walls, so almost everything I saw through the window was new to me. I was amazed, completely blown away by the wonder of it. Everything was so green. I'd never seen large wooded areas before or fields full of crops or meadows. There were sheep in the grassy fields, black-and-white cows and, occasionally, pigs – and I'd never seen any of those before either, not even in pictures. There were no animals in the convent, and I don't remember seeing any picture books. At the age of eight, possibly the only animal I could recognise, apart from a cat or a dog, was a donkey. And that was only because Jesus had ridden one into Jerusalem.

Some of the girls had talked about horses, and I wondered if there would be any at Tom's farm. I loved the idea of horses. I tried to imagine the farm and the rest of Tom's family. Tom seemed to like me, but would they? I hoped so. I was enjoying being out of the convent and didn't want anything to spoil that feeling.

The journey seemed to last ages, and I was glad when the train arrived at Moira. Tom told me that it was a bit of a walk to the farm, but that it would do us good and on the way we could stop at the shops. He said that he wanted some tobacco for his pipe and that I could buy sweets with the money I'd been given. I didn't mind the walk, especially when we got on to the country roads. I loved looking at the cows and sheep in the fields on the way. Soon we came to a row of houses, one of which had been converted into a shop. The shopkeeper seemed to know Tom really well.

'Is this the wee orphan, Tom?' she said, as if I couldn't hear.

They chatted for a while before Tom bought his tobacco and some sweets for his niece, nephews and me. From here, he told me, it was now only a ten-minute walk to the house. We made our way through open farmland past several small farms. I couldn't believe how different – how full of life – the landscape was, compared to the drab, dark brick walls of the convent. The greenness of the fields dazzled my eyes; I wanted to study every animal we passed.

'Here we are, then,' said Tom, pointing to a bungalow at the end of a long drive. Next to the bungalow was a farmyard complete with small outbuildings, barns and several animal pens. He took me by the hand and led me up a path towards the front of the house. Brightly coloured flowers lined both sides of the path, and a sweet fragrance filled the air. As we came closer to the bungalow, I saw young faces peering through the windows.

Tom walked me round to a door at the back. 'Only friends and family come through the back door,' he said with a warm smile.

The hot kitchen was filled with the lovely smell of home cooking. Freshly baked loaves and rolls rested on cooling trays on a large table. I'd never smelt anything so good in my life and suddenly felt extremely hungry. A jolly-looking plump woman was bending over to put some pies into a very hot oven.

Straightening up, she said, 'Ah, you must be Frances. Come over and sit yourself down here. I'll get yous a wee tea and something to eat. You must be starving after your journey. I'm Siobhan, and I'm sure we're going to get on just fine.' She pulled a chair out from under the table.

Smiling shyly, I sat down. Tom pulled out a chair for himself, took a wooden pipe from his pocket and began to fill it with the tobacco he'd bought. He seemed wonderfully content as he struck a match and puffed to keep the pipe lit. I couldn't help staring. I hadn't realised that a pipe could bring someone so much pleasure. I found myself liking the pipe smell because it wasn't a convent smell.

Siobhan and Tom discussed the whereabouts of the other members of the family while she buttered bread and filled the kettle. Her round face was red from the heat of the kitchen, and her apron was covered in flour, which sprinkled over the stone floor whenever she moved. Her light-brown hair was held up in a bun at the back of her head, and after an afternoon of hot baking, loose strands were now stuck to her perspiring face and neck. It wasn't long before she'd prepared sandwiches, scones, cakes and mugs of tea.

'Eat up now, Frances. You look like you could do with a bit of meat on you,' she said, pushing a plate across the table.

Careful not to show up the nuns, I blessed myself and thanked God for the wonderful food. Then, very politely, I began to eat my sandwiches and drink my tea.

'Your manners are wonderful. The good sisters are doing such a good job with all these wee orphans they take in, don't ye think so, Tom?'

'They're doing a grand job, Siobhan. I hope the girls appreciate it. Where would they be if it weren't for the Church?'

I said nothing, not wanting to be sent back to the convent.

For me, the food was a feast. Everything tasted so wonderful compared to the convent food, and I ate until I couldn't fit any more in. I blessed myself again and thanked God for providing the food. Then I took my cup and plate to the large square sink under the kitchen window.

'Just put them on the draining board,' Siobhan said.

The back door opened, and a man walked

in, banging the door behind him. He panted and puffed as he struggled to remove his wellies.

'This is Barry, my husband,' Siobhan told me. 'He's been working on the farm. Tom will show you around later. Do you like animals?'

'Yes, I think so. I'm not sure.' I felt embarrassed and went red. It seemed such a simple question. Surely I should know if I liked animals or not, but the fact was, I'd never come into contact with any.

'Never mind,' said Barry. 'You'll like them well enough before you go back to the good sisters.' He sat down, still breathing heavily.

Siobhan poured him a mug of tea and put it on the table in front of him. Barry was different to his brother. Both men were big, but much of Barry's bulk was clearly the result of overeating, and he obviously loved his wife's cooking. His belly pushed his braces so far apart that they sat on either side of it, instead of going over his shoulders and straight down the front.

I listened while the two men talked, mostly about horse-racing. Tom said he'd put the bets on and that the bookies had been packed. Barry looked excited as Tom reached into his inside pocket and brought out some slips of paper. He said had a really good feeling about them.

I could hear children shouting in another

part of the bungalow. It sounded as if they were playing. Suddenly, Tom got up, disappeared out through a door and shouted at the kids to stop the racket and come and say hello to their visitor. He came back closely followed by three young boys. I put their ages at about six, seven and ten. All three were dressed in a similar fashion, with tank tops over their shirts and patches on the knees of their brown corduroy trousers.

'Hello,' said the oldest boy, smiling.

'Hello,' said the two younger ones.

'Hello,' I said. For a few seconds we stood around, staring at each other and feeling awkward.

'This is Jimmy, Sean and Jerome, my youngest three boys,' said Barry, pointing them out. I could see he was very proud of them. 'You'll meet Edward and Declan and Maggie later. And this is Frances,' he added. 'She'll be staying with us for a wee while. Now put on your wellies and we'll show her around the farm.'

The boys raced across the room and, after much pushing and shoving, recovered their boots from a pile next to the back door. Meanwhile, Barry pulled himself to his feet using the kitchen table for support. Jerome brought over his dad's wellies and put them down in front of him. Still gripping on to the table, Barry stepped into them. It seemed to take a huge effort, and he was out of breath by the time he'd walked out of the back door with the boys in tow. Tom tagged along, holding my hand.

The first thing I noticed was a loud squealing, the second was an awful smell. Tom explained that this was a pig farm and that there were a lot of newly born piglets. The squealing got louder as we approached a sty – and the smell became almost un-bearable. I put my hand up to cover my nose, which helped a bit but not much. The baby pigs were lovely, but I didn't like the look of the big ones. Some of them looked really mean. None of the Murphys seemed to notice the smell or the noise.

Next to the pigsties were two large old barns full of bales of hay. The bales were stacked up high, with a gap at the top. Rest-ing up against one of the haystacks was a long wooden ladder.

'Do ye want to go up and see where the cat has its kittens?' Jerome asked me.

'Yes!' I followed him up the ladder and across the hay. 'They're just here,' he said, pointing.

A black cat was curled up on a tartan blan-ket with five tiny kittens nestled around her.

'They're only a week old,' said a voice behind me. Not wanting to miss out, Jimmy and Sean had climbed up to join us.

I loved being up so high on the hay, and the smell was much cleaner. 'They're lovely,'

I said softly, so as not to disturb them.

Jerome picked two of them up and handed them to me. They were so tiny and warm. I stroked them for a minute and handed them back. Then Tom called for us to come back down the ladder again. I was down first, and as I watched the boys come after me, I was surprised to realise that I already felt comfortable with them. It was years since I'd even seen a boy, let alone talked to one.

Outside the barn, some hens and a few roosters ran freely, but the majority were secured in the chicken coop across from the barn.

'You can collect the eggs with me in the morning if you want,' said Tom, like it was a really exciting thing to do.

I smiled but said nothing; I didn't know if I wanted to get that close to the hens.

'Let's get inside. The racing will be on soon,' Barry wheezed.

The boys led me through the kitchen into the living room, where they got up onto a long brown-and-beige sofa that ran along the wall facing the fireplace. The fire was lit and framed by a tiled mantelpiece. To the left of the fireplace was a comfy armchair with cushions. To the right, in the corner of the room, there was a relatively new black-and-white television set. I'd never seen a television before, although some of the daygirls at the convent had them and talked about the programmes. I couldn't wait to watch some-thing.

Barry came in, pulled out a chair and sat himself down facing the television, with his betting slips beside him. Siobhan whispered to me that the chair by the fire was Tom's and he didn't like anyone else sitting in it. Then Tom came in, switched on the television and started messing about with the aerial. A crackly voice announced that the racing was coming up next.

'That's the best I can do,' he mumbled a minute or so later, returning to his chair by the fire. After rearranging his cushions and relighting his pipe, he looked over at me. 'Come and sit on my lap,' he said, holding out his arms.

I did as he asked and walked across to him. He lifted me up onto his knee. It was nice and warm over by the fire, and I sat contentedly, watching the telly. When the racing started, the boys rushed off to their room to play, but Tom and Barry couldn't take their eyes off the fuzzy screen, and soon both men grew tense and excited. The horses were being led into their boxes, ready for the start; they'd spotted the ones they had bets on and their eyes were glued to them.

The race began, and they shouted encour-agement, urging their horses to win. Barry looked as though he wouldn't be able to contain himself until the end of the race.

His face was flushed bright red and sweating. 'Come on boy, come on!' he kept shouting at the telly.

I couldn't tell who was winning but hoped that one of their horses won or else they might get into a bad mood. Suddenly, I became aware of Tom rubbing his hand up and down my leg. It made me feel very uncomfortable, especially when his hand went up under my dress. Turning to look at him, I was surprised to see his eyes still fixed on the television screen, as if nothing unusual were happening.

'I need to go to the toilet, please,' I said, jumping down off his knee.

'I'll show you where the bathroom is,' shouted Siobhan, coming in from the kitchen. She wiped her hands on her apron and led me out of the room.

When I got back, a smartly dressed young man in his early twenties was sitting on the couch – Edward, one of the older Murphy sons.

'And you must be Frances.' He shook me by the hand and began to tell me about himself and his job in town.

I had no idea of what to say back but found myself liking him straight away. He told me that the beautiful flowerbeds along the path to the bungalow were all his work. He spent the weekends tending them – plants were his passion, and he came to life when he spoke about them. I enjoyed listening to him talk and sensed that he was going to become a good friend.

Our conversation came to an abrupt end when Barry shouted, 'I've won, I've won!' and waved a betting slip around in front of Tom. One of his horses had come in first.

'Well done, Dad,' yelled Edward from the couch.

The younger boys all came running in, shouting, 'How much did you win, Dad?'

I wasn't used to this level of excitement around me. With everything else that had happened that day, it was becoming hard to take it all in. Barry wasn't saying how much he'd won, just that it was 'a good bit of money'. Siobhan came in to calm everyone down and tell us that dinner was ready.

Edward and his brothers ran to the kitchen, but Tom and Barry stayed to wait for the next race. I didn't know what to do, so I stayed on the couch. A few moments later, Siobhan arrived back with Barry's dinner and put it on the living-room table. She went out and reappeared with Tom's dinner, which she put on his knee.

'Would you like yours on a tray, Frances?' she said.

'Yes, please,' I said, although I was really quite reluctant to be left in the room with Tom.

A few moments later Siobhan came back

to the living room with a rather solemn-looking, overweight teenage girl.

'This is my daughter, Maggie. She's just back from town.'

I smiled at the plump teenager. 'Hello, I'm pleased to meet you,' I said politely.

Maggie tried to crack a smile, but it was clearly an effort. She didn't seem happy with the idea of me being in her home.

Siobhan told Maggie to go and have her dinner before it got cold. Mother and daughter disappeared into the kitchen. After such a long day the smell of good food was making me feel really hungry, so I was delighted when Siobhan returned with a tray for me. The large plate of real Irish stew looked and smelt great, and after a quick blessing I was soon tucking into it. It was scrumptious, a world away from convent food. I enjoyed every mouthful, and before long my plate was scraped clean. I sat for a while with the tray on my knee, feeling bloated and very happy to be out of the convent.

Barry and Tom finished their dinners and began shouting again at the telly. 'Come on boy! Come on, come on!' The race was nearly over, but I couldn't see the screen because they were both on their feet right in front of it. 'Come on, boy!' they shouted.

The race ended and their horse came in second, but they seemed happy enough. Edward came back and congratulated his father and uncle. Siobhan followed him in but didn't seem the least interested in the result. She took away my tray and praised me for eating all my dinner. 'That should fatten ye up,' she added.

Edward sat down next to me. 'There's a film on now,' he said. 'Would ye like sit on my knee to watch it?'

The boys came in from the kitchen and sat down wherever there was an empty space. I had no idea what a film was, but everyone seemed excited about it, so I felt sure it must be something good. In fact, I couldn't wait to see it. I liked Edward and would much rather sit with him than be anywhere near Tom, so I climbed onto his lap, and we made ourselves comfortable. I couldn't remember ever having felt so content.

Tom started messing around with the aerial again. The picture was perfect when he held it above his head, but as soon as he set it on top of the television, it went fuzzy again. This pantomime went on for several minutes, until eventually he was satisfied that the picture wasn't going to get any better. By this time *Singing in the Rain* had already started.

The film amazed me. The singing, dancing and music; all of it was new to me. In fact, almost everything that day had been a new experience. Everyone, except for Maggie, appeared engrossed. She, on the other hand, was sulking at the other end of the couch, wearing the same discontented expression she'd worn when she met me. Every now and then she'd let out a sigh and look at her parents for some sort of reaction, but they were either too caught up in the film to notice or deliberately ignoring her. At one point, our eyes met and she gave me a really bad look, as if to say, 'What are you doing here, with my family?' I quickly turned my attention back to the film.

It had been an exciting but exhausting day, and I found myself falling asleep on Edward's lap before the film had ended. I tried really hard to keep my eyes open but eventually gave in and let myself go, missing the final scenes. It was my first day out of the convent and my first day on a farm, and the sense of space and freedom had at times felt overwhelming, much as I had loved it. What's more, new faces were rare at the convent – the new girls generally arrived in ones or twos at irregular intervals – and today I'd met more people than I might normally meet in several months or even a year.

I loved the countryside, and of course the food was delicious. I'd never imagined that food could taste so wonderful. Apart from that brief incident with Tom, it had been an almost perfect day. But it had also been physically and emotionally exhausting, and I was so tired that I didn't stir when Edward lifted me up and carried me to bed.

CHAPTER 10

The Swing

Sometime during that first night my sleep was disturbed by a rocking motion, and I had a weird sense of something moving between the tops of my legs. Terrified, I opened my eyes. It was very dark, and for a minute or two I couldn't think where I was. Then I remembered that I was at the Murphys' farm. But obviously I wasn't asleep on Edward's knee any more. Instead, I was in bed with someone, and I didn't know who it was, although something told me it was either Tom or Barry, Whoever it was, they were naked and so was I.

I was petrified. Pretending to be asleep, I rolled over to the edge of the bed, away from whoever it was, but that just made things a whole lot worse. Suddenly, I found myself being lifted up and twisted around until I lay face down on the man's belly, my head resting on a musky, hairy chest. I wanted to scream out but was too frightened to make a sound. Instead, I rolled back onto the bed and lay as far away from him as I could get, hoping that he would just leave me to sleep.

'Frances, it's Uncle Tom, darling. Come on now, come for a nice cuddle.'

I said nothing. I felt his breath on my neck and shoulders. It smelt of stale tobacco and whisky, and I wanted to be sick. Once more I felt myself being lifted up and placed on his belly. His calloused hands stroked my back and buttocks, and he began to rock me, quite roughly, backwards and forwards against something long and hard between his legs.

'There now, that's my good girl.' He kept saying it, but everything about what was happening felt bad and wrong and nothing like a cuddle.

'No, I'm going to be sick in a minute,' I pleaded several times, but he took no notice. Instead, the rocking got faster. The springs in the bed made loud squeaking noises. I started to panic, and it felt like I was going to suffocate with fear and disgust.

'Just a wee while longer,' he said, still rocking me back and forth on top of his revolting sweaty body.

A few minutes later he rolled me onto the bed, where I lay quietly crying to myself. The bed went on rocking, and the springs continued to squeak – he was obviously still doing something. I didn't want to think about it. I shut my eyes really tight and tried to think about something else, but it was impossible to blank out what had just happened, even though I was used to being treated like I didn't matter. Oh, why was I born a Reilly? I wondered if life might have been different if I'd been called something else. Perhaps this was the reason bad stuff kept happening. The nuns always said, 'Reilly!' as if referring to a piece of shit, and that was exactly how I felt right now.

The bed stopped moving. I lay very still, praying that he wouldn't touch me again. He got up and left the room. The light shining from the hall made it easier to see around the room, and I took a good look at my surroundings. The furniture was old and didn't look right in the new bungalow. I made out a patchwork pattern on the bed cover. On a rickety bedside locker next to the bed was a collection of some of Tom's pipes, along with an ashtray and a mug. In the corner of the room, his clothes had been spread over a worn green armchair. Seeing them, I felt sick again. I heard the toilet flush and the sound of his footsteps coming back, so I closed my eyes and pretended to be asleep.

He shut the door, and the room returned to darkness. He fumbled about before he got back into the bed and then moved around, making himself comfortable. Finally, he began to snore, and I relaxed a little bit, although I knew that with everything that was going on in my head, sleep would come much harder to me than it had to Tom. Also, I was afraid to sleep, in case he woke up. But he didn't stir. He just lay there, snoring.

When daylight started to peek through the curtains, I sat up and scanned the room for my clothes. I really needed to get dressed. Unable to locate them, I started to panic. I had to find them before the house started to wake, before I could go to the toilet and, most importantly, before Tom woke up. I decided to sneak out of bed and have a better look around. My feet touched the floor, and I felt some bunched-up material beneath my soles. My clothes! I hadn't thought to look down there. Relieved, I dressed quickly and crept out of the bedroom down the hall to the bathroom, where I slid the lock across the door. There was no way I was leaving until the rest of the house got up.

With nothing to do but sit and think, the time passed really slowly, I was shattered and kept dozing off, so I grabbed one of the boy's dressing gowns from a hook on the back of the door, wrapped myself up in it and lay down on the floor to sleep. It didn't feel like I'd been there long when I heard the handle of the door being turned.

'I'll be out in a minute,' I shouted, jumping up and quickly returning the dressing gown to its hook. It was much lighter outside now. I smoothed down my hair and flushed the toilet.

'Is that ye in there, Frances?' Siobhan said.

I unlocked the door and was relieved to see her standing outside.

'Wait in the kitchen and I'll be there in a minute,' she said, stepping inside.

I moved as quietly as I could through the living room into the kitchen. No one else was up, which suited me. I wasn't ready to face the rest of the family yet. Careful not to make any noise, I sat on one of the chairs at the big kitchen table. I still felt very tired and fought to keep my eyes open and hold back my yawns. Lifting my arm onto the table, I used it as a pillow for my head, thinking that I would just rest for a few minutes until Siobhan came back. But by the time she returned, I was sound asleep.

'Come on now, wake up, Frances,' she said, gently shaking me.

I rubbed my eyes and tried to focus.

'Have ye had any sleep at all?' she asked, but I was too tired to respond.

She guided me into the living room and lay me on the couch. 'I'll get ye a cover and ye can lie here for a wee while.'

A few minutes later she tucked a blanket tightly around me.

When I woke up again, almost everyone was up. I heard voices in the kitchen – it sounded like Siobhan, Edward and Barry – and the younger boys were playing in the back bedroom. The gorgeous but unfamiliar smell of sizzling bacon wafted in from the kitchen. Silently raising my head, I surveyed the room. A fire had been lit, but thankfully I was alone. I snuggled back under the blanket, not wanting anyone to know I was awake yet. I definitely didn't want to face Tom. I felt dirty, used and guilty after what had happened in the night. I was also fairly certain that it was my fault it had happened because I was a Reilly, How was I going to get through the day? I didn't feel I could say anything to the family. It would be really embarrassing, and they probably wouldn't believe me. They might even call the nuns, and then I'd be in big trouble. And, anyway, for the moment it was nice where I was. I felt cosy and warm all snuggled up under the blanket.

It was almost lunchtime when I felt Siobhan shaking me again.

'Wake up now, Frances, there's some food for you in the kitchen.'

She'd prepared a proper full Irish breakfast of potato bread, soda bread, eggs, beans, sausages and bacon, with a big mug of tea to wash it all down. There didn't seem to be anyone else about. Siobhan explained that Edward was at work, Maggie had gone into town, and the others were working on the farm. I got tucked into my food, feeling sure that Siobhan must be the best cook ever.

'Did you have a problem sleeping in a

strange house?' she asked, sitting down next to me.

'Yes, I did.'

I carried on eating, unable to look her in the eye. I felt my ears burning and huddled over my breakfast, hoping that my face hadn't turned bright red – or that if it had, Siobhan wouldn't be able to see it. She didn't seem to notice and asked me what I'd like to do later.

Suddenly, she came up with the idea that I could go into town with Tom.

I smiled, struggling to hide my horror. 'Couldn't I stay here and help you?' I said.

But she insisted that I wouldn't want to be hanging about the house all day and that I should get some fresh air and exercise, which would help me sleep better. I hated the idea. I didn't ever want to see Tom again, but I couldn't get out of it. Siobhan had decided. Instantly losing my appetite, I put my knife and fork down on the table. I sipped my tea, hoping that it would stop me throwing up.

The back door opened, and Tom and Barry walked in, stopping to pull off their wellies.

'So you've decided to get up, then, lazybones,' said Tom in a jovial voice.

Excusing myself from the table, I rushed to the bathroom and locked the door behind me. I felt awful. My stomach churned, beads of sweat broke out on my face, and very soon I threw up my breakfast. Siobhan knocked at the door asking if I was OK. I called out that I was fine and heard her walking back to the kitchen. I cleaned the splashes from around the toilet seat and tried to make myself look more presentable, brushing my teeth and hair and rinsing my face with cold water. I felt a little better now, but seeing Tom in the kitchen had filled me with disgust, and I couldn't shake the feeling off. Someone tried the door.

'Just finished!' I shouted, flushing the toilet. I opened the door. Barry was outside.

On my way back to the kitchen, I passed the living room and saw Tom through the doorway sitting in his chair by the fire, a mug of tea in one hand and his pipe in the other. I tried to walk past unnoticed, but he called out to me just as I reached the kitchen door. Reluctantly, I turned around, my head bowed. I peered at him from beneath my fringe, unable to bring myself to look at him directly.

'Come and sit for a minute,' he said, patting his lap. Feeling helpless, and very alone, I walked slowly towards him, despair and disgust coursing through my body. He leant forward and lifted me onto his knee. 'So we're going to town. If you're a good girl, I'll buy you something nice, what do you think you would like?' He bounced me up and down on his lap.

'I don't know,' I whispered, without meeting his eye.

I was hoping that Siobhan would appear when I felt his hand rubbing up and down my leg. I froze. He paused for a second and then slid his hand up under my skirt, pushing up between my legs until his fingers were inside my knickers. He began touching and rubbing me. I wanted to scream out, but instead I sat there paralysed, unable to move a muscle.

Barry came into the room, and Tom immediately removed his hand and relit his pipe as if nothing had happened. Barry switched on the television to see the news and weather. The younger boys came in from playing outside. Everything seemed happy and normal again.

The whole family seemed to love and respect Tom. I found the courage to climb down off his knee and sit with the boys, who were planning to make a swing with some rope and an old tractor tyre. They'd picked out a good tree and were really excited about it. Jerome said that I could have a go when I got back from town. It sounded like great fun, and I couldn't wait. Barry offered to help put it up after lunch.

Before long, Tom and I set out along the narrow country roads to Moira. Tom held my hand as we kept to the grass verge on the side of the road, even though there was little traffic. I felt awkward and desperately wanted to pull away, but it was impossible. My childish hand was tiny, and he had a very strong grip. Being out in the country-side again should have been wonderful, but being with Tom dampened my spirits, and I felt unable to enjoy the experience. Neither of us said much as we walked along.

The town was packed with shoppers. Everyone seemed to know Tom, and he stopped to talk to quite a few people. Once again I had to listen to him explaining that I was from Nazareth House Convent. Once again people looked down at me with sympathetic expressions on their faces. It was humiliating. A woman gave me a half-crown and a man gave me sixpence. Tom said that I could hold on to the money while we decided what I should buy.

First we stopped off at the butcher's shop. Tom obviously knew the butcher well, and they chatted for some time. As before, Tom began by telling him about me. Meanwhile I inspected the shop. I liked the look of the meat in the trays and the smell of sawdust, which was thickly layered on the floor. I noticed the butcher had given Tom some extra sausages, free with his order.

'God bless ye,' said Tom as we walked out.

It was much the same story in every shop

we went to. By now I'd stopped listening, instead focusing on the shops and the other shoppers. I was fascinated. This was my first glimpse of how normal people lived, and it was very different to my own reality. These people had so much more than I did, and I envied them that, but most of all I envied them their freedom. No one here was being forced to do anything they really didn't want to do, and I wished I could be free like the children around me, who were nicely dressed and asking their parents for things I could never dream of having. How well off they all were. It was hard not to be jealous.

Finally, we came to a clothes shop. Tom added some money to the money I'd been given and I bought two pairs of white ankle socks, one to wear to Mass in the morning. They looked so much better than the socks I had on. Thrilled, I carried them all the way back to the farm.

Back at the bungalow, Siobhan was in the kitchen with Maggie, who was sitting at the table, her face screwed up, giving me the dirtiest looks she could manage. I couldn't understand what I'd done wrong. Tom sat down on one of the kitchen chairs and lifted me onto his knee, at which Maggie gave me her worst look yet and stormed out of the kitchen in a really foul mood. Shortly afterwards, Siobhan followed her out.

I asked Tom if I could see the boys' swing.

'They'll be in the field past the pigsties,' he said, adding that he'd come along in a while to have a look himself.

I jumped off his knee and ran out through the back door, past the barns and pigsties towards a tree in the next field, where I could just about make out the boys. It felt fantastic to be running because it was forbidden to run in the convent. For the first time in my life I felt as if I'd been set free. As I got closer to the tree, I saw a big tractor tyre swinging back and forth, with Sean sitting inside it.

Sean hung onto the rim of the tyre, shouting at his dad to give him another push. Barry obliged as best he could but was soon out of breath. Excusing himself, he huffed and puffed his way back to the house for a drink. I watched him go, wondering if he'd make it, but the boys didn't seem concerned. They were obviously used to seeing their dad like that, so I relaxed and turned my attention back to the swing.

'Do ye wanna go?' said Sean, jumping off. 'We'll push ye.'

I inspected the swing. The rope looked strong and was securely attached to a thick branch of the tree. 'OK, then.'

The boys helped me up, and I grabbed hold of the tyre, then they gave me a push and I began to swing through the air in great swoops. It was scary at first, but once I'd got used to it, I couldn't get enough, even though sometimes they pushed so hard that I thought I was going to smash into the tree trunk. Jerome said they weren't doing it on purpose. It was just that I was so light and easy to push. I laughed and screamed as I sped through the air. It was the most exciting thing I'd ever done, and such fun. For the moment, at least, I wasn't worried about the convent, Tom, my sisters or anything. I wished that life could be like this all the time.

Eventually, I got down and sat on the grass to watch the boys have a go. Hearing voices behind me, I turned and saw Edward and Tom, who'd come to see the swing. In his collar and tie, Edward looked as though he'd arrived straight from work. He was impressed with the swing and offered to give anyone who wanted it a push after dinner. The boys replied with an immediate and very excited 'Yes!'

'Come on now, your dinner is just about ready,' said Tom, steadying the rope and tyre.

Edward smiled at me and held out his hand, which I willingly took. I chatted happily to him as we walked back to the house, telling him all about my trip into town, the shops, the people, the money and, most importantly, the socks, which I was very pleased with.

Edward smiled down at me. 'Uncle Tom is very fond of you. I'm glad you had a good day,.

I dropped my gaze, suddenly silent and solemn. I really wanted to say how I felt about Tom but sensed it would mean that Edward and I would no longer be friends – and I didn't want that to happen.

'Are you OK? You've gone really quiet.'

I nodded.

When we got to the bungalow, the back door was open, and we went into the kitchen. I could see straight away that Siobhan had been busy. Her face was red, her apron ruffled and stained, and a wonderful smell filled the room. I felt instantly hungry and was delighted when she put my dinner on a tray and told me that I could have it on the couch with Edward. Edward carried my tray into the living room and then went back to fetch his own.

I inspected the contents of my very full plate – potatoes, vegetables and homemade meat pie with loads of gravy. It looked and smelt delicious.

'Don't just look at it! Eat it up before it gets cold,' Edward said, coming back into the room with his own dinner.

Tom and Barry arrived, followed by Siobhan, who was carrying their trays. Tom turned on the television, and we watched a western while we ate.

When he'd finished his meal, Edward announced that he was going to look over his flowerbeds.

'Would you like to come with me, Frances? I'll tell you the names of some of the flowers.'

I had about as much experience of flowers as I did of animals, but I didn't hesitate. 'I'd love to!'

The flowerbeds were blooming and didn't look as though they needed any attention, but Edward checked through them carefully, ripping out a weed here and there. He showed me where the weeds were so that I could help. I was thrilled. I was already very fond of Edward, and it was exciting to be allowed to help with something that was obviously very important to him. But my euphoria ended the instant I encountered a worm. Screaming, I jumped backwards out of the flowerbed. Edward laughed when he realised what all the commotion was about. I hadn't known until then that I hated – in fact positively detested – worms.

'I'll just watch from here,' I said, feeling rather embarrassed.

Edward carried on weeding, and I looked on from the relative safety of the path. I loved the colours and fragrances of the flowers and enjoyed listening to him talking about them. I thought that he must be really clever to know so much. By the time he'd finished, it was starting to get cold, and I was happy to go back inside. The others were still in the living room watching the western, and apart from gunshots and whoops, the house was quiet. Edward and I stayed in the kitchen. We'd missed most of the film, and he didn't want to disturb the others with our chatter, so he made a pot of tea and cut us both a big piece of Siobhan's homemade cake.

'I wish my sisters were with me,' I said. 'They would love this cake.'

'Maybe you could take some back for them.'

I didn't explain that the nuns would confiscate it and my sisters would never get to eat it.

'No, that's OK,' I said, thinking how hard it would be to conceal. It wasn't like I could put it down my shoe or in my dress; there would be nothing left but crumbs. The thought made me smile, and I took another bite.

Siobhan came in and said that I should have a bath so that I was clean for Mass in the morning.

'I'll call you when I've run the water. Meanwhile you can find your nightdress,' she said as she left the kitchen.

Suddenly, I felt awful. Consumed by the horror of the previous night, all I could think about was bedtime and Tom. How, I wondered, could I avoid another night like that? In my desperation I blurted out, 'Can I sleep at the bottom of your bed tonight, Edward, please?'

He looked a bit surprised and explained that his was just a single bed and there wouldn't be enough room for me, as he took up most of the space.

'Uncle Tom doesn't mind you sleeping in with him. He has a nice big bed. Anyway, you don't want to hurt his feelings, do you? He might think you don't like him any more.'

My heart sank to the pit of my stomach, but I tried to force a smile.

Siobhan called me, and I hurried off to find my nightie. In the bathroom, she helped me out of my clothes and lifted me into the water, which was warm and clear, nothing like the dark-brown convent water I was used to. This was the first bath I could re-member having where the water hadn't stung. Cupping it in my small hands, I poured it over my head, trying to wash away the horror of the night before. It helped, but only a little. Siobhan went away saying she'd come back to make sure I'd washed properly.

I lay back in the water. It felt luxurious to be alone in a hot bath. I moved my feet to create small waves that washed over my body. Sliding further down, immersing my ears and my eyes, which were tightly shut, I began to relax as the warm water washed away the grime of a day on the farm.

I didn't hear Barry letting himself into the bathroom to use the toilet. Alone, so I thought, enjoying the privacy, enjoying the feel of warm water on my body, I was startled and distressed by the touch of a hand between my legs. I shot up into a sitting position, rubbing my eyes. I'd expected to see Tom and was shocked to see Barry's huge belly above me, his braces hanging down the sides of his legs. His flies were undone, and his left hand was inside his trousers, moving about quite fast. I was horrified.

'Shh!' he whispered, rubbing me with rough chubby fingers. 'There now, that's a good wee girl.'

As with Tom the previous night, I found myself powerless to react to what was happening. My small body stiffened and tears filled my eyes as Barry continued to touch me and rub himself.

Someone tried the bathroom door. Panicked, Barry rushed to sort himself out, washing his hands and stuffing his shirt into his trousers. Within seconds he was flushing the toilet. He opened the bathroom door and found Siobhan waiting outside, holding a towel. Explaining that he hadn't been able to wait for the toilet, he left as if nothing had happened.

I was so relieved that he'd gone. I splashed

water on my face to hide my tears, and again I wondered what I'd done wrong for all this to be happening to me. Now I was going to have to avoid Barry as well as Tom. Much as I hated the convent, it was obviously going to be very hard to come back to the farm if the nuns sent me here again.

Siobhan helped me out of the bath and wrapped a towel around my body, I dried myself and slipped into my nightie as quickly as possible so that the younger boys could have their baths. We all had to be clean for Mass in the morning. Once I'd brushed my teeth and hair, Siobhan told me that I could go and watch television for a while. I asked if I could sleep on the couch, but she didn't think it was a good idea and said that I wouldn't get a good night's sleep unless I was in a proper bed. So I went off to the living room, where Barry and Tom sat watching television.

'Come and sit with me,' Tom said, tapping his knee.

I wanted to die. 'I'm just getting a drink of water,' I said, rushing out of the room.

Edward was in the kitchen reading the paper. 'Would you like some milk, Frances?' he said.

'Yes, please.' I pulled out a chair and sat next to him, still trying to think of a way to avoid sleeping in Tom's bed again. It wasn't looking good.

Edward put a glass of milk down in front of me. 'Don't look so unhappy. Is it because you're going back to the convent tomorrow?

I burst into tears. He picked me up, gave me a cuddle and sat me on his knee.

'You'll be able to come back and stay with us again soon, I'm sure of that. We're already very fond of you, you know.'

His comforting words only made me more upset, and tears dripped into my glass as I tried to drink the milk he'd given me. I couldn't do anything to control them, and putting the glass back on the table, I sobbed and wiped my eyes on the sleeve of my nightie. Edward hugged me and asked what was wrong again, but how could I tell him what his father and uncle had done to me? I was embarrassed and not at all sure that he would believe me. And I was too frightened to say anything about the nuns for fear of what they would do to me when I got back.

Just then Maggie came in to get a drink. She seemed annoyed that her brother was comforting me and clearly thought I was putting it on. Edward was unaware of his sister's dirty looks, but I tried hard to stop crying and pull myself together because I wanted to get on with Maggie, even though she'd taken such a dislike to me. She poured out some lemonade and left the kitchen.

Again Edward asked me what was wrong, and again I didn't reply.

160

'Come on, let's see what's on the telly. It might take your mind off things.'

He gave me a piggyback to the couch, and I climbed onto his knee before Tom could call me over to sit with him. The news was on. I found it boring and started to flag, but I was worried about falling asleep. Hoping that if I stayed awake until Tom went to bed then perhaps he might be too tired to disturb me, I struggled to keep my eyes open. I lasted out through the news and part of the next programme, which was also rather boring.

CHAPTER 11

The Family

Eventually, I must have fallen asleep, as the next thing I remember was waking up in bed next to Tom. He had a firm hold of my little hand and was rubbing it up and down against the hard thing between his legs, which was wet, sticky and horrible. I tried with all my strength to pull away, but it was no use. His grip on me tightened, and he moved my hand up and down even faster, breathing heavily now and grunting like a pig. I tried to blank out what he was doing, but it was impossible, and I broke into quiet sobs. How could this be happening all over again?

'Ye're OK, it's Uncle Tom,' he rasped, continuing to rub himself with my hand. 'Now come and lie on me for a cuddle, and I'll tell the nuns how good ye've been. I'll say that we'd love to take ye out for holidays, wouldn't ye like that? Ye get on with us all, don't ye? And we like having ye here. Now come and be nice to Uncle Tom, that's a good wee girl.'

He tried to lift me up onto his sweaty

belly. I was so terrified that I thought I might go mad with fear.

'I really need the toilet!' I said, trying to push away from him. If I could make it to the bathroom, then I could think about what to do next.

He rolled over and grabbed me. 'Quiet! Or you'll wake everyone up.'

'But I need the toilet,' I insisted, even more loudly.

He seemed angry but loosened his grip on me, and I scrambled off the bed. Relieved to be free from him, I headed towards the crack of light that crept in through the bedroom door. My hands shook as I turned the handle, praying he wouldn't call me back. Slipping out of the bedroom, I ran to the bathroom and locked the door.

Still shaken, but hugely relieved, I reached up to the basin, turned on the hot water and washed my hands over and over again. But however much soap I used, they still didn't feel clean. Feeling disgusted and dirty; I stood by the sink sobbing. But I had to pull myself together and think quickly. I needed an excuse for not getting back into bed with Tom. As I calmed down, I noticed that the house was completely quiet. All that could be heard was the gurgle of water running through pipes.

I sat on the toilet feeling cold, tired, lonely and miserable. It occurred to me to wake

Edward up and say I was sick, but he would probably tell me to get back into bed where Uncle Tom would look after me. I thought about waking Siobhan, but she was sleeping with Barry; and I didn't want to be near him, either. There didn't seem to be a way out.

It was still a long time till morning, and I knew I'd have to think of something soon. I prayed to God for help, even though I'd asked for his help lots of times and he'd never come. I hoped this time would be different, but deep down I knew I was on my own. I heard Tom outside the door.

'If you're finished in there, come back to bed.' He sounded very impatient and was obviously waiting for me.

'I can't come out yet. I'm not feeling very well and I might be sick soon,' I whispered through the door.

'Try coming back to bed and you'll feel better,' he said.

His words made me cringe. 'I can't go back to bed; I'll be sick,' I insisted.

Just then I heard Siobhan's voice. She asked Tom what was going on, and he explained that I was feeling ill. My heart leapt. Maybe I'd be able to convince Siobhan that I shouldn't get back into Tom's bed. There was a knock on the door, and she asked if she could come in. I unlocked it just as Tom was going back to his room.

Siobhan was standing outside the bath-room wearing a long pink nightdress with frills around the bottom.

'How are you feeling?' she asked, putting her hand to my forehead. 'You're not very well, are you?' She took a good look at me. I was pale and shaking with fear. 'Come with me and I'll get you some hot milk.'

On the way to the kitchen I started to worry that I might go to Hell for pretending to be sick but decided that if I confessed to the priest when I got back to the convent, then perhaps it would be OK.

Siobhan began to heat up some milk in a saucepan. I was surprised that she didn't seem annoyed at being woken. She gave me a bowl in case I was sick and couldn't make it to the toilet.

'Tell me when you're well enough to go back to bed. If you're too sick, I'll sit with you until we can see a doctor in the morn-ing. I hope you're not coming down with something serious.'

Siobhan really seemed to care about me, and I couldn't remember any adult caring about me before. I guessed that this must be what it was like to have a mother. It was a good feeling. But somehow I had to con-vince her that I was too sick to get back in bed with Tom, without the doctor being called. Siobhan put the hot milk and some dry biscuits down on the table.

'There now, this should help you get back to sleep.'

I sipped the milk and nibbled at the biscuits. Siobhan made herself a cup of tea, cut a large piece of homemade cake and sat down beside me to keep me company.

'You're going to have lots to tell your sisters when you get back, Frances. I bet you miss them,' she said, to distract me.

I looked at her sadly, trying to smile. 'Yes, I do miss them. They'll want to know everything as soon as I see them.'

When we'd finished our drinks, we moved into the living room. Siobhan made me up a bed on the couch and wandered back into the kitchen, returning a few minutes later with a hot-water bottle. I snuggled up and felt much better when I realised that I wouldn't have to go back to Tom. Siobhan sat at the end of the couch and chatted until exhaustion finally overtook me and I fell into a deep sleep.

The next morning I woke to the smell of bacon again. I heard Siobhan ask, 'Who wants black pudding?' I had no idea what black pudding was, but everyone seemed to want some.

I listened to them tucking into breakfast. They sounded like a very happy family who got on well with each other most of the time. I thought how much I would like to be part of the family if it hadn't been for Tom and Barry. After breakfast there was a lot more noise from the kitchen as they got ready to leave for church.

The back door slammed for the last time and the house was quiet. At first I thought I was the only one left, but then I heard the sound of someone moving about in the kitchen. There was little noise and no talking, so I guessed it was probably just one person. I hoped it wasn't one of the men. Suddenly, I felt very uncomfortable. If it was one of the men and we were alone in the house, then they would probably come in and see me soon. I shut my eyes, pulled the blanket over my head and lay rigid, listening out, afraid to move or even breathe aloud.

A feeling of complete and utter relief swept over me when I heard the sound of Siobhan gently humming. I got up and went to the toilet. When I came back, she handed me a big mug of tea. It was hot, sweet and just what I needed.

'How are you feeling now? Could you eat some breakfast?' she asked maternally.

'I still feel a bit sick, but I'm much better than I was last night... I think I could try some breakfast, please.'

She looked pleased, obviously concluding that if I was well enough to eat, then I must be on the mend. It struck me that I'd better eat as much as I could, as this was my last day out of the convent and Siobhan's cooking was great. Unfortunately, now I knew how proper food tasted, the awful convent food would seem twice as disgusting, if that were possible. It was hard to imagine eating that slop again. I couldn't wait to tell Loretta and Sinéad about Siobhan's food, although I hoped they wouldn't be too jealous.

Before long she was calling me into the kitchen and placing a full cooked breakfast in front of me. It looked and smelt wonderful. She followed up with a large mug of hot tea and a plate of toast. I was determined to enjoy every mouthful and take the memory of this amazing meal back to the convent with me. The food tasted every bit as good as it looked. The kitchen was warm and homely, and for the moment I felt content.

Siobhan asked if I'd enjoyed my stay and whether I might like to come back again. I said I'd had a great time, which in many ways was true. She looked so pleased that I didn't want to upset her by saying anything about the sleeping arrangements, and I simply couldn't say anything about how Tom and Barry had touched me. Anyway, I would be back at the convent by nightfall, so I wouldn't have to worry about them for some time. On the other hand, I was anxious about going back because it meant having to concentrate on keeping on the right side of Sister Thomas again, as if that were possible. And the girls who normally picked on me were likely to be worse than usual because I'd been out for a few days. At least my bed would be a relatively safe place.

After breakfast I went off to get dressed. Siobhan gave me back my clothes from the previous day, washed and ironed, and made sure that my case was neatly packed, ready to go. Suddenly, I was overcome by emotion and started to cry. She gave me a hug and said that I could come back again soon. I couldn't speak and just stood there sobbing, not knowing why I was crying but unable to control it. I was glad that no one else was around to see me. Then she took me into the bathroom to clean up my face before the others came back from church. Fortunately, I'd stopped crying by the time the back door opened and they all piled in.

'Is there any tea?' they asked.

Siobhan sorted out mugs and poured tea for Edward, Tom and Barry.

Edward asked if I was feeling better now. I nodded and said that I was. Barry suggested that I should get out for some fresh country air. Tom lifted his mug and went off to the living room. He seemed to be in a bit of a mood and didn't say anything to me.

'Can we play on the swing?' one of the boys asked, and they were on their way out of the back door before Siobhan had managed to say yes.

'Why don't ye go, too?' said Edward. 'I'll follow ye down in a while and give ye all a push.'

I ran to put on my shoes and caught up with the boys by the barn, where they were throwing stones at an old tin can. I picked up some stones and joined in. Sean soon tired of the game and concentrated on showing me how to throw properly. Eventually, I managed to hit the can a few times. I'd never done anything like this in the convent, and it felt great.

'Race ye to the tree,' said Sean, running towards the field.

The other boys dropped their stones and dashed off after him, but I was having too much fun developing my stone-throwing skills to stop just yet. I thought I was getting pretty good, but with no one there to see me I eventually got bored and decided to join the boys on the swing. They were probably having loads of fun by now.

I ran through the field to the tree, where they were all on the swing trying to push each other off. I sat on the ground and watched for a while, but soon I was swinging back and forth. It was great. I was going to miss this sensation when I got back to the convent, so I shut my eyes and enjoyed the moment. The wind blew through my hair and over my face as I went higher and higher. I'd never imagined it was possible to feel so free. But then I heard Tom's voice, bellowing out across the field, and my happiness evaporated. He sounded really cross.

'Stop that now!' he shouted at the boys.

I opened my eyes and saw him striding towards me with a scary look in his eyes. Reaching out his arms, he pulled me off the swing and chastised the boys for pushing me too hard. 'What if she'd fallen off? She can't go back to the convent hurt. What would the nuns think? Yous boys have no sense.'

'Sorry, Uncle Tom,' they said one after another.

I tried to stick up for them and explained that I was holding on really tight so I couldn't fall off. But Tom was having none of it.

'I'm going to the shop. Ye can come with me.'

It sounded more like an instruction than a request, and not wanting to disobey him, especially when he was so cross, I fell in beside him, and we wandered off past the bungalow and out through the gate.

I was worried that he might say something bad about me to the nuns, which would get me into awful trouble, especially with Sister Thomas. He might still be cross with me for not getting back in bed with him during the night. He hadn't said anything, but he was acting differently towards me now. I just wanted to be back with the boys on the swing.

Neither of us spoke the whole way to the shop. Suddenly, he switched and was nice to me again. Putting his arm around my shoulder, he asked me what sweets I'd like. He seemed in a much better mood on the way home, and I was relieved that he'd relaxed his grip. My hand was quite sore by now.

'Will you tell the nuns you had a nice time?' he asked as we approached the bungalow.

'Yes, I will. I have enjoyed myself.'

That seemed to please him, and he told me to go back and play on the swing but to be careful. I dashed off, and after I'd had two turns, Barry called us in for Sunday dinner.

We ate at the kitchen table, while Barry and Tom sat with their trays in front of the telly. Siobhan looked all hot and bothered from the cooking and seemed relieved to be sitting down at last. As I munched through my lovely roast dinner, I listened carefully to the way the members of the family spoke to each other. The boys chatted freely and comfortably, talking mainly about the rope swing but also about anything else that popped into their heads, while Edward talked to Siobhan about plants that he wanted to buy for the flowerbeds, but Maggie sat quietly and didn't contribute anything to the conversations going on around her. Although she seemed close to Siobhan, I couldn't detect much of a bond between her and any of her brothers. They seemed to just ignore each other. It was strange. I thought they'd be protective of their only sister, but that didn't appear to be the case. Now and then she sent me dirty looks across the table, but I ignored them.

I ate until I was so full that I thought I would pop. Siobhan asked Maggie to clear away the plates while she served up pudding. Large portions of apple pie and custard took the place of the dinner plates. There was steam rising from my bowl; the portion seemed huge, and I wondered how on earth I was going to eat any of it. I relaxed back into my chair as the rest of the family got tucked in. By the time I'd got round to trying mine, everyone else had left the table and headed off into the living room to watch the Sunday matinée. I had a few spoonfuls before emptying the rest into the kitchen bin, hoping that Siobhan wouldn't notice. After stacking my bowl, I went to join the others.

Tom told me that I should be ready to go once the film had finished. The thought of leaving caused a flood of mixed emotions in me again. I needed to cry and left the room, closing the bathroom door behind me just as the tears started to flow. Again, I didn't know exactly why I was crying. Part of me wanted to stay, but another part of me wanted to go.

I felt a lot of hurt inside, and the tears were the only way I could let the pain out.

The sound of laughter drifted in from the living room. The film was obviously really funny. The laughter died down for a few minutes and then started up again. I tidied up my face as best I could and slipped back to see what I was missing. It was a hilarious film, and within a few minutes I was totally engrossed. I didn't even notice Edward pulling me up onto his knee. Like everyone else, my eyes were fixed on the two funny men on the screen.

When the film was over, Siobhan said she'd make a nice pot of tea before Tom took me back. The younger boys looked upset at that, and so did Edward, although he was better at hiding it. I was going to miss them, too, and said my goodbyes as we drank our tea.

Finally, Tom got up and said, 'Are you ready, then?'

I took one last sip of tea. Siobhan hugged me and said she'd see me soon. Then Edward hugged me. Barry shouted, ''Bye!' from the other room. Maggie was nowhere to be seen. The boys followed us to the gate and waved until we were out of sight.

Tom and I walked together along the quiet country roads back into Moira. It made me miserable to think about going back to the convent. With little conversation between us, and fewer distractions, the journey back seemed to take much longer. Moira was much quieter than it had been when I'd arrived. Being a Sunday, all the shops were closed and the streets were practically deserted.

At the train station, Tom bought two tickets and led me to the platform.

'Come on. This is our train.'

As we pulled out of the station, Tom began to question me about what I was going to tell the nuns. He seemed obsessed with it.

'You might want to come and see us again to get away from the nuns for a break. So you will have to tell them that we treated you really well, or they might not let you come again.'

'I will tell them I had a great time and what a good cook Siobhan is,' I said, guessing exactly what it was that I wasn't supposed to say.

Tom seemed satisfied. He talked to another man in the carriage while I stared out of the window, trying to blank out my thoughts. My feelings were all mixed up, and I knew that if I thought about anything at all, I was going to burst out into tears. Eventually, we arrived back in Belfast.

'Come on now, this is our stop.'

His voice startled me out of my daze. I jumped up quickly and followed him off the train. We weren't far from the convent, and I felt a horrible sinking feeling in my stomach.

I didn't want to go back, but neither did I want to stay with Tom. I wanted the impossible – to go back to the farm without Tom or Barry being there. We walked quietly along, but when I saw the high red bricks of the convent walls I started to cry. Suddenly, it was all too much.

'There, there now,' said Tom as we approached the convent gate. 'Don't upset yourself. What will the nuns think I've done to ye?'

He handed me a clean linen hankie, and I wiped away the tears. I didn't want anyone to see me crying because I knew that some of the girls would see it as a sign of weakness and make me pay for it. If there was one thing I'd learnt in my years at the convent, it was not to appear weak. If you cried in front of others, it would soon get around and provide fuel for the bullies, who picked on the weakest girls, the ones that wouldn't fight back. Sometimes they left me alone because Loretta was my sister, but Loretta couldn't always be around to defend me, and as one of the smallest girls for my age, I'd been picked on and beaten up a lot in the past, which had forced me to toughen up.

Tom rang the bell. Sister Kevin opened the gate.

'Ah, Frances Reilly, go straight to your dormitory and let Sister Thomas know you're back.'

Tom bent down, gave me a hug and handed me my suitcase. As I turned and walked away back towards the main convent building, I heard Sister Kevin offer him a cup of tea. Glancing back, I saw them coming through the gate and moving to a different part of the building, but by now they were too far away for me to hear any of what was being said. I walked along the corridor and up the stairs to the dormitory, hoping that Tom wasn't saying anything bad about me.

The dormitory was busy. Girls just back from a weekend out were sharing stories about what they'd done and catching up on convent gossip. Sister Thomas wasn't about, and no one knew where she was, which was a relief, as I didn't feel up to facing her yet. Everyone was asking if I'd had a good time when Loretta burst in and gave me a huge hug.

'Did you bring me something back?' she said, squeezing me tight.

I took the sweets out of my pocket and gave them to her. She looked really pleased and put a few in her mouth.

'Were the people nice?' she asked, with that look on her face that meant she wanted to know everything.

I told her a bit about the farm, the Murphys and the food, but then Sister Thomas came in and we stopped talking and made ourselves look busy. She came straight over to Loretta.

'Are you supposed to be here, Reilly, or should you be doing something?'

'Sorry, Sister, I'll go and do it right now!' Loretta hurried out of the dormitory.

'So, you're back, Reilly,' Sister Thomas said, turning her attention to me. 'Change into your normal clothes and let me have everything you took with you. It all has to go back to the storeroom.'

CHAPTER 12

Doubting Thomas

For weeks afterwards, memories of the farm kept swirling around my head. I'd think about the good things – playing on the tree swing, Edward's flowerbeds and, best of all, Siobhan's cooking, and I'd smile to myself, but then Tom and Barry would creep into the mix. I tried to push them out by replacing them with better memories, and sometimes it would work. But all too often it didn't, and my mind would fill with images and sounds of the awful things they'd done to me. A cold, penetrating shiver would slowly pass through my body and nausea would rise up from the pit of my stomach. Sometimes, mostly at night when the lights were out, when no one could see me, I'd cry about it.

I carried on like this for days. One minute I'd think about something really good – like seeing the kittens in the barn – and I'd be on a real high. After all, in just a couple of days at the farm I'd had more fun than I'd had in all my years in the convent. But the next minute I'd remember one of the men and be filled with disgust. When I was having nice thoughts about the Murphys, I almost wished I was still at the farm, but when thoughts of Barry and Tom came into my head, I felt relieved that I wasn't.

Up until now I hadn't thought there was anything good about being in the convent, but I'd found something: at night my bed was my own.

It was recreation hour. Sister Francis was on duty and had handed out balls and skipping ropes to her pets. The rest of us either tagged along with them or did our own thing. I sat alone on a cold stone step. An image of Tom waking me jumped into my head. I wished that I could stop thinking about it because the pain was becoming almost unbearable. I looked up at the sky to distract myself and saw a plane flying high above me. Wherever it was going, I wanted to go there, too.

It wasn't long before I was crying. I brushed the tears away with my hand, but they kept on coming. Rita, a senior and friend of Loretta's, came over to see what was wrong.

'Are you OK?' she asked, sitting down next to me. Her tone of voice was so sympathetic that it just made me cry even more. 'You don't want to let things get to you, especially the nuns – otherwise they win.

You know that, Frances.'

I stopped sobbing for a moment but wouldn't meet her eye. 'It's not just the nuns,' I said in a whisper.

'What else is it, then? You tell me and I'll see if it's worth worrying about. How's that?'

Cringing with embarrassment, I kept my voice down as I described my time at the Murphys' farm. Rita listened carefully to every word. The nuns would have to know about it, she said, which made me wish that I hadn't said anything, but she reassured me that everything would be OK and offered to tell the duty nun on my behalf. I agreed as long as she didn't tell Loretta. I didn't want my sister upset.

Nervously, I watched Rita speaking to Sister Francis and looking over at me. They talked until the bell rang but were too far away for me to make out what was being said or how the nun was reacting. The bell went and we lined up.

Sister Francis shouted, 'Everyone carry on, except Frances Reilly.'

As the others marched off, I dropped out of line and stood beside her. I sensed immediately that it had been a mistake to tell her.

'I believe you have been telling stories about the Murphy family, who very kindly took you out for the weekend!' she said, her eyes flashing. 'Why have you been telling such filthy lies? What sort of dirty minds do you Reillys have? Go to your dormitory and wait for Sister Thomas. And while you wait, ask God to forgive you. He might, if you turn that filthy mind of yours to prayer instead of filthy lies!'

Wishing I'd trusted my instincts, I walked slowly off to my dormitory. If Sister Francis didn't believe me, then there was no way Sister Thomas would. I tried not to think about what would happen next, but it could only be bad, very bad.

I slumped on the edge of my bed and thought about what she'd said about praying. Once, long ago, or so it seemed, I would have prayed as hard as I could for forgiveness, and for Sister Thomas to believe me, but now I just sat silently and waited.

Soon I heard brisk footsteps, and Sister Thomas hurried into the room, her face distorted with rage and her features screwed up as if she were in acute physical pain. This was the expression that she reserved for her deepest moods, an expression I had come to dread. Without saying a word, she stormed down the central aisle of the dormitory and slapped me across the face with such force that she knocked me to the floor and half-way under my bed.

'You're a liar, Reilly! How dare you accuse the Murphys?' she screamed.

I was still trying to get myself together from the fall when I felt myself being dragged out from under the bed. Some of my hair caught in the metal springs beneath the mattress, and as she pulled me out, large clumps were ripped out at the roots. Bashing my head against the hard, metal bed frame, she hauled me to my feet and dragged me off to the bathroom.

'I think you know what we do with liars, Reilly,' she said.

Grabbing a large piece of carbolic soap from the sink, she pushed it into my howling mouth. I struggled hard, barely able to breathe. My arms thrashed around, but she kept a tight grip on my hair with one hand and used the other to ram the soap ever deeper into my mouth. At that moment I wanted to kill her.

I went on struggling, even though I knew there was little point. I could never win. Suddenly, I retched violently and the soap slipped out of her reach. With a look of disgust, she let go of my hair and stepped back. I held on to the sink as I vomited. I had soap stuck to my teeth and bubbles coming out of my mouth and nose.

'Get yourself cleaned up, Reilly, and get back to the dormitory.' She stormed off.

I rinsed out my mouth but couldn't get rid of the taste of soap. Splashing water onto my face, I sobbed into the sink until eventually no more tears would come. Then I dried my face, cleaned up the sink and got myself back to the dormitory well before Sister Thomas returned.

My head was still really hurting. My face felt bruised all over, and there was a red handprint on my cheek, hot and stinging. Worse than the physical pain of the attack, though, was the emotional pain. Sitting on the edge of my bed, I felt dejected and extremely vulnerable.

My hair was a mess, and I needed to get a comb through it. Reaching down into my locker for my comb, I burst into tears again when I saw bunches of dark-brown hair hanging from the springs beneath my bed. Clumps of hair fell away from my scalp as I gently eased the comb through the matted mass that remained. I put them on the bed and rolled them together into a hairball, which, as I added more strands, began to resemble a small furry animal. My head hurt so much that I decided not to bother putting my ribbon back in yet. Weeping and rocking, trying to hug myself better, I lay on top of the bed and listened out for Sister Thomas.

About half an hour later I heard footsteps in the hall. I was so tired that I'd almost missed them and quickly jumped up. But I needn't have panicked. It was only Rita.

'Jesus, Mary and St Joseph, what happened

to you?' she asked. She looked shocked at the sight of me. 'Is it because of what I told Sister Francis?'

'Yes. They think I'm lying about the Murphys.'

'Oh God, I'm really sorry. Do you want me to get Loretta for you?'

'No! I don't want her to know. She'll go mad and then she'll be in trouble again. Anyway, Sister Thomas will be back soon.'

'OK, then, if you're sure. I'll come back later and see if you need anything. I could try to get you some food, if you're not allowed down to tea.'

'Thanks.' I tried to smile because she really did look sorry for the trouble she'd caused, and I didn't want her feeling bad. After all, she'd only been trying to help.

When she left, I flushed the hairball down the toilet. Sitting carefully on my bed so as not to crease the sheets, I wondered what was going to happen next. I didn't have long to wait. Soon I heard Sister Thomas's heavy footsteps on the stairs. Once more I jumped off the bed and smoothed the covers.

'On your knees, Reilly, and start praying for God's forgiveness for all your wicked lies! You will remain praying until I tell you to stop, and you will not be going to tea with the others.'

Dropping to my knees, I made the sign of the cross and whispered my prayers as

185

quickly as I could, with my hands pressed tightly together and my eyes firmly shut. I probably looked quite devout, but in fact I was just trying to blank out Sister Thomas, the convent and all the pain I felt inside.

'I can't hear you, Reilly!' she shouted from the other side of the dormitory.

I prayed louder, longing for something to eat or drink to take away the taste of soap in my mouth. I carried on with 'Hail Marys' and 'Our Fathers' until well after she'd left the dormitory and her footsteps had faded. Then, just in case she'd secretly crept back again, I prayed for a little bit longer until I sensed that she really had gone.

I sneaked bravely out into the corridor to the top of the stairs. Picking a spot with a good view, where no one would be able to see me first, I sat down and got comfortable. From experience I knew that I could run back to the dormitory in plenty of time if I heard anyone coming. It was much better than kneeling by the bed praying, especially because I was cheating the nuns. It felt good to get one over on them for a change, particularly Sister Thomas.

From my vantage point, I could see all the way down several long flights of stairs to the corridor below. Far below me I could hear people talking. Someone started singing a sweet, soothing song. I could just about make out the words. 'Sad movies always make me cry,' she sang. 'He said he had to work, so I went to the show alone...'

The bell rang and it was time to move. I dashed back to the dormitory. The familiar noise of girls making their way to the refectory for tea was followed by ten minutes of silence, and then I heard footsteps again. I fell to my knees and closed my eyes. 'Hail Mary, full of grace, the Lord is with thee...'

'This was all I could get,' Rita said, handing me a few rounds of dry bread.

'That's dead on; it'll get rid of the soap taste in my mouth,' I said gratefully.

The first few mouthfuls tasted of nothing but soap, but by the time I'd finished eating, I could just about taste the bread.

Rita hurried from the room. I hoped she'd be OK. I didn't want her getting in trouble for trying to help. All went quiet again. The boredom started to get to me, and I began pacing up and down the length of the dormitory. Now and then I stopped and stared out of the window. Far below, I could see some nuns talking in a huddle, but they didn't look up. I paced a bit more, all the time listening out for Sister Thomas. Still feeling very sore, I longed for bedtime so that I could lie down, go to sleep and try to forget about this awful day.

It was dark when the others came back. I was pleased to see them; I was tired of being alone. They arrived in small groups, and from the way they were chatting to each other, it was obvious that there weren't any nuns about.

'Can you believe it?' someone said. 'Kathleen and Mary have just seen a ghost in the refectory!' Most of the girls were a bit spooked, but a few of them seemed excited. It wasn't hard to guess what sort of a night lay ahead of us. This was bound to trigger off a round of ghost stories.

I loved ghost stories, as did most of the girls, but there was sure to be one or two who wouldn't be able to sleep afterwards, so nights like this often ended in trouble. With what had happened to Kathleen and Mary, plus a few good spooky tales, they'd be screaming at the slightest thing, which would bring Sister Thomas back in a rage.

As far as I could make out, Kathleen and Mary had seen the ghost of a girl with a long plait in her hair. Someone said that she must have lived ages ago because it sounded like she was wearing really old-fashioned clothes. I was just beginning to wonder if they'd made it all up when Kathleen came into the dormitory. She looked awful. Her hair was a complete mess, her face was pale and drawn, and she was struggling to get her breath. She really did look like she'd seen a ghost.

'Sister Thomas is on her way up,' someone whispered.

I dropped back to my knees, while the other girls busied themselves getting ready for bed. Sister Thomas marched in. She kept her eyes on me throughout prayers, and I became convinced she was planning my next punishment. Her staring eyes were making me panicky and nervous, so I concentrated on praying and tried to block her out. All I wanted was to be allowed to go to bed.

After prayers the others got into bed, but I carried on praying, and Sister Thomas carried on staring. After a few tense moments she told me to go and get the chamber pot before returning to my prayers.

'Reilly is praying for God's forgiveness for all her lies,' she announced to the room as I walked off. 'She is praying not to go to Hell, although I doubt there'll be space in Heaven for any of the Reillys.'

I returned with the large chamber pot and carefully placed it in the centre of the aisle between the beds.

'No one's to talk to Reilly,' she added.

Everyone's eyes were on me as I knelt beside my bed. The lights went out, and for a moment or two, until the dimmer light came on, it was pitch black. After a few minutes I'd adjusted to the gloom enough to see the chamber pot sitting in the centre of the room. I hated the chamber pot. Forcing us to use it, when the toilets were just outside the dormitory, was deliberately degrading.

Sister Thomas left, and we waited until we were sure she had really gone. Eventually, one of the girls started whispering about the ghost. Kathleen said she thought it had been trying to tell her something. Maybe a girl had died in the convent building and wanted to tell someone how it had happened.

'Maybe the nuns battered her to death,' suggested Margaret, 'then buried her body in the convent grounds.'

I shivered. I had a horrible feeling that something spooky was under the beds, and suddenly, I didn't want to be kneeling alone on the cold floor. I told the others to stop scaring me. 'It's not fair. You're not on the floor in the dark,' I said.

But soon the whispering started up again, so I got up and sat on the edge of my bed with my feet tucked under me so that nothing could grab at them from below. We took turns telling each other ghost stories, all of them true, of course, and some of them really quite brilliant. A few of the stories had been told before, but no one seemed to mind. Nights like these didn't come around very often, and we weren't in the mood to sleep.

We heard footsteps and the whispering stopped. I fell down onto my knees again. Sister Thomas swept back into the room and began to walk along the rows of beds, checking to see if anyone was awake. I was convinced she'd heard us, but she appeared to be satisfied. She came to a halt at the end of my bed.

'Get in bed now, Reilly.'

'Thank you, Sister.' I climbed under the covers. It was such a wonderful feeling to be able to lie down at last. I realised that I was much more afraid of Sister Thomas than I could ever be of any ghost and wondered if the ghost Kathleen had seen had been beaten to death by a nun like her. Remembering some of the beatings I'd taken, I was filled with sadness and sympathy for the long-dead girl.

The next morning the incessant ringing of the morning bell ripped through my sleep, tore me out of my dreams and dumped me back into reality. Not for the first time I was overcome by an urge to grab the bell from the nun and chuck it out of the window. I hated that awful sound. This particular morning, with my head still aching from the night before, the bell jarred more than ever. Each peal seemed a thousand times louder than usual, reverberating through my brain until it felt like it might explode.

At last morning prayers began, and then we rushed to get ready for morning Mass. I did my best to keep up, but I was in a delicate state. While I was washing my face,

I heard Sister Thomas call, 'Reilly!'

My heart thumped wildly, as it always did when she called my name. I hurried to see what she wanted. 'I don't care whose turn it is, Reilly. I want you to empty the chamber pot right now.'

I looked across to the middle of the room. The chamber pot was full and it was going to be extremely difficult to move it without spilling its contents, which, I thought, was just how she wanted it.

'Come on, Reilly, I haven't got all morning.'

The menace in her voice made me tremble. I leant over the pot to get a good grip of the sides and began to lift it up. The stench made my stomach turn, and I was on the verge of gagging, but I knew that she was ready to pounce if I spilled a single drop and was determined not to give her that satisfaction. She made it obvious that she found it amusing to watch me struggle. She was hoping I'd stumble – better still, I might vomit and then she could give me a beating and get me to clear up the mess. Focusing all my powers of concentration, I took small, shuffling steps towards the bathroom and, to my relief, made it to the toilet and managed to pour the contents of the pot away without any spillage. Just as I was cleaning up with Jeyes Fluid, she called out, 'Reilly, make sure you're ready for Mass before the bell goes.'

'Yes, Sister.'

She hovered behind me as I rushed to get ready, watching my every move. Soon all that was left to do was my hair. I'd deliberately left it until last because my head was so sore and tender. I gave it a few tentative strokes with a brush, but even the lightest pressure hurt. Seizing her opportunity, Sister Thomas grabbed the brush from my hand.

'Like this, Reilly,' she said, pulling it vigorously through my hair.

I fought hard to hold back the tears and screams as she forced the brush through the bloody, knotted clumps of hair. The hard bristles scraped my scalp, reopening the scabs left by the previous day's wounds. She was really getting into it when, thankfully, the bell rang for Mass and she ordered me into line. My head hurt like crazy, and I still wanted to cry out with pain, but I was proud that I hadn't screamed in front of her and wasn't going to break down now.

Sister Thomas woke us earlier than usual the next day.

'This morning,' she said, 'I want to read you the story of Doubting Thomas. This story reminds us of what happens when we doubt what the Bible tells us and fail to keep our faith in God the Father, Son and Holy

Ghost. Of what happens when we stop believing that God sees us all the time and
knows when we're lying.'

She turned and looked directly at me. I
was sure this must be about the Murphys.
She opened the book and started to read,
while the rest of us held back our yawns.
We'd heard the story so many times that we
could recite it off pat. After the first few
lines I was no longer listening. Instead, I
started to think about what to say if she
started on me again. I didn't want another
beating, but saying I'd been lying about the
Murphys might not save me from that. I
tried to figure out what would get me into
the least trouble, but Sister Thomas was so
horrible that she was probably going to hit
me again no matter what. I couldn't win.
My concentration wandered back to the
story just as she was explaining again that
doubters would go straight to Hell.

I was always being told I was going to Hell,
often just for being a Reilly. I'd been condemned to Hell so many times that I couldn't
see any way of getting to Heaven, no matter
how hard I prayed or how good I tried to be.
I tried not to think about what an eternity in
Hell would be like, but there really was no
escape from it. The Bible was full of refer-
ences to it, and the nuns continually threat-
ened us with it, especially when they were
telling us off. In chapel, we were told that if

we did wrong we would 'burn in the fires of Hell' and that there was no escape from the pain of it. It was too horrible to imagine, especially for a child. Every now and then I even dreamt about it, waking up in a sweat and frantically praying to God not to send me there. Most of the time I tried hard to be a good Catholic girl and do what was right. But I was never sure if it was going to be enough. After all, I was still a Reilly.

The story ended, and Sister Thomas said morning prayers. Physically, I was feeling worse than I had the day before. On the way to Mass I felt weak and couldn't stop thinking about going to Hell. At Mass the priest's sermon was about the Devil and Hell and how only the chosen would get into Heaven. I couldn't bear it and tried to switch my mind off, but suddenly, it felt like someone had switched off all the lights instead. When they came back on, Loretta was standing over me.

'Are ye all right now, Frances?'

I tried to get up, but I was dizzy and disorientated.

'Ye'll be OK now, Frances. Ye just fainted.'

Sister Kevin told Loretta to take me to the dormitory. Loretta helped me up, and slowly we walked away.

'Do ye hate being a Reilly, Loretta, and are ye scared of going to Hell?' I asked her shakily.

'There's nothing wrong with being a Reilly!' she said. 'I'm proud of it, sure. If I wasn't a Reilly then I wouldn't be yer sister, and I love being yer sister.'

I lay on my bed and sobbed. Loretta gave me a hug. 'What is it, Frances, what's wrong?'

When my sobs had subsided, I blurted everything out – what had happened at the Murphys' house and Sister Thomas's punishment. 'And now I'm going to Hell!' I said.

Loretta looked upset. She told me to hang in there until she could think of a way to get us out. 'They'll have to let us out one day, anyway. They can't keep us here forever. And when we're out we can let people outside know what goes on in this place. I promise you, Frances, we'll think of something. I'd better go now. I'll try to bring you some breakfast.'

I felt some relief at having shared my story and feelings with my sister but hoped she wouldn't do anything that would get her into trouble with the nuns. Then I reasoned that she wasn't stupid and knew better than to confront them directly. I relaxed a little.

After she'd gone, Bernadette and Chrissie sneaked in to see me.

'Are you OK, Frances?' Chrissie asked.

'I should be used to it by now, but I'm not,' I said through clenched teeth. 'I hate

Sister Thomas so much. I wish I could get back at her.'

Chrissie had never seen an expression like that on my face before. 'Ye won't do anything stupid, will ye, Frances?' she said.

'Don't worry. I'll keep my head together. But people should know what goes on in this place!'

Bernadette sat on the end of my bed. 'Ye're right, Frances, but how do we tell them without getting into trouble?'

I thought for a while. Then it hit me. 'Ye can make paper aeroplanes, can't ye, Bernadette?'

'Yes, but–'

'We could write messages on them and send them flying over the wall for people on the road to Belfast to read. If we could just get the truth out, the papers might get hold of it and the convent would be shut down. Then we'd be sent to a better home.'

Bernadette and Chrissie fell silent. I watched their faces for a reaction.

'Ye might be right, Frances,' Bernadette said thoughtfully. 'I'll try to get some paper later on.'

The dormitory felt unnaturally quiet and peaceful after they left. With nothing much to do, I found myself staring at a sacred-heart picture of Jesus hanging on the wall. It was the only colourful thing in the room. Soon I had the strangest feeling that the eyes in the picture were staring straight at me. I thought back to the previous day and the ghost girl. Perhaps there was a ghost or spirit inside the picture. I felt a bit spooky and goose bumps appeared on my arms as I let my imagination run wild. Something kept drawing me back to the picture, and I was now convinced that Jesus's eyes were watching me through it. It was a really uncomfortable feeling. I shut my eyes, hoping that when I opened them, the picture would look normal again, that the eyes wouldn't look so real. But it didn't work. When I opened them again, Jesus was still staring down at me. But where was He when you really needed Him?

CHAPTER 13

The Inspectors

I met up with Bernadette and Chrissie at recreation. Bernadette had some paper and a pencil under her cardigan to make the paper planes with. She'd taken them from Sister Francis's class.

'What shall we write?' I asked, wondering how we could get people to take us seriously. We found ourselves a place to sit far away from the rest of the girls and the two nuns on duty.

'We could write, "Please help us. The nuns are cruel," Chrissie suggested.

'That's good. Can you write it, Chrissie?' Bernadette said, knowing that I would struggle to spell the words.

Chrissie didn't have to be asked twice. She picked up the pencil and began writing on the paper in large clear letters. I laughed at the way she poked her tongue out of the side of her mouth as she concentrated. After she'd written the same message on both sides of eight pages, Bernadette started folding the paper into planes.

We went behind a tree near the wall.

Chrissie was on lookout, and when the coast was clear, she gave the nod to Bernadette and me, and we threw the paper planes as high as we could into the air. One of Bernadette's went over the wall, but the rest fell to the ground. Laughing at our lack of skill, we gathered them up quickly and waited for a few moments to make sure we weren't being watched. I said I would be lookout next time to give Chrissie a go.

When I thought it was safe, I gave them a nod and they tried again. None of the planes made it this time, but they were having a great laugh trying. Bernadette suggested that as I was the smallest and the lightest of us, I should stand on someone's shoulders and throw the rest over. It seemed like a good idea. I loved any chance to climb, and I had a good sense of balance.

'You can stand on my shoulders, Frances.'

'OK, Chrissie, but don't let me fall. You'll have to stand very still!'

Some girls walked by, and we pretended to be picking up leaves from the ground and stripping the green from them. We got some strange looks, but the girls went on past.

Bernadette took her place at the other side of the tree to keep watch. When Chrissie and I heard the words 'All clear!' we moved closer to the wall, and Chrissie clasped her hands together to form a makeshift step. I swung my leg up, placed one foot on her hands and was up on her shoulders in a few seconds.

'Still clear!' said Bernadette, from the other side of the tree.

I steadied myself and threw the paper planes with all my strength. I managed to get five over the wall, but one fell back to the ground and another got stuck in the barbed wire. I reached up and pulled it out.

'Seniors coming!' warned Bernadette.

I jumped down, and we pretended to be looking for something on the ground again. The seniors paid us no attention whatsoever.

'I think we've done enough,' Chrissie said.

We spent the rest of recreation wondering if anyone would bother to pick up the planes and read them.

'I hope whoever finds them doesn't hand them into the nuns,' I said.

But there was no going back now. All we could do was hope that the plan would work and that the convent would be investigated and shut down.

After recreation we went to our classrooms. I'd been moved from Sister Kevin's class to Sister Francis's, and I hated it because Sister Francis had a big blackthorn stick that she would use on girls she didn't like. We weren't taught a lot. The subject was nearly always religion, and if one of us couldn't answer a question about the Bible, Sister Francis would make an example of her in front of the class by hitting her with the stick.

I'd been in her class a few weeks and had been beaten nearly every day. Unusually, Sister Thomas hadn't called me out of lessons for a while, but I felt sure she'd be summoning me soon because she'd much prefer me to be scrubbing floors than learning anything. Still, for the time being I was stuck in a class where, because I'd missed so many lessons, I couldn't answer all the questions, and I was getting whacked for my ignorance. Quite often I did actually know the answers, but when I was asked and everyone looked at me, I'd find myself flushing red and my mind would go completely blank. And the more that I couldn't answer, the more questions I was asked. It was yet another no-win situation.

I didn't want to be in this class. I just didn't seem to fit in. Like all the nuns, Sister Francis had her pets, and they were never punished. After just one day in the classroom I knew who they were. It seemed that they couldn't do anything wrong, or if they did, Sister Francis was completely blind to it. Incredibly, I started hoping that I'd be sent off to do some dirty job instead of going to class. It was what I was used to, and at least I wouldn't be embarrassed.

Sister Francis warned everyone to be on their best behaviour because the ministry inspectors were coming around. We had to make sure that the classroom was tidy, then we had to wash, do our hair and change into our Sunday clothes. Back in the classroom, she went through what we should say if the inspectors asked us any questions. Her instructions were to be followed exactly or we'd be severely punished after they'd gone.

If asked, we were to smile and say that we enjoyed being in the convent and that 'The nuns do their very best for all of us.' Sister Kevin came in and whispered something to Sister Francis.

'I want you to all to recite the Ten Commandments, and keep in time!' Sister Francis barked at us. 'The inspectors are on their way and I want them to be impressed. Now, look like you're enjoying your lesson. I'll be watching all of you!'

The inspectors – two men and three women – came in just as we'd got to the fifth commandment, 'Thou shall not kill.'

Sister Francis shook their hands. They waited in silence until we'd finished.

'Good afternoon, girls,' they said.

'Good afternoon,' we chorused, smiling politely, just as Sister Francis had told us to.

They looked around at us as if they were studying animals in a zoo, while Sister Francis kept a close eye on us to make sure that we were behaving well. Then they walked around the classroom asking questions at random. One of the men stopped at my desk.

'What's your name?'

'I'm Frances Reilly, sir,' I answered meekly. My face felt hot. Out of the corner of my eye I could see Sister Francis staring at me, hanging on to my every word in case I said the wrong thing.

'Do you like it here in the convent?'

'Yes, sir, I do,' I lied, forcing a smile. I wished that Sister Francis would leave so I could tell him that I really didn't like it one bit.

'So you have a lot to thank the good sisters for. For taking you all in and caring for you?'

This made my blood boil. 'Yes, sir,' I said, nearly choking on the words.

'Very good.' He patted me on the head and moved on to another girl.

The others gave similar answers to similar questions, and we all did an excellent job of creating a false impression of convent life, especially Sister Francis's pets, who couldn't praise the nuns enough. The inspectors seemed happy with what they'd seen and heard, but just as they were about to leave the classroom, one of the women spotted the long blackthorn stick in the corner of the room, Sister Francis's pride and joy. How she loved to walk about the room threatening and beating the girls with it!

'What do you use this for?' the woman said, picking it up.

Sister Francis went red in the face and faked a smile. 'Oh, that's my pointing stick,' she said, holding out her hand to take it. The woman handed it over with a quizzical look, and Sister Francis made a show of pointing to some writing at the top of the blackboard. To me, it was obvious that she was lying, but the inspector seemed satisfied. I couldn't help thinking that the nuns were a bunch of hypocrites. There appeared to be one rule for them and another for us. It should have been Sister Francis reciting the Ten Commandments. What about the eighth commandment, 'Thou shalt not bear false witness...?'

'Goodbye, girls,' the woman said.

'Goodbye, miss,' we echoed.

Sister Francis looked at us proudly as they left. We'd put on a good performance.

Later, in the line to go to chapel for the Rosary, I heard Chrissie's voice behind me. 'Do you think that those inspectors were here because someone found our paper planes?'

It hadn't occurred to me and I thought for a moment. The visit had the appearance of being prearranged, but it was a bit odd that the inspectors had turned up on the same day that we sent our messages over the wall. If they'd come because of our pleas for help, I thought, they'd been really quick to act. Then again, if they'd wanted to find out the truth, they should have talked to us without nuns being present.

All through the Rosary I thought about the paper planes lying on the other side of the wall. I tried to visualise people picking them up and reading them and thought about what I'd do if I were in their shoes. It was hard to think about anything else and I couldn't wait to get a chance to talk to Bernadette and Chrissie again. Sharing a secret with my friends was great, and it really helped get me through the day.

CHAPTER 14

The Cubbyhole

At the top of the stairs, next to one of the dormitories, there was a storeroom. It wasn't really big enough to be called a room; it was more of a walk-in cupboard. The first thing you noticed when you entered it was the strong smell of cleaning materials, a pungent mixture of floor polish, Vim and Jeyes Fluid. The walls were lined with large wooden pigeonholes that contained cleaning products and utensils such as hand brushes, deck scrubbers and cloths. The room was also known as 'Sister Thomas's cubbyhole'. She held the keys, and she controlled what – and who – went in and out.

I'd been to the cubbyhole many times, but my visits usually had nothing to do with cleaning. This was where Sister Thomas took me, and others, to be punished. I hated the cubbyhole. It was the very worst part of my living nightmare. Today I was in trouble for looking at Sister Thomas on the way to Mass. A few weeks earlier I'd been in trouble for not looking at her. Originally she'd accused me of not being able to look people straight in the face. She'd said that when I looked down I was gazing into Hell. So this time I'd looked directly at her, but she'd taken offence at that, too. It was another lose-lose situation, I thought, as I walked ahead of her up the stairs.

Just the sight of that door from the top of the stairs was enough to fill me with the deepest sense of dread and despair. My small frame trembled, my limbs grew heavy, and each step was more difficult than the last. I knew what lay ahead and wished with all my heart that it was already over.

Sister Thomas racked through her large set of keys, searching for the one that would unlock the cubby. She met my eye before opening the door. I recognised the look on her face, it was the look that said, 'I've got you, Reilly, you're mine.' I'd seen it almost every day since I'd moved up to the juniors. My heart sank.

Following me inside the cubby, she switched on the light and locked the door behind her. In one corner of the small room there was an old wooden crate. She pulled it into the centre of the space and sat down, staring long and hard at me. Beneath my brown convent-issue dress, I began to quake with fear.

'Undress and face the wall, Reilly!'

Sister Thomas's orders were to be obeyed at once, or things could get a lot worse, so I turned my back to her and started to take off my clothes. My body was shaking and my fingers fumbling as I struggled to remove the garments.

It struck me as odd that whenever we undressed in the dormitory we had to do so underneath our long nightdresses and that even a glimpse of bare flesh would have been enough to provoke the severest reprimand from the nun now staring so intensely at my body. But I was in no position to ask questions. I carefully folded each item of clothing I took off and placed it in a neat pile on the floor, until I was naked, still facing the wall. There was no sound from Sister Thomas. I knew that she was playing games – making me wait as long as possible before starting my punishment – and I let out an anguished sob.

'No one will hear you, Reilly, so you can stop that at once!' she shouted.

In an attempt to stop crying, I took a deep breath and held on to it for as long as I could, standing perfectly still and in silence. Tears streamed down my cheeks and dripped off my chin, forming wet patches on the dark wooden floor. I couldn't see Sister Thomas, but I could feel her eyes boring into me. This was part of a regular pattern that she followed, and it was obvious that she got some kind of thrill out of seeing me like this.

I was used to the brutal punishments

dished out by many of the nuns, but what happened here, with Sister Thomas, went well beyond that. I lowered my head and waited. Almost at once, an intense, excruciating pain filled my backside. The force of the blow threw me against the pigeonholes. Crying out, I tried to keep myself upright and pushed away from the wall.

'I'll beat the Devil out of you, Reilly! Get your eyes to Heaven!' Sister Thomas screamed.

I raised my eyes, hoping that if I did as I was told, the punishment wouldn't be as bad this time.

'Turn around and face me, Reilly.'

I turned, trying hard not to lower my gaze, but my eyes were full of tears, and I didn't know where to focus them. As I peered forward, I could just make out the blurred black and white robed figure towering over me, a heavy wooden clothes brush raised high above my head, poised to strike. The brush moved, and I instinctively shrank from the blow and dropped to my knees, putting up my hands to shield the back of my head.

'Take your eyes off me, Reilly!' she shrieked.

I felt another explosion of pain as the brush head smashed into my back. Again and again she laid into me. Huddled on the floor, I lacked the breath to scream, and if I had, it would have made no impression. Even now she continued to taunt me.

'You haven't had enough yet, Reilly,' she laughed, smashing the brush down again.

I lay on the floor sobbing hysterically, my back, bottom and legs racked with pain, shivering as much from cold as from fright. My suffering was made all the worse by the certain knowledge that no one would come and rescue me.

Finally, it dawned on me that the beating had stopped. It had probably only lasted several minutes, but it felt like an age. I moved my head out from behind my hand, just a little, and watched Sister Thomas pacing up and down the confined space of the cubby. I tried to sit up but couldn't find the strength, so I lay there at her mercy; hoping the punishment was over. Unfortunately, it was not.

'Get up, Reilly. I'm not finished with you yet.' Once more I tried to get to my feet. 'Move!' she shouted.

Slowly, I managed to pull myself up into a standing position. Shaking with fear, convulsing with sobs, I turned to face her.

'I'm leaving you in here, Reilly, to think about whether you want to be a child of God or a child of the Devil. You will not move from this spot until I come back. And you will not make a sound!'

I heard the door being locked and her

footsteps on the stairs, but I dared not move yet. Everything was quiet. Frozen to the spot, my body aching all over, I noticed that there were hot-red weals rising on my legs and on the cheeks of my backside.

I wrapped my arms around my body for comfort and warmth. There was nothing to do now but wait. In some ways this was the worst part of the punishment, as I never knew how long she'd leave me. Sometimes she'd return within the hour – but often many hours, or occasionally even days, would pass before she came back. The sister in charge of you could do what she liked with you. The other nuns wouldn't dream of intervening. And when Sister Thomas eventually returned, she might not necessarily broadcast her approach with the pounding of thick convent shoes on the stairs or the clanging of heavy iron keys. Instead, she often crept back in silence, with her shoes in her hand and the keys carefully restrained. I knew I had good reason to be afraid and that no matter how cold or cramped I became I must not move from my spot. I wasn't about to make things harder for myself by giving her an excuse to prolong or intensify my punishment.

Sometime later I heard the bell ring for dinner, followed by the sound of girls moving towards the refectory. I wondered if Sister Thomas would come back to let me out or, more likely, to check that I was still standing on my spot. But there was no sign of her. All I could hear was the fading sounds of the last few girls settling behind their seats, ready for grace. After grace a deathly silence pervaded the convent. Nowhere was that silence felt more than in the cubby.

There was no heating in the cubby, and I shivered and sobbed as I tried to rub some warmth into my goose bump-covered flesh. Time passed slowly while I waited for the sound of the after-dinner bell. The bells were my watch, but they seemed to ring untrue, because it always felt like hours were passing in the cubby when only minutes had elapsed outside.

I paced up and down on the spot, trying to get some feeling back into my legs. Soon, pacing turned into jigging, and then I realised with horror that I needed to go to the toilet. As much as I loathed the sight of Sister Thomas, I now prayed for her to return before nature took its course. I couldn't hang on for very much longer, and I knew that she would be furious if she came back to find I'd wet myself.

By the time the bell sounded for the end of dinner, I was bursting to go. Perhaps if she came directly up from the refectory, I might hold out long enough to beg to use the toilet – and surely she would let me go. Not that she would be concerned about my plight, but she wouldn't like to see her sacred floor soiled by a wretched Reilly. But then I thought that perhaps this was exactly what she was hoping for. It would prove what a vile child I was and give her every reason to punish me further. Just then I heard footsteps approaching. Please, please, please, I begged in silence, but the footsteps moved on and faded slowly, and with them went all hope.

I wasn't aware at first that my struggle was over. First the tops of my legs felt pleasantly warm, then the pain in my stomach eased, and I felt an almost euphoric sense of relief wash over me. Warm fluid poured down my legs, and a puddle spread rapidly outwards from my feet. There didn't seem any point in holding back now, so I just let go until I'd finished. Eventually, when the flow had stopped, I found myself standing in a puddle of urine. An overpowering stench filled the small room.

Sister Thomas is going to kill me, I thought, staring at the puddle of wee. 'Oh my God, what am I going to do?' I whispered into the darkness.

Stepping out of the puddle, I shook each foot dry. The urine had felt warm on my bare legs and feet, but now, as they dried, I grew colder than ever. I searched the pigeonholes for something to clear up the mess without the nun noticing. But this was Sister Thomas's private space. If I touched anything, she was bound to notice, and then I would get punished for stealing as well. As I racked my brains for an idea, I heard footsteps outside in the corridor, followed by the jangling of keys. The heavy wooden door swung open.

Sister Thomas walked in with her arms folded in front of her. She was clearly about to say something, but instead she turned quickly, slammed and locked the door behind her and swung round to face me again. I was back on my spot now, with my eyes downcast. Whack! My head flew back with the force of a powerful slap, and I fell to the floor, into the puddle.

'You filthy dirty brute, Reilly!' she yelled as she hit me again, careful to avoid the wee. Eventually, when she'd tired of slapping and punching me, she ordered me to my feet.

'I'm sorry, Sister,' I pleaded with her. 'I couldn't help it.'

'Shut up, Reilly!' She grabbed a handful of my hair and forced my head down into the puddle. Using me like a mop, she rubbed my head back and forth across the floor until my long, loose hair was dripping wet and my face and nose were scratched raw. Finally; with a powerful tug, she forced me to my feet.

'Get dressed and get this cleared up right

now, Reilly, and don't think I've finished with you yet.' She released her grip on my hair.

I wouldn't meet her eye as I put my clothes back on, but I was aware that she was watching my every move. Once I was dressed, she told me to go to the bathroom and get a mop and a bucket filled with water and Jeyes Fluid. I did as I was told and was quickly back to clean the floor. Once the job was completed, she locked up the cubby and ordered me back to the bathroom.

Walking on ahead of her, my hair still dripping with wee, I wondered what would happen next. I quietly prayed that I had the strength to bear it. As I put the bucket and mop away; my thoughts were distracted by the sound of running water. Turning towards the noise, I saw Sister Thomas pouring Jeyes Fluid into a bath. As usual, the smell of it turned my stomach. I knew the bath was for me and watched her pick up a wooden scrubbing brush. I didn't like the way she was staring at me and froze with fear as she began to bellow at me again.

'Get yourself over here, Reilly. You filthy animal!' I slowly shuffled towards her. 'Undress and get into the bath,' she said.

I began to undress.

'Quicker than that, Reilly!'

Terrified, I tore at my clothes.

The cold water was still running as I stepped into the freezing bath. The Jeyes

Fluid, which stung at the best of times, was like a dagger to my wounds. Just as I was lowering my battered body into the cold, murky water, she clamped her hands onto my shoulders and tried to force me under the water. I barely knew what had hit me and was completely disorientated. Panicking, I grabbed hold of the side of the bath and tried to keep my head up, but my strength gave out, and slowly she forced me down. Underwater, unable to breathe, I was convinced that she wasn't going to let go of me in time. I was going to die. I started freaking out, and she lost her grip. I pushed myself up, gasping for air. Looking behind me, I saw her drying her hands. Thank God, I thought, it's over.

She turned towards me again, her face flushed red from her exertions. The front of her habit was soaked, despite her best attempts to dry it, and she was clearly in as bad a temper as ever. She put the towel on the floor and picked up the scrubbing brush.

'You will stand up, Reilly, and I will teach you that cleanliness is next to godliness and that there's no room in Heaven for filthy animals like you Reillys. You'll all be going straight to Hell.'

I stood up, shivering with cold and in terror.

'Turn around, Reilly; and bend over.'

I began crying again, pleading. 'Please,

Sister! No!'

But she only got angrier. 'Now, Reilly!' she shouted, clearly losing her patience.

I turned my back to her and bent over, holding on to the side of the bath.

'Spread your legs wide apart.'

I obeyed. I could hear her rubbing the scrubbing brush on a large block of carbolic soap and could guess what was coming next. I was right, and soon I felt rough bristles scratching the private parts between my legs and bottom. The pain and humiliation seemed unbearable, but somehow I had to bear them. What choice was there? Again and again I begged her, 'Please, Sister! Please stop...' but she carried on until she was completely satisfied that the job was done.

When it was over, I sat in the water, sobbing. The pain in my private parts was excruciating, and my whole body hurt from the damage inflicted over the course of the day.

'Finish yourself off now, Reilly; and when you're dressed, stand outside the storeroom door till I get back.'

'Yes, Sister,' I whimpered, trying to hold back the sobs until her footsteps had faded into the distance. I got out of the water, wrapped myself in a towel and sank to the floor, weeping and trembling uncontrollably.

CHAPTER 15

Girls on the Run

When Loretta heard on the grapevine that I'd been in the cubbyhole again, she sneaked away from her work and came to see how I was. She found me lying on my bed in the dormitory, racked with pain and dazed from the trauma of what I'd been through.

'I just want to die,' I sobbed when I saw her. 'What's the point in going on? Nothing's ever going to change.'

Shocked by my scratches, weals and bruises, she was trying to comfort me with a hug when her best friend Bridget rushed in.

'Ye'd better get back to work,' Bridget warned. 'Sister Austin's coming to check on ye soon.' Seeing me, she added, 'What's wrong, Frances?'

'That old witch Sister Thomas took her up to the cubbyhole again,' Loretta said.

'Oh no,' said Bridget. 'Did she hurt ye bad?'

Unable to speak, I nodded.

'Jesus, Mary and St Joseph, this can't go on.'

'But we can't do anything about it!' I burst out as she turned to leave.

'We could try and break out of this dump,' Loretta said.

That stopped Bridget in her tracks. 'How?' she said.

'I know some girls who got away,' Loretta said. 'Some got caught, but there were a few who made it to Dublin. Once you get to the South, there's nothing the nuns can do – or the police for that matter – because you're over the border, in another country.'

Loretta sounded serious and had obviously given it some thought. We fell silent for a few moments as the idea that we could actually escape began to take root. The thought of being free was enough to block out the likely consequences of being caught, and before long we were completely absorbed in planning our escape. Just talking and thinking about it breathed new life back into us, and I all but forgot about my aches and bruises.

'I could get some nuns' clothing from the laundry,' said Bridget, who'd been working mornings in the nuns' laundry for some months.

'Yes! We'll get dressed up and go out by the back gate, where the tradesmen come in,' Loretta said. 'Friday would be best, when the bin men come, but someone's gonna have to distract whoever's on the gate.'

'It's usually Sister Francis. Surely we can think up something to distract her for a minute or so,' Bridget said.

We heard footsteps.

'Shhh! Someone's coming! Let's get out of here, Loretta.' And then they were gone, leaving me to dream of life beyond the walls, far, far away from Sister Thomas.

When the bell rang the next morning, I felt awful. My head throbbed, my back was stiff, and my knees ached more than ever. Somehow I managed to get through prayers without crying. As I washed and dressed for Mass, I kept reminding myself that I had to be OK today so that we could continue planning our escape. We'd be out on Friday; I was sure of it. I visualised the three of us, dressed as nuns, walking straight out of the back gate. It didn't occur to me that we wouldn't be convincing nuns. I thought that no one would know the difference if we were dressed in flowing habits.

'Come on, Reilly, get a move on,' shouted Sister Thomas.

With a start, I realised that everyone else was lined up for Mass. I jumped into line, and we proceeded silently to chapel. That morning I paid a lot of attention to how the nuns wore their habits. I scrutinised their veils and tried to work out how they put them on. Some of them seemed to notice me staring, and I looked quickly away; worried they might somehow guess our plan.

It was hard to keep my mind on Mass or anything else that morning. All I could think about was getting away from the convent forever. I was definitely ready to take my chances outside on the streets. Anything was better than this – and if I didn't leave soon, then I might die here. I couldn't wait to see Loretta and Bridget again so that we could come up with a really good plan of action. As the morning moved on and I imagined my new life, I became incredibly excited. By morning recreation, I could hardly contain myself.

'When are we going to run away, Loretta?'

'We could go this morning,' she said. 'If we had the clothes.'

'I could get them later on,' said Bridget. 'And there are a few more girls who want to go, so there will be about eight of us.'

Loretta gaped at her. 'What do you mean, eight? Eight is too many. We'll be noticed.'

Bridget seemed unconcerned. 'I just told a few girls who were up for it that they could come with us. They told some more girls, and now there's eight of us.'

We stared at her in disbelief.

'Can you get eight sets of nuns' clothes, then?' I asked.

'No problem, I'm on nuns' laundry duty today.'

She sounded so confident that we forgot about numbers and concentrated on getting the rest of the plan together. After some discussion we agreed that if Bridget could get the clothes, we'd go that evening. Loretta would get someone to distract the nun on duty, and we'd slip out of the back gate together.

I hoped with all my heart that Bridget would get the outfits we needed. I had to get out, I had to. Suddenly, Sinéad flashed into my mind. The thought of leaving her behind made me sad, but Loretta and I had to escape first, and then we could think about how to get Sinéad out later. I was sure she'd understand, but I had to try to talk to her before we left.

It was going to be difficult because she'd been quarantined with suspected mumps and wasn't allowed any visitors. I crept up the stairs to the infirmary and sneaked in through the door. Luckily, the nun on duty had her back to me, so I slipped into the next room, searching for Sinéad. I found her in a bed by the window. I really hoped she wouldn't be too upset at my news because her tears might be enough to put me off going.

She smiled when she saw me. There was still a close bond between us, despite the very limited time we spent together.

'How are ye?' I asked, hugging her. She

certainly didn't look too ill.

'I'm fine,' she said, returning the hug and was clearly very pleased to see me.

I listened to her news, then I told her about our escape plan and how we'd be back for her.

'We're not going to forget about ye,' I said.

She didn't seem the least bit upset. In fact, she seemed pleased that we were trying to escape, proud even, and didn't think for one minute that we were going to forget about her.

'Good luck,' she said.

I was surprised and relieved by her reaction. We had a final hug, and as I crept away, unseen, I looked back and saw a big grin on her face.

I tried to hold this image of Sinéad in my head but felt so emotional about saying goodbye that tears started to fill my eyes. However, this was no time to be weak. I turned away from the door and rushed back to join the others before the bell sounded for the end of recreation.

I was glad the visit had gone well. At least now it wouldn't come as a shock when she heard that her sisters had run away. I was sure that once Loretta and I found our mammy, we'd tell her what the convent was like and she'd come back for Sinéad.

I was so nervous and excited that I was finding it really hard to act as if nothing was going on. I had to be vigilant, though. Too much was at stake now to make any slips. It was crucial that the nuns didn't get suspicious, or they would start watching us very closely.

I could almost taste freedom. No more beatings or disgusting convent food and no more Sister Thomas. I imagined myself waking up under a tree in a park feeling absolutely free, and that's what kept me going.

Later, as we left the chapel and headed towards the refectory for tea, Bridget whispered, 'I've got them, Frances! Meet me in the toilets in a few minutes' time.'

I was careful to keep my head facing forward and carried on marching as if nothing had happened. When we arrived at the refectory, I asked Sister Kevin if I could be excused to go to the toilet.

'Yes, Reilly, but be quick about it,' she said abruptly. She appeared to be in a foul mood, but I wasn't going to let that bother me, not today, and I rushed off to the toilets.

Bridget was waiting for me. 'I've got them!' she said again.

'We're getting out!' I hugged her, jumped up and down and ran around in circles. I couldn't help it. I'd never been so excited. 'We're getting out of here! We're getting out of here!' I kept repeating.

Loretta rushed in and warned us to be quiet, as we could be heard all the way down the hall. 'How many have you got?' she asked.

'Enough for seven of us – that's all I could get.'

'So we'll just have to tell someone they're not going. It can't be helped.'

'Who won't be going?' I asked.

'We'll have to think about that. But for now, get back to the refectory before Sister Kevin wonders what you're up to.'

'You took your time, Reilly. Now say grace and get seated.'

Sister Kevin's mood hadn't improved. I quickly found my chair, blessed myself and started to pray over my food, thanking God for the horrible slop I had to eat.

'What is it with you Reillys?' I heard Sister Kevin say. Thinking she was talking to me, I turned and saw Loretta and Bridget walking into the refectory together. Bridget apologised and explained that they'd been late getting off laundry duty. When they were seated, they winked and smiled over at me, looking very pleased with themselves. I assumed they'd come up with a plan and hoped we were going after tea. I was desperate to see the other side of the wall.

After tea, Sister Kevin sent us to the hall for Irish dancing practice. Normally I would have been happy to go, but I knew that there would be a head count to make sure everyone was present, and that meant we'd have to delay our escape. Sister Thomas counted us in and walked over to the stage, where there was an old record player and a small pile of records. She took an ancient LP from its cover, placed it on the turntable and lowered the needle. A long, loud crackle was followed by the sound of Irish music.

'Pick a partner for the two-handed reel,' she told us.

'You can be my partner,' Loretta said, taking my hand.

I was delighted, not only because I needed an excuse to talk to Loretta but also because it meant I wouldn't be stuck with someone without any timing. Loretta and I were good dancers, but some girls never got the hang of it and could make even the best partner look bad. Then you'd both be in trouble with the nuns. Sister Thomas paired off the stragglers, returned to the stage and set the needle back to the beginning of the record.

'Toes pointed and begin,' she said.

While we danced, she watched us carefully for mistakes, and although she couldn't find anything wrong with our technique, we had to be on our guard. Fortunately, she started picking on other girls, but all the same, it would have been too dangerous to talk about our plan just then.

We finally managed to catch up with each

other in the dormitory. All the girls involved were gathered around my bed, which worried me because a nun might appear from nowhere and guess what we were scheming. We kept our voices to a low whisper. With only seven sets of clothing, one of us was going to have to stay behind, but no one volunteered. We were all desperate to leave.

'Well,' Loretta said, breaking the silence. 'Frances, Bridget and I are definitely going, so it's got to be one of the rest of yous.'

But still no one offered to stay.

'Bernadette is getting out soon, anyway,' I said tentatively. 'And the nuns don't pick on her as much as the rest of us, so perhaps she should stay.'

Bernadette couldn't really argue. She didn't seem to get things as bad as the rest of us, even if she did hate the convent just as much, and her family were taking her back home in a few months' time.

'All right, then,' she conceded. 'If it's got to be me, is there anything I can do to help the rest of yous get out?'

'We need a distraction,' Loretta said. 'It needs to be good, or we won't have time to get away.'

'I can do that. When are yous going?'

'Tomorrow morning,' Loretta said, apparently deep in thought. 'We'll just take a chance and go when it feels right.'

It wasn't much of a plan, but it was better

than nothing. Sister Thomas came into the dormitory and we scattered to get ready for bed.

I was the first one out of bed when the bell sounded for morning prayers. I'd been awake most of the night, anxiously trying to hold down my excitement. I watched the other girls stirring at the sound of that awful clanging bell. Maybe today I would be free. The cold floor didn't bother me today, nor did the fact that I was really tired. I just wanted to get on with the morning as quickly as possible.

Sister Thomas started the prayers, even though Rita was still getting out of bed. She was nearly always last. Normally, prayers wouldn't start until everyone was kneeling on the floor, but this morning Sister Thomas's mind seemed to be elsewhere. She rushed us through prayers and dashed out of the room, leaving us to get ready for Mass. The atmosphere in the dormitory was much nicer in her absence, and I took a moment to breathe it in before getting ready. I had a feeling that this was the start of a really good day.

We were ready with about five minutes to spare before Mass. Sister Thomas hadn't returned, and people were wondering whether something had happened. I wasn't bothered, though. Nothing was more important than escaping, and it was convenient that she wasn't around.

When the bell sounded, we got into line and walked in single file to the chapel. Sister Thomas appeared on the stairs, looking flustered. She did a head count as we passed and then followed us inside. I prayed really hard that we'd manage to get away. As I took one last look around the chapel, my stomach bubbled and I felt a bit sick. It was a familiar sensation, the one I always experienced when there was a chance of getting into trouble.

At breakfast Bridget and Loretta told me we'd be going as soon as we could. The nuns' clothes were in Loretta's hall locker, next to the toilets, and we were going to have to try to get there at roughly the same time.

'What about right now? We could do it now if we had a good distraction,' I said, not wanting to wait another minute.

A message was relayed in whispers from one girl to another until it reached Bernadette. We needed a distraction straight away. A couple of minutes later Bernadette looked across at me and nodded her head.

'She's going to do it, Loretta,' I said nervously. I could feel myself trembling with anticipation. Just then a fight started at Bernadette's table, drawing in the duty nun and a crowd of girls. Now was our chance. We stood up and slipped away to the hall.

Loretta opened her locker, and we started pulling at the clothes.

'I'm the smallest,' I reminded the others,

examining them for size.

Bridget took charge and allocated the disguises. This caused a bit of whingeing, but there wasn't time to waste. Bernadette's distraction was working a treat, and the noise of fighting in the refectory was increasing by the minute. It sounded like everyone was joining in. We fumbled with the clothes, trying to get them to fit. Mine completely drowned me. The veil practically reached my hips and I had to double up the skirt and tuck it into my waist so that I didn't trip up.

'We're going to have to be quicker!' Loretta said. 'Try helping each other to get them to look right.' Soon we were as ready as we were ever going to be.

It was pretty funny to see each other in habits, and some of us started mimicking the nuns. Bridget pretended to be Sister Thomas. She was very good, and we guessed straight away who she was trying to be, but then I started to get annoyed.

'There will be plenty of time to muck about once we're out of here,' I said.

I opened the door, just a crack. I couldn't see anything, but I could hear the commotion going on in the refectory. I opened the door a bit more. The coast was clear.

'Come on, let's go.'

We left in single file and made it all the way to the changing rooms without being seen. This was a good place to stop and check out the back gate. To our surprise, we found Bernadette waiting with the key.

'How did you manage that? I thought you were in a fight,' Loretta said.

'Not me, I just told the girls on my table that some other girls were saying nasty things about them, but that they weren't to say that I'd told them. That did the trick, and yous got your distraction.'

'How did ye get your hands on that?' I said, pointing to the key.

'Don't ask; it wasn't easy. Come on, you have to go now.'

We walked calmly to the back gate. Bernadette opened it as quickly as she could.

'Good luck,' she said, hurrying to close it again before anyone saw.

At last we were on the other side of the wall. We stood on the pavement watching cars go past in amazement – finally, the real world, the world outside, freedom. We started hugging each other with glee, but then I noticed that we were being stared at by passing motorists.

'Come on, people are looking. We've to behave like nuns, or someone will call the cops.'

We lowered our eyes, clasped our hands together and bustled along the pavement, doing our best nun impersonations. Five minutes later we came to Ormeau Park, where a crowd of people were gathered at the gates. The moment they saw us they started to laugh, and I felt my face grow hot and flushed. For the first time it occurred to me that maybe we weren't very convincing nuns. In fact, going by the reaction of the people outside the park, we probably looked ridiculous.

'Let's go through the park,' I said.

I wanted to get away from the main road. Hopefully, there would be fewer people in the park at that time of the morning. The others agreed that we might draw less attention there, and we walked past the laughing crowd and through the gates. I distinctly heard a man say, 'They're probably on the run from the orphanage up the road.'

It was quiet in the park. We found some trees and bushes to hide behind and sat down to talk.

Loretta said that we shouldn't stay long, because the people at the gate would probably tell the police. 'This will be the first place they'll look.'

'Wouldn't we be better hiding here until it gets dark?' Bridget said. 'It'll be easier to move on without being seen at night.'

It was hard to know what to do. I said that I thought Loretta was probably right and we should get out of the park. I trusted her instincts and didn't want to sit around all day, waiting to get caught. We were outside the walls but still dangerously close to the convent.

We went on trying to weigh up our chances. Around twenty minutes had passed since we'd stepped out of the front gate and it struck me that by now Sister Thomas and the other nuns would have noticed our absence. I hoped that Bernadette hadn't got into any trouble for helping us. A chill went through me at the thought of the punishment we'd face if we were taken back to the convent. The others went on arguing about whether to stay in the park or move on.

'Let's take a vote on it,' I said, trying to move things along. Everyone except Bridget voted to leave the park.

'I'm not sure about our clothes,' I said. 'We look really stupid. Let's get rid of the veils so that it just looks like we're wearing long, black dresses.'

We took off our headwear, and I shook out my hair with relief. How could the nuns bear to be confined by their veils all the time? I'd heard rumours that their heads were shaved when they became novices. Gathering up the discarded veils, I hid them in a nearby bin.

'Come on, now,' Loretta said. 'Let's get away from the park before the police turn up. You can come with us if you want, Bridget, or you can take your chances staying here.'

'OK, then, I'll come with you.'

She still sounded unsure, so we set off before she changed her mind. We passed a few people out walking their dogs and said good morning to them. They smiled and said good morning back, which made us feel a lot more confident. Soon we were walking briskly down the Ormeau Road, trying to appear like we were going about our daily business while keeping a good lookout for policemen.

'I can't believe we're doing this, Loretta,' I said. 'Sister Thomas will know we've gone by now, and she'll be going nuts. I bet she'd love to get her hands on us right now.'

Loretta laughed. 'You're right, Frances. She's probably having a fit and telling everyone, "The Devil is in those Reillys and they'll burn in Hell."'

'Do you think we'll burn in Hell?'

'No,' Loretta said. 'But I hope she does!'

Soon we arrived in Belfast town centre, where the traffic was busier and there were a lot more people around. We walked past rows and rows of shop windows, marvelling at all the beautiful things we saw. I wondered if I'd ever be able to have nice stuff, like normal people. We passed a café. The gorgeous smell of sizzling bacon wafted out through the entrance.

'The slop we get never smells like that,' Bridget said.

It was nice to see shops and smell good cooking, even if we didn't have any money, but we didn't hang about in the town too long. Soon it would be getting even busier and there would probably be quite a few policemen about. A few minutes later we found ourselves walking along the River Lagan, where it was much quieter, and we began to relax a bit. After all, Loretta said, we'd come quite a long way from the convent, even if we didn't really know where we were going.

'Let's stop here for a while,' she suggested. 'It's the safest place for the moment.'

We found a place to sit, no longer feeling so vulnerable. It was the best feeling in the world, I thought, to sit looking at the water, without a care in the world. I jumped up. 'We've done it! We're free!' I shouted at the others.

'Yes, we have!' Bridged shouted back. 'We'll head out of Belfast after it gets dark. Then we'll cross the border. They can't touch us once we're over.'

It was so exciting. Soon we were laughing and joking about. I collected a load of stones and threw them in the water. Then the others were up and searching for anything they could find that would make a splash, competing to throw further and higher. In went stones, sticks, beer bottles and even an old shoe that Bridget found. It was a lot of fun.

Loretta started singing 'Santa Lucia' and we all joined in. It was one of the songs we'd had to sing at the annual concert when the ministry came to visit. We sang in harmony, and one song led to another, and then another. But our voices trailed off when we saw a man with a small dog walking slowly along towards us.

'No, don't stop!' the man said, quickening his step. 'That was just lovely.'

So we started up again, singing to a rapt audience of one man and his small dog. The man closed his eyes as he listened, as if swept away by the music. He was middle-aged, with distinguished grey hair and smart clothes, and I imagined that he probably had lots of money and a really nice family. He thanked us when we reached the end of our repertoire. Once again he told us that we sang beautifully. He reached into his pocket and we heard the sound of jingling coins. Taking out a handful, he sorted through them and picked out a big silver one.

'Here's a half-crown. Get some sweets for yourselves,' he said, handing the money to Bridget, who was closest to him.

Bridget had no problem taking the money because we didn't have a penny between us. We thanked the man and gave him grateful looks.

'What should we get with it? Sweets, chips or something else?' Loretta said.

The rest of us thought for a minute.

'We could go to a shop and see what we can afford,' Bridget suggested.

It seemed like a good idea and soon we were inside a shop, surrounded by a dazzling array of sweets, biscuits and cakes. The man behind the counter kept a very close eye on us. He obviously thought that we were going to steal something.

'Can I help yous?' he said.

'We're just deciding what to buy, we'll be ready in a minute,' Bridget replied politely.

'Are yous girls from the convent?'

We shook our heads. 'No.'

I could feel myself blushing again. I wasn't comfortable about lying and was sure that God would punish me for it. Loretta tried to bluff it out by telling him that we were doing a play and were still in costume, but he didn't seem at all convinced. She asked him for a selection of sweets and handed over the half-crown. He poured sweets out of big jars onto a set of scales and then tipped them into small paper bags. It seemed to take ages, and we started to get nervous. We just wanted to leave the shop and get back to the river, where we felt safe. Eventually; he passed the sweets over to Loretta.

'So what school are yous at, then?' he said.

'Sorry, we're in a hurry and haven't got time to chat,' Loretta said.

We rushed outside and she passed the sweets around.

'I didn't trust him. He was too nosy,' she said. 'Let's get back to the riverbank. He's probably phoning the police right now.' We scurried along, sucking on our sweets. We were nearly at the river when we spotted a policeman. He'd already seen us and was running straight towards us.

'Run!' I shouted. No one needed telling again. Picking up our long, heavy skirts, we sprinted away as fast as we could. But the policeman was catching up fast. I was out in front of the others, even though I was the smallest, and my heart felt like it was going to burst right out of my chest.

I heard Bridget shout, 'No! Get off me!' and I glanced back. The policeman had grabbed her arm, and she was struggling to shake him off. By now we were running through Belfast town centre. People stopped and stared as we flew past, out of breath and panicking, our skirts billowing out behind us.

I can't go back, I was thinking. I just can't. Suddenly, from out of nowhere, a policeman grabbed me. My heart stopped.

'I can't go back there!' I screamed at him. 'You don't know what they're like!'

He said nothing, just walked me to a car and told me to get in. Bridget was already inside. I burst into floods of tears.

'Don't give them the satisfaction of crying, Frances,' she said.

The policeman started the engine. 'Let's get you two girls back where you belong,' he said in a sarcastic tone.

I wanted to jump out of the car. The thought of going back to the convent was unbearable. 'I wish I was dead,' I said, hoping, with all my heart, that Loretta had got away, that maybe she'd find our mammy and come back for Sinéad and me.

The Reverend Mother was standing by the main door. She gave us a furious look as we arrived.

'Thank you for returning them, Officer,' she said.

'The others will be back soon enough, too,' the policeman said. 'They're being chased all over the town at the minute. I'll be off now, in case I'm needed to bring back any more.'

The Reverend Mother saw him to the door before turning to face us again, her cheeks red and her eyes swivelling madly. She looked like she was going to go berserk at any moment. 'You will stand there until the rest of the girls have returned. It will give you time to reflect on what you have done and to consider what would be a suitable punishment.'

I thought I was going to be sick with fear. Glancing over at Bridget, who was pale and visibly shaking, I realised that I probably looked just like she did. After what seemed like ages, the policeman returned with the others. I lost all hope when I heard Loretta's voice among them. They were sent in to stand with us while the Reverend Mother talked to the policeman.

We didn't need telling how much worse things would be if we were caught trying to talk to each other, but no one had forgotten the sweets. The Reverend Mother's back was turned, so Loretta managed to pass them around without being noticed and we shoved them furtively into our mouths. But sweets were only a temporary comfort, and we gave each other worried looks as we quietly sucked the luxurious flavour out of them.

The Reverend Mother went off some-where with the policeman, and Loretta shared out the rest of the sweets.

'Well, at least they won't be able to deprive us of them now,' I whispered.

'We're probably not going to get anything else to eat today,' she said.

'I expect that will be the least of our worries by the time they're finished with us,' Bridget added.

'The next time we get out, we stay out,' Loretta vowed.

'That's if we survive that long,' I said, shivering with fear.

CHAPTER 16

The Premonition

For three weeks I tried to be everywhere Margaret was. I followed her around at recreation times and kept reminding her not to go up any ladders, even if a nun told her to. At first Margaret was flattered that I should be so concerned for her safety, but now it was beginning to annoy her that wherever she went, I went.

It all started in chapel one day, at Mass. While we were chanting prayers, I had a really clear vision of Margaret falling off a high ladder. It felt like a flashback, except that I had a strong sense that it was a flash-forward, and Margaret appeared to be quite badly hurt. But three weeks later nothing had happened, and she was getting so fed up with having me around that she insisted I stop following her.

I was relieved in a way, because I was beginning to tire of it myself. When I'd first had the vision, I was sure it must be some kind of a warning and that it was up to me to make sure that I prevented a disaster. But now that nothing had happened for so long,

I couldn't understand why I'd seen it and decided I'd just have to let it go. Margaret was fine, so I could forget about the ladder and get on with other things. Some girls were beginning to think that I'd become obsessed with the whole thing, and I could sort of understand why, when I thought about it. It was all rather creepy, and anyway, it would be great to spend my recreations with Chrissie again instead of following Margaret around.

Chrissie was glad to have me back. She'd been beginning to think that it might be months before I finally realised that nothing was going to happen, as I could be very stubborn. It was good to talk about other things instead, especially our lives when we left the convent – of big houses, open spaces, horses and friends. By the end of the day I'd put Margaret out of my mind.

The next few days passed without incident. Then one evening, when we were getting ready for bed, Mary came running into the dormitory shouting that an ambulance was on its way for Margaret. Apparently, Sister Francis had asked her to climb a ladder and retrieve some balls that were stuck on top of a high cupboard, and she'd fallen down.

I was amazed. 'Is she badly hurt?'

'I think so. But Sister Francis won't let anyone near her till the ambulance gets here.'

'Oh my God.' I sat down on my bed, feeling stunned.

Chrissie came over to see if I was OK. 'It's not your fault, Frances. You tried to warn her, and she thought you were going a bit mad. Maybe next time people will listen!' My friend was trying to reassure me, but it wasn't working.

'I hope she's going to be all right. I feel like it is my fault. I saw it all happen so clearly – and just think, Chrissie, I was right about it. If I have another vision, and I hope that I don't, I will just have to trust it to be true. But I don't know why I would have seen Margaret falling off a ladder a full month before it happened. It seems weird. Now I'm going to seem like even more of a freak to the others.'

'Well, you're not a freak to me. I think it's great that you saw it and tried to stop it. I wish I could do that. Anyway, don't worry what people think; you're better than a lot of people in here.'

Chrissie sounded like she meant every word, and I began to feel a little better. Bernadette rushed in to tell us that the ambulance had arrived for Margaret. Some of the girls ran over to the window to see if they could see anything, but Chrissie and I stayed where we were.

Sister Thomas arrived, shouting, 'Get away from those windows and kneel down for prayers!'

'Is Margaret going to be OK, Sister?' asked Rita.

'It looks like she's broken her nose,' she said briskly. 'We should know for sure when she gets back from the hospital. I'm sure she's in good hands.'

After we'd washed and lined up for inspection, she scanned the dormitory. 'Now, are you ready for prayers?'

She made the sign of the cross, and we said our prayers quickly. Then she turned out the lights and left in a hurry.

'Frances, have you had any visions about me?' whispered Kathleen.

'No, I haven't, Kathleen,' I said, hoping that would be an end to it because I was still feeling disturbed by what had happened. But that was just the beginning of it.

'What about me?' asked another girl. 'Have you had any visions about me?'

'No, just the one about Margaret. I'd never had one before and didn't even know if it would come true, but now it has.'

'Well, if you ever get any about me, let me know because I will definitely believe you after this,' said Mary. Followed by a chorus of 'Yes, me too!' from the other girls.

'I really hope I don't get any more, but if I do, I will tell whoever it is,' I said.

There were more questions, and more after that. Still, at least none of them were calling me a freak any more. In fact, most of them seemed genuinely interested in my vision, which turned out to be one of the many premonitions I've experienced in my life. So before we finally went to sleep I tried, once more, to describe exactly what I'd seen and how it had felt.

CHAPTER 17

Back From the Farm

I'd just arrived back at the convent from a holiday at the Murphys' farm. I'd been there several times now, but this time Sinéad had been allowed to go with me. We shared some good times. Sinéad got to sample Siobhan's wonderful cooking and to play with me and the boys around the farm. She'd had a fantastic time and looked upset to be back.

After two weeks of Siobhan's wonderful cooking neither of us was looking forward to the convent food. Fat, gristle and vegetable slop simply wasn't enough to keep us going. Often we were so hungry that we ate handfuls of grass to fill ourselves up, like cows or sheep.

It had been a real holiday for our taste buds, but of course it ended the moment we got back and Sister Kevin searched us. She found some new socks and a few packets of sweets that we'd desperately been trying to conceal in our clothes.

'I'll be confiscating these. Now get yourselves to your dormitories at once.'

Sinéad looked as if she was just about to

cry, and I could easily have joined her, but I wasn't going to give Sister Kevin that satisfaction.

'You'll have a lot to tell your friends,' I said, hoping to cheer her up.

She managed a weak smile, and I smiled back, proud of my brave little sister.

In the dormitory, the other girls were telling each other about their holidays. I listened with envy to the ones who'd gone home to their real families. Sitting quietly on my bed, I decided that this time I wouldn't tell anyone about what Tom and Barry had done to me. There was no point. I just had to accept that they were allowed to do whatever they wanted to me and nobody would stop them.

Suddenly, I flashed back to the farm. The dormitory vanished, and I was in the barn with Barry. He'd lured me there by pretending to have something to show me. 'A surprise,' he'd said, breathing heavily as he led me behind some bales of hay. Something in me sensed what was about to happen, and I tried to get away, saying that I needed to find Sinéad, but Barry wouldn't let me go. Keeping a tight hold of my arm, he told me that Sinéad was fine. He hemmed me in against the hay and started touching me under my dress. I began to cry, but he didn't take any notice. I felt his dirty hand inside my knickers, his fat fingers rubbing me.

'I have to go now!' I shouted, my head

exploding with panic. But I was no match for the large man who was now pushing his finger into me. Panting loudly with excitement, he seemed unaware of me, even though I was sobbing and telling him that he was hurting me. At one point he stopped, but only to undo the zip of his trousers and to try to force my hand inside them. I made a fist, knowing now exactly what he wanted, and shut my eyes so that I wouldn't have to look at him.

He froze at the sound of the boys playing with Sinéad nearby and quickly pulled away from me.

'Clean your face!' he snapped. 'You can't go out looking like that.'

Then, just as suddenly as it had vanished, the dormitory reappeared, and I became aware that the others were still telling their stories. Sister Thomas's footsteps came into earshot. Everyone scattered. I jumped to my feet, patted down the creases on my counterpane and stood by my bed, terrified that she'd start on me as soon as she saw me. This time she wasn't creeping about like she sometimes did, trying to catch us out. Instead, her footsteps came hard and fast, which meant that she was in a terrible mood. She entered the dormitory like someone possessed, her facial features distorted with rage. Her large rosary beads, which she wore around her waist with the huge crucifix hanging down at the side, were rattling as she stormed into the room, glaring maniacally.

'Who brought the Devil back with them?' she screamed, her face a picture of fury and disgust. She bent over and began to look under our beds.

'Not me, Sister!' I said.

The other girls joined in, one after the other. 'Not me, Sister!' they chorused, peering under their beds.

Hunched down so that she could see under each bed, she began running down the dormitory as if chasing something. 'There he is!' she shouted. We watched in terror as she ran back along the rows of beds and dived to the floor.

'Open a window, I've got him, I've got Nick!' she yelled, emerging from under one of the beds. Nick was the name she used for the Devil. She'd often told us that he was under our beds, knowing that it would scare us.

She appeared to be having a terrible struggle with someone or something that none of us could see. Moving to the window, she made a big show of throwing the Devil out. 'Get out, Nick, get out!' she shrieked.

We watched in silence. Even though we were used to this kind of behaviour from Sister Thomas, it was always hard to cope with it because we were never sure what she was going to do next. She began to walk along the rows of beds, inspecting each girl, staring into her eyes. When she got to me, her face twisted up with hatred, and I knew that I was going to get the blame for bringing the Devil back with me.

Just as I was thinking about what I could say in my defence, she lifted her hand and slapped me across the face, knocking me against the bed and banging my head on the iron frame. Dazed, I pulled myself up again. Pain mushroomed inside my head. Tears dripped down my cheeks.

'It was you, Reilly! You brought Nick back with you. Tears aren't going to save you from the fires of Hell. Now here's something to cry about!' She began to slap and punch me around the face and head.

'I'm sorry, Sister!' I pleaded. It occurred to me that perhaps I'd brought the Devil back because of what Tom and Barry had done to me. Maybe I really was evil – a child of the Devil – and Sister Thomas could see it in me. It would explain why Tom and Barry did the things they did to me; maybe they saw it, too. But I didn't want to believe it. I didn't want to go to Hell.

'Get up, Reilly, or I'll give you what for!' she screamed. She'd stopped punching me and was now standing over me as I lay on the floor with my hands over my head.

Some of the other girls met my eye as I tried to get to my feet, but none of them were able to help, even if they'd wanted to. Sinéad stood by her bed, her head turned away from me. She couldn't bear to watch me being used as a punchbag, but there was nothing she could do that wouldn't make things worse.

Sister Thomas raised her hand to strike me again. 'Had enough yet, Reilly?'

'Yes, Sister,' I said, wiping my face with my hands.

She lowered her arm and told me to kneel by my bed and pray until further notice.

'Yes, Sister. Thank you, Sister.' I knelt on the hard cold floor and blessed myself, using every ounce of energy left in me to hold back my sobs.

Sister Thomas stomped out of the dormitory. Some of the girls gave me sympathetic looks. Others, especially some seniors, carried on as if nothing had happened at all.

'Are you all right, Frances?' Kathleen asked, once the nun's footsteps had faded into the distance.

I couldn't reply. There was a lump in my throat, blocking my voice.

'Don't let her get to you. She loves picking on you. You're not the Devil's child. Take no notice of her.'

I gave her a nod and tried to force a smile to show that I appreciated her comforting words. The bell rang, and everyone lined up and walked out of the dormitory, leaving me alone. I was relieved, in a way, as I no longer had to put on an act and pretend to be OK. My tears started to flow freely, rolling down my face onto my dress and arms.

Using the bed for support, I pulled myself up off the floor. My head hurt and so did my body. I wiped my eyes and paced up and down between the rows of beds, trying to make sense of everything, but I couldn't understand any of it. Why did Tom have to keep taking me into his bed when it was so obvious that I didn't want to be there? Why didn't the rest of the Murphys know what he was like and stop him? Why did Barry find any opportunity to get me alone and to touch me where he shouldn't touch me, and why was I stuck in Nazareth House taking abuse from the nuns? I didn't have any answers, just more and more questions. Eventually, I lay on my bed and closed my eyes tight, trying to calm my swirling head and blank out all the emotional and physical pain.

After about half an hour I was disturbed by the sound of voices. Whoever it was, they weren't close yet, but I thought I'd better get myself back on the floor just in case. My face felt hot from the slaps and punches I'd received, but because mirrors weren't allowed, I had no way of seeing the damage. Stiff with pain, I moved slowly around the bed, removing all signs that I'd been lying on it. I could still hear movement and voices, but nobody came near the dormitory for at least another hour.

With nothing to distract me, I found it impossible not to think about the farm. Once more I flashed back to it. This time I was at the sewerage works in some fields nearby, where the Murphy children often played. There was a whole group of us – Maggie Murphy, some of her brothers and a few local children – and as usual we were playing on the pipes, which spouted water out of small holes as they rotated. The trick was to stand on the pipes and hold on to the thick wire that linked them to a pole in the middle. Using one foot to push off, it was possible to make the whole contraption move around like a merry-go-round, faster and faster. We were all having fun, except for Maggie, who wouldn't join in. She was in one of her grumpy moods. Jerome told her to stop acting jealous and come and play, but she plonked herself on the grass and refused.

After we'd tired of the merry-go-round, we moved on to a rectangular brick wall surrounding a small reservoir. Inside the wall, quite a way down, was a large warning sign that said, 'Depth 13 Feet'. We started throwing large stones and broken bricks into the water, enjoying the glooping noises they made. Maggie was still giving me dirty looks and wouldn't join in. She was only there because Siobhan had told her to go out and play, like everyone else.

I climbed up onto the wall and started walking along it, using my arms to balance. The others sat on the grass and watched. I loved having an audience, and while I had everyone's attention, I decided to give them a song. Just as I'd begun singing, Maggie got up, lifted an old brick from the ground and threw it at me. I disappeared over the side of the wall and landed in the water with a huge splash.

I held my breath as I sank, but panic soon set in. I couldn't swim and I couldn't see the top of the water. I didn't know how deep I'd gone and began to worry about having enough breath to get me back into the air. Thrashing my arms and legs about frantically, I tried to scramble up to the surface. My lungs felt like they would burst, and I began to think that I wasn't going to make it, which made me panic even more.

I was about to give up the struggle when I saw daylight above me. Doing something that resembled the doggie paddle, I broke the surface and gasped fresh air into my lungs. I could hear voices above me, shouting at me, and looked up to see a row of faces watching.

'Hang on, Frances, hang on!' they shouted.

I searched the walls for something to grab

on to, but the surfaces were too smooth to get a grip of. My arms and legs were beginning to tire.

'Hang on, Frances, we're going for help. Hang on there.'

I tried to stay above the water for as long as I could but soon felt myself being dragged back under. I gulped a desperate last breath of air before I sank again. I'm going to die, I thought. If I didn't get a breath very soon, I'd be gone forever. My arms and legs thrashed about as I struggled to stay alive, but they were beginning to feel heavy.

I heard a voice in my head telling me to calm down and make a last effort to rise up. 'Don't panic, keep calm,' it said. I raised my arms above my head and brought them down again, pushing against the water. With each stroke I began to move slowly upwards. The voice in my head kept saying, 'You can do this. Don't give up. Keep going, keep going.' Eventually, I reached the surface and took in some air.

The others were still shouting, 'Hang on, Frances, hang on.'

I couldn't understand why none of them were helping me. Why didn't they throw something down for me to hold on to? They're going to watch me drown, I thought.

Just before I sank again, I heard someone say, 'We're getting help!' I surfaced and sank, surfaced and sank again, until finally I ran out of energy. All hope of rescue faded as I plunged downwards. This is it, I thought. I had no more strength left in me. I was giving up the fight, and images of my sisters, the convent and my drowned friend Josephine flashed through my mind. But worst of all was my fear that the Devil would take me now. Sister Thomas had told me nearly every day that I'd go straight to Hell when I died, and I believed her. Deeper and deeper I sank, holding on to my last breath. Water shot up my nose and began to seep into my mouth and down my throat.

Suddenly, I felt my hair being tugged. I was moving, being pulled upwards. There was someone else in the water with me. I willed myself not to open my mouth yet, even though it felt as if I had no breath left. Now I was being pulled by my dress and began to move faster. At last I was back on the surface, coughing and spluttering. Above me I heard shouting and cheering. With my head supported by an unknown arm, I looked up and saw the other children's faces. I couldn't see my rescuer yet, but I totally trusted whoever it was not to let me sink back into the water, so I allowed myself to be held for a few minutes until I'd regained my strength and was breathing properly.

The next thing I knew a voice was asking, 'Frances, are you all right?' and I felt my wet hair being pushed back off my face. I opened my eyes to sunlight. The other children were kneeling around me. There was no more need for panic. I was out of the water and breathing normally. I could relax.

Shivering with cold, I looked around at the worried faces and managed a small smile. Then I caught sight of Maggie, who seemed to be more concerned about the trouble she was in than anything else. I heard her say to her brothers, 'What am I going to do? Please don't tell anyone.' I looked away. Right now I didn't want to have anything to do with her. And then my eyes were drawn to a teenage boy, about fifteen years old, who was also dripping wet. I recognised him as Francy who lived next to the shop.

'Thank you so much,' I said.

He smiled and shrugged his shoulders. 'Ye're welcome, but ye shouldn't go playing around there any more!' He sounded kind, concerned.

'Don't worry, I won't! I don't want to be anywhere near water ever again!' I said.

'Ye're shivering, Frances,' he said. 'Stay there, and we'll collect some sticks and make a fire. Yous boys, get as many sticks as ye can carry! I'll go to my house and come back with some towels and matches.' The boys went off to gather wood.

Francy was soon back wearing a dry set of clothes. He handed me a large bath towel.

'Here ye go, put this round ye and get yer wet things off till we get them dry for ye.'

I did as he said and soon felt much better, wrapped in the big dry towel.

'I'll wring these out for you, Frances,' said Maggie, trying to sound like she cared. She began squeezing the water out of my clothes, and when she was done, she shook them hard to remove the creases.

The boys arranged their sticks and logs into a pile, and a fire was soon blazing, crackling and sparking to start with, before flaring up and giving off a glorious heat. I warmed myself, while the boys went off to gather more wood.

Maggie held my wet clothes close to the fire, turning them occasionally. She kept smiling at me, trying to suck up, but I wouldn't look at her. I knew she wasn't being genuine because she'd never been nice to me before. It was just that she didn't want to get into trouble for throwing the brick. As I watched the steam rise from my clothes, I kept thinking how lucky I was to be alive.

Francy came back with some more wood and built up the fire. I admired him for his bravery and wished I had some way of thanking him. I didn't have anything to give him – no money or belongings – so I promised myself that I'd remember what he'd done forever, and maybe one day I'd be able to repay him.

Siobhan was beaming when we finally arrived at the back door for dinner. 'Yous have been out playing for a long time, I bet ye're all starving.'

'Yes!' we yelled, pulling off our shoes. I slipped to the bedroom and changed my clothes, and then we all sat down to one of Siobhan's lovely dinners.

'Sinéad has been helping me make a pie,' Siobhan said.

I looked over at my wee sister, whose hair and dress were covered in flour. She definitely looked like she'd been having fun.

Suddenly, I was jolted back into the present by the sound of girls coming back from the refectory. I was still kneeling by the bed, and my knees ached. Sinéad came over to see how I was doing.

'Why don't ye get up and stretch your legs for a while? Sister Thomas isn't here yet,' she said.

'Yeh! I'll look out for her, Frances,' Mary said. 'Get yerself up for a wee while.'

I struggled to my feet. It was hard to straighten my legs. Slowly, I felt the blood beginning to circulate again, the sensation of pins and needles. 'Oh my God, that's better!' I sat on the bed rubbing my legs with Sinéad next to me, while Mary kept watch at the dormitory door.

'Are ye OK, Frances?' Sinéad said.

'Yeh. I should be used to it by now. I hate

her so much. I wonder how she'd like it.'

'Ye won't do anything stupid, will ye, Frances?' Sinéad said.

'Don't worry. I don't want another beating. I just wish we could get out. I hate this place.'

Bernadette joined Sinéad and me on the bed. She chatted away endlessly, trying hard to distract me and to make me laugh.

'Quick! She's coming,' Mary shouted.

I got back onto my knees, and the others moved over to their beds.

Sister Thomas told everyone to get ready for bed, so I stood up. 'Not you, Reilly! Get yourself down to the porch, where you'll find shoes to be polished. That should keep you busy for the night. And if I can't see my face in them when you've finished, you'll do them all again. You will not go to bed until they are done. Do you understand me, Reilly!'

'Yes, Sister.'

I left the dormitory and went downstairs to the bottom landing, which felt eerie with no one around. I walked through the dark hall past the stage and lockers until I came to the cold, dimly lit porch. Before me was a mountain of black shoes. Alongside them were shoe polish and brushes.

The sight of all those shoes made me cry. I was never going to finish polishing them by morning. I sat on the cold stone floor and pulled my dress down over my knees.

Remembering a story that Siobhan had told me about Rumpulstiltskin, I felt a bit like the miller's daughter who was set the task of spinning straw into gold.

'I'd better get started on these before Sister Thomas comes to spy on me,' I said aloud. My voice echoed, and it struck me that I might be going a bit mad, talking to myself like that.

Picking out six pairs of shoes at a time, I applied the polish and left them in rows to dry before I shined them off later. I worked hard to get them done properly. I was determined not to give Sister Thomas a reason for making me do them again. I took care to apply the polish evenly on each shoe, checking and rechecking it before putting it down. It was tiring work, but I had to keep moving to keep myself awake. As I got into a rhythm, I began humming a song, rocking from side to side to keep warm. Inevitably, the floor's coldness seeped through my body to my bones. It was going to be a long night. Still, I just had to get on with it. There was no point in feeling sorry for myself.

I kept up a steady pace as the hours passed, brushing shoes till they shone and finishing off with a rag to get that extra gleam. The rows of shoes I'd already done looked as good as new, but there were still loads more to do.

I finished another row and tried to stand

up, but my legs had stiffened up painfully with the cold. I needed to stop working and move around to get some feeling back into my legs, but Sister Thomas would go mad at me if I didn't finish in time. I tried to stand up again. Unbearably sharp pains shot through my legs. I rubbed them hard to get the life back into them and, once I'd got to my feet, tried running on the spot. It seemed to be working; the pain was less intense. I'll just have to go faster when I sit back down, I thought to myself.

I polished shoes all night, with occasional breaks to get my circulation going again. I was numb with cold, exhausted and aching all over by the time I'd finished. Standing up and stretching, I noticed that there was daylight coming in through the windows. I had no idea what time it was. Taking one last look to make sure I hadn't missed anything, I turned out the light and made my way back to the dormitory, hoping to get some rest before the morning bell rang. Creeping in, I put on my nightdress and got into bed. In no time I was asleep.

When Sister Thomas rang the bell, I struggled out of bed and onto the floor for prayers. My eyes were stinging and watering. During prayers I found it hard to focus, but I was aware of the nun's eyes on me so did my best to keep up.

'I'm surprised you managed to get to bed, Reilly!' she said when prayers were over. 'I hope you did a good job of polishing those shoes. I'll be inspecting them after Mass, and I expect them to be perfect.'

'Yes, Sister.'

I knew that I wouldn't be able to take much more abuse without cracking up. I wasn't sure what would happen if the nuns thought I'd gone mad. It wouldn't be good, that much I knew. I could end up in the Muckamore nuthouse, and I'd heard some terrible stories about what happened to the girls who were sent there. So, whatever I did, I had to stay sane, even though I was living in an insane world.

Over the next few weeks I struggled to keep the farm out of my mind. I didn't want to lose the good memories because I had so few of them in the convent, but the other memories were so awful that I had to try to block them out. But much worse than the memories were the flashbacks, which I couldn't control. Whenever I had a flashback, I relived the pain I'd felt at the time all over again. There seemed to be nothing I could do. Finally, I told the priest about Tom and Barry's abuse at confession. He told me to say the Rosary as a penance, which made me feel even more like it had been my fault.

CHAPTER 18

Taking on a Senior

It had been pouring with rain all day, and Sister Kevin, who was on recreation duty, told us to go into the hall because it was too wet to play outside. Chrissie and I were first in, and we sat down on a row of chairs at the back. Soon the other chairs were all taken by seniors.

Now, there was an unwritten rule in the convent that if a senior wanted a chair, then a junior got up without being asked. Everybody knew it, and most of the juniors automatically sat on the floor.

Sister Kevin patrolled the hall with her arms folded, listening in on our conversations. All the nuns eavesdropped, and we'd learnt to change topic whenever they were near and then change back when they were out of earshot. It was like turning a switch on and off.

Ann and one of her friends – two seniors – were staring at Chrissie and me across the room. They didn't look happy.

'What's wrong with them?' I whispered.

'We're in their chairs,' said Chrissie.

We were still juniors – just – and Ann was a bit of a bully who loved picking on juniors. She especially loved picking on me but was careful not to go too far for fear of what Loretta might do. Loretta was now one of the oldest seniors, but even when she'd been younger, few girls had been willing to take her on.

'Come on, Frances, let's get up,' Chrissie said.

I grabbed her arm. 'No! Sit yourself down, Chrissie. It's not a rule, and I'm fed up of having to jump for seniors. Who do they think they are, anyway?'

Chrissie was totally shocked. She looked at me as though she half expected me to say I'd been joking, but she could tell that I wasn't. Her face puckered with fear. As Ann closed in on us, she got up and moved without thinking.

'Come on, Frances, it's not worth it!' she pleaded. Not only was Ann older than I was, she was much bigger. Also, I was generally rather timid, and although I'd fight back if attacked, I avoided fighting whenever possible. However, despite Chrissie's pleading, I wouldn't move. Instead, I sat still and stared straight back at the two seniors. In the past, yesterday even, I'd have been too afraid of Ann not to move away well before now, but for some inexplicable reason I wasn't scared any more. I was absolutely determined not to give in to these bullies.

'Get out of my chair!' Ann demanded.

'I don't see your name on it,' I shot back.

Poor Chrissie couldn't believe what she was hearing, and neither could anyone else. Ann's face registered shock, and for a moment she didn't seem to know what to do.

'Get out of that chair. Now!' she shouted angrily.

I felt my heart race as adrenaline rushed through my body, but I remained sitting, stony-faced and resolute. I didn't know what would happen next, but I knew that I'd have to see it through. There could be no backing out.

By now a small band of girls had gathered around the chair. Sister Kevin was at the far end of the hall near the stage, completely unaware of the situation. Ann reached out and grabbed hold of a handful of my hair. Then, pulling it as hard as she could, she tried to force me up and out of the chair, but I clung on tight to the sides of the chair and stayed put. Infuriated, Ann tugged harder, this time trying to pull my head down towards the floor.

My head began to hurt a lot, and I knew I'd soon have to let go. Then I saw my chance: Ann's hand was right in front of my face. I sank my teeth into it, near the thumb, and bit down as hard as possible. Ann screamed and loosened her grip. I bit deeper, afraid to stop because as soon as I did she'd be on me in a flash. I could hear some of the other girls cheering me on. I heard Chrissie shouting, 'Come on, Frances!' and suddenly, I felt great.

With my teeth clamped firmly on Ann's thumb, I looked up into her face. Her expression was murderous; she definitely wanted to kill me. So I knew that I was going to have to finish this fight off properly if I wanted to survive in the convent. It was bad enough having the nuns pick on me. I couldn't afford to have the seniors after me as well. As more of the girls began shouting, 'Come on, Frances!' I went for it. With Ann's thumb still between my teeth, I laid into her legs, kicking them furiously with my hard convent shoes. The cheering got louder.

Sister Kevin forced her way through the crowd to break things up. I felt her hand on my arm pulling me away from Ann.

'Stop this fighting now!' she insisted.

Immediately, I released my grip on Ann's thumb. It was bleeding, and Ann was crying. I couldn't believe it – I'd made her cry in front of all her friends! This was either really good or really bad. I wasn't sure which yet, but it certainly felt fantastic. Sister Kevin sent us to stand outside the Reverend Mother's office.

We didn't look at each other while we waited to see the Reverend Mother. Ann was still sobbing slightly as she nursed her thumb, and I stood and stared at the wall, thinking that even if the Reverend Mother caned me, it would still have been worth it. I tidied my clothes up and fixed my hair, and within a few minutes I was confident that it didn't look at all as if I'd been in a fight. I looked over at Ann, who really did look a mess. I was amazed that I had it in me to inflict so much damage on someone, but it was clear, looking at her, that I had. Just then the heavy office door swung open, and the Reverend Mother appeared.

'Why have you been sent here?'

Ann stared nervously down at the floor. 'Sister Kevin sent us here for fighting, Reverend Mother.'

She said, 'Is that so? Then you had better come in.'

The Reverend Mother appeared to scrutinise us as we stood facing her desk. She looked puzzled. Perhaps, I thought, she's surprised that I've been sent here for fighting. Or she could have been shocked that I'd clearly come off better. Either way, I knew I was in serious trouble. She continued her inspection. Then, with a rare smile – or was it a smirk? – she sat down at her desk.

'Now, I would like an explanation as to why you were fighting.'

Ann and I said nothing.

'Who is going to tell me?'

I looked nervously at Ann.

'I'm waiting,' said the Reverend Mother impatiently.

I thought I'd better say something or the punishment would be worse. 'Ann tried to pull me out of a chair by my hair because I'm a junior and I wouldn't give the chair up when she told me to.'

I couldn't help thinking how stupid it all sounded. The Reverend Mother took a few minutes to think. 'Is this true, Ann?'

'Yes, Reverend Mother.'

Silence again. After a minute or two the Reverend Mother got up and walked over to Ann. She inspected her legs and asked to see her hand, which she was still nursing. Ann held out her hand to show the wound on her thumb, which was swollen and still weeping blood. It looked nasty, and for a moment I felt ashamed of myself. I now expected my punishment to be bad. The Reverend Mother glanced down at Ann's legs again. The marks on them were looking worse.

I'm dead, I thought. I was sure my punishment was going to be awful and was now so nervous that my right leg started shaking uncontrollably. The Reverend Mother examined me more closely. She seemed surprised that there wasn't a single mark on me. I nearly fainted with shock when I realised she was trying to hold back a grin. By the time she'd returned to her desk and sat down, she was actually smiling.

'You can go and get back to what you were doing,' she said to me. 'It's good that you've started standing up for yourself, although I am not condoning fighting.' Turning to Ann, who looked really annoyed, she said, 'You stay here.'

I couldn't believe my luck. 'Thank you, Reverend Mother,' I said, quickly leaving the room.

I was elated and couldn't wait to get back to recreation to tell the others what had happened. I was on a real high. For the first time ever it felt as though I had some control over my life, and particularly over how people treated me. I felt invincible because if I could stand up to Ann then I needn't be afraid of anyone, not even the seniors who normally picked on me. From now on, no one was going to get in my way.

When I got back to the hall, a crowd of girls, mostly juniors, gathered around me. I took great delight in telling them that the Reverend Mother had let me off and that Ann was still in the office. They laughed and told me it was brilliant the way I'd challenged Ann. It struck me that I'd really gained their respect. Up to now I'd been a victim, but finally, I'd been pushed too far and for the first time in my life I'd fought back, I'd won, and in future people would look at me differently. It felt absolutely wonderful.

CHAPTER 19

A Strange Relationship

I wondered why Doreen and Sister Francis were so close. Doreen had always been the nun's favourite girl and was much better treated than the rest of us. For this reason, no one wanted Doreen hanging around. We didn't quite trust her motives and wouldn't confide anything to her for fear of her telling Sister Francis, who gave her gifts. Doreen pretended that her visitors bought the gifts in for her, but we knew they were from Sister Francis.

On my way to the toilet one day I passed a classroom that was supposed to be empty and saw Doreen and Sister Francis hugging and giving each other a kiss. I couldn't understand why anyone would want to kiss Sister Francis and was glad that it wasn't me she liked. The sight of them made my flesh creep. I'd never before witnessed that sort of contact or affection between a girl and a nun. It was unthinkable.

I thought that maybe Sister Francis was trying to be a mother figure to Doreen. But Doreen already had a mother who loved her and visited her every Sunday. I tried to push the horrible image of the two of them out of my head, but I couldn't. I'd always felt that there was something strange about their relationship and now it had been confirmed.

Recreation time was spent in the hall because it was raining. I was sitting on the side of the stage watching the others talking and playing in their little groups. I wasn't in the mood to join in with any of them.

Sister Francis was on duty and she walked around the hall watching what everyone was up to. Doreen was by her side, smiling and talking. I found myself staring at them and wondering what they could possibly find to say to each other.

'Ye don't mind if I sit with ye, do ye Frances?' Rita said.

'Go on ahead,' I said, smiling at her. None of us liked to hang around with Rita because she quite often smelt of wee – and worse. But it wasn't like she could help it. There was obviously something wrong with her. Girls made rhymes up about her and teased her about it, and I could tell how miserable it made her. Normally I wouldn't have been able to sit next to her because of the smell, either, and I would have made some excuse to move away. But she was all right for the moment because she hadn't had one of her accidents yet.

'Why are ye sitting here by yourself?' she asked.

'Oh, I'm just thinking,' I said.

'What are ye thinking about, then, Frances, or don't you want to tell me?'

I felt sorry for Rita. She obviously just wanted someone to talk to. 'I was thinking about Sister Francis and Doreen. They walk around like they're family or something. I saw them in the classroom earlier, hugging and kissing each other. It made me feel sick. I mean, who'd want to kiss Sister Francis?'

Rita pulled a disgusted face. 'Well, ye won't find me giving Sister Francis a hug. I'd rather die, but ye know Doreen's her pet. She sometimes goes and sits on Sister Francis's bed with her in her cell at night. I've seen her coming out of there a couple of times really late, and she had sweets. I could hear her eating them. She doesn't know I saw her. I pretended to be sleeping. I thought it was a wee bit weird because we're never allowed in the nuns' cells, but Doreen's not treated like us.'

'I wonder what they talk about. I really don't trust Doreen, but at least I'm not in her dormitory,' I said.

'I wish I wasn't in her dormitory' Rita said. 'She's become a bully to some of the juniors. Kelly said that Doreen makes her take her knickers down, and she touches her on her private parts when no one is around.

I think that she does it to some of the others, too. Only the wee ones, who can't say anything because they're afraid of her. But don't say I told you that, Frances, or I'll get into trouble.'

I was horrified at what I was hearing, but Rita seemed really relieved to get it off her chest. I had the feeling that she hadn't told anyone else about it.

'She's a dirty bitch, Rita. Why would she want to do that?'

Rita shrugged. 'I don't know. Maybe she's just sick in the head.'

'Well, she'd better not come near me, or I'll go mad on her. I wouldn't care if I got into trouble for it.'

'God, this place gets to ye. I sometimes wish I was dead.' Rita sounded like she'd really had enough.

'Try not to think that way, Rita. You'll be out of here one day. But I know what you mean. I've felt like that loads of times. We just have to get on with it the best we can.'

The bell rang.

I kept my promise to Rita and didn't discuss our conversation with anyone, but after that I found it hard to look Doreen in the face. And the situation got worse when I walked into the toilets one day and glimpsed her in one of the cubicles with two of the girls from her dormitory. The door was half open, and I saw Doreen quickly snatch her hand away from one of the girl's knickers and pull her dress down. There was an awkward silence as I walked to another cubicle and closed the door. I could still hear them fumbling around. 'Just wait there, till she's gone,' Doreen whispered.

When I came out to wash my hands, the cubicle door was closed. Glancing underneath it, I saw three pairs of feet and left with the feeling that Doreen was doing something very bad. I hadn't seen much, but I could sense that I'd disturbed something. I decided to get back into my work and forget it because I couldn't figure out what they were doing, and I didn't want to imagine what it was. I would definitely be keeping clear of Doreen from now on.

A couple of weeks later some of us stayed up late into the night telling ghost stories. There didn't seem to be any nuns around – Bridget had heard that they were all in a meeting.

Orlagh, the new girl in the bed across from me, was getting spooked. 'Please stop it now! You're scaring the life out of me,' she said.

Some of the girls giggled.

'Put yer fingers in your ears like the other scaredy cats do,' Margaret said. 'Anyway, we're only whispering.'

'This is all that some of us have to look forward to,' I explained gently. 'Ye'll soon get used to it. Ye have to toughen up to be in this place.'

I'd no sooner got the words out when Orlagh screamed, 'Oh God, there's someone under my bed!' She jumped out of her bed and got into Margaret's.

Margaret looked panicked. 'We'll be in trouble if Sister Thomas comes in. We're not allowed to get into each other's beds!' she said.

'I can't go back!' Orlagh said, her teeth chattering. 'There's something under there, sure. I'm really scared.'

'It's only me, Orlagh, I was mucking about,' Bernadette said, sliding out from under Orlagh's bed and going back to her own.

Unfortunately, Sister Thomas chose this moment to throw open the dormitory door and turn on the light. Her face was bulging and red.

'Who's been squealing in here?' she howled, scanning the room. Her angry eyes zoomed in on Margaret's bed.

Margaret and Orlagh were sitting up straight, side by side, rigid with fear. Looking as if she were going to burst a blood vessel, Sister Thomas stormed across to them.

'Get out!' she shouted, yanking Margaret out of bed by the hair. She dragged her along the floor and around to the other side of the bed.

'I wasn't doing anything, Sister, I swear to

God!' Margaret cried.

But Sister Thomas was obviously in no mood to listen. Grasping a handful of Orlagh's hair in her other hand, she pulled her out of bed. Orlagh screamed.

'Quiet!' Sister Thomas screamed back, even louder. 'Girls do not share beds in God's house! I know exactly what you filthy girls need for your filthy thoughts!' Still clutching their hair, she dragged them along the dormitory and out of the door. 'The rest of you get to sleep and turn off that light,' she called back. 'I don't want to hear a sound.'

No one said a word for awhile, for fear that she might return. Then we heard cries and howls coming from a nearby room. 'Please, Sister. No, Sister!' Margaret begged.

I cringed. I knew only too well what Sister Thomas's punishments were like and began to feel sick. "What's happening to them? They sound like they're being murdered!' I whispered. 'Oh God, help them!'

'I'm going to sneak nearer and have a listen,' said Bernadette. She opened the door a crack. 'Sister Francis is in there, too. I can hear her voice.' She opened the door another fraction, and we all strained to hear the nuns' voices and the girls' pleas, but it was hard to make out what was happening.

Eventually, Bernadette closed the door and jumped back into bed. 'I think they're throwing them into a cold bath, and I heard quite a few slaps as well. I'm not sure how many nuns are in there with them.'

I couldn't get to sleep that night. I kept wishing the punishment would end, but every now and then I'd hear a shout or a scream that told me it hadn't. A deep feeling of hatred for the nuns welled up inside me. Tears of frustration rolled onto my pillow.

CHAPTER 20

The Nuns' Pets

For nearly ten years I'd woken up to the awful sound of that morning bell, my daily reminder that I was still living out my nightmares in the convent. And today was no different. The bell woke me again. But as my eyes flickered open and I focused on the ceiling high above me, I became aware that there was something gooey stuck to the roof of my mouth. I couldn't imagine what it could be. Frantically I cast my mind back to the moment before I'd gone to sleep. Nothing unusual had happened, so maybe it had crawled into my mouth during the night.

Sister Thomas started morning prayers, and I tried to make it look like I was joining in, but I couldn't speak properly for fear of my tongue touching the thing in my mouth. I felt I couldn't swallow, either, in case some of it went down my throat. I hoped prayers would finish quickly so that I could make a beeline for the toilet and spit it out. Luckily, Sister Thomas didn't seem to notice that I was holding my clasped hands in front of my mouth while I pretended to pray. In fact,

I was so terrified that I probably appeared intensely serious. Wondering if someone was playing a practical joke on me, I quickly glanced around the dormitory. But no one was paying me any attention, and I couldn't see anyone grinning. It was just morning prayers as usual.

When prayers finished, I slipped away to the nearest toilet cubicle and closed the door. I dreaded having to put my finger in my mouth and poke around. What if it was a slug? I braced myself for the worst. Leaning over the toilet, I opened my mouth wide and scraped away at the roof with my fingertip, making sure to remove everything at once. Cringing, I held my finger at a distance to examine what was there, but instead of a slug on my fingertip, to my delight, I saw a large red jellied sweet. I quickly popped it back into my mouth and began to puzzle over how it had got there. As the morning went on, I became more and more intrigued. I asked around, but no one knew anything about it.

That afternoon Sister Austin made me scrub the kitchen floor instead of going to recreation with the others. This was my punishment for taking too long to eat the lumps of fat in the stew at dinner. While I was on my knees scrubbing, two of Sister Thomas's pets – Gertrude and Agnes – came in. I immediately sensed trouble. They were big girls, much stronger than I was, and I'd had run-ins with them – and others like them – from the day I'd started in the juniors. They were always picking on me and putting me down, and often their aggression was physical. It never got any easier to cope with. In some ways it was harder to take than the nuns' abuse, because the way I saw it, we girls were all in the same boat and should stick together.

They sauntered towards me. I tried to ignore them and kept my head down as I scrubbed the floor, but then Gertrude kicked the bucket over, and they broke into gales of laughter. Don't react, I told myself. Keep calm. I tried hard not to show how furious I was because it would only make things worse.

They'd spilt dirty water all over the kitchen floor, and my legs were soaked. My shoes and tights squished as I got to my feet. Knowing that the nuns would delight in blaming me for the mess, I swallowed the insults on the tip of my tongue, bit my lip and began to clear it up before anyone came along and saw it.

My blood boiled as I wrung out the cloth. I felt pathetic, not standing up for myself, and wanted to get up and throw the bucket at Gertrude. But I didn't look at either girls and managed to hold down my temper, even though I could feel their eyes on me and hear them sniggering.

It took a good twenty minutes or so to clean up the floor, by which time they'd left the kitchen. I thought that I'd try to visit Loretta later on, if I could manage to slip away unnoticed. I hadn't seen very much of her since she'd started to work in the old peoples' section of the convent, and I missed her a lot. It occurred to me that she might be able to give me some advice on how to deal with Gertrude and Agnes.

I tiptoed along the edge of the kitchen to avoid getting footprints on the floor and took one last look back to make sure that the job had been done properly. Suddenly, Gertrude, Agnes and two other seniors pushed me back inside the kitchen. I slipped on the wet floor and fell over. My legs and hands stung on impact, and I noticed that a load of shoeprints had already messed up my work.

All I could think of was how I'd have to wash the floor over again, but that was the least of my problems. As I stood up, the four girls grabbed me and pushed me up against the sink. They began to taunt me, calling me names and telling me I was 'a little scrubber' and 'a dirty little bitch'.

One of them started poking me hard on the chest. 'Tell me, Reilly, that ye're a dirty little scrubber. Say it, Reilly! Say it!'

They were trying to provoke a reaction, and they got one. I started to fight back, pushing and screaming, 'Get away from me ye bastards. Get away!'

One of them grabbed me and pulled me down onto the wet kitchen floor, forcing my arms up over my head. I kicked and shouted, but soon someone else's hands were pinning down my head and covering my mouth and part of my nose, blocking off my air supply. Panicking, I struggled even harder. I managed to wriggle enough to breathe through my nose, but I knew I was in trouble. Pinned down like that, all I could do was kick out frantically, but then someone pulled at my legs and sat on them. I was completely helpless. I may as well have just given in then, but I couldn't bring myself to. My instinct was to make things as difficult as possible for my attackers.

'Let's see how much this wee bitch can take,' one said. The others laughed.

I was horribly aware that my dress had ridden up to my waist, and now someone was trying to pull my knickers down. I tried to fight back with every last bit of strength I could muster, and for a moment it seemed to be working and I managed to break free, but they pushed me down again. I felt a hand covering my mouth again. I bit into it as hard as I could.

'Stop fucking biting, ye wee bitch!'

I bit down harder. The girl screamed and pulled her hand away.

My mouth was free. 'Someone help me! Get my sister. Get Loretta!' I yelled, hoping that one of Loretta's friends would hear. Then there was a tea towel over my mouth.

'She fucking bit me! Me hand's bleeding, the wee bitch.'

'Don't worry; we'll give her what for.' More laughing.

I felt my knickers being pulled down to my knees. Out of the corner of my eye I saw Sister Austin looking on from the doorway. She walked away, smirking. The girls went on laughing. One of them was holding a large ladle. Now she was trying to force its handle between my legs. I strained to keep my legs tightly closed. The handle of the ladle jabbed my thighs painfully, digging into my skin. I screamed and fought back, but it was useless. Then, just as I thought I was losing the fight, the bell went. The girls backed away from me.

'This isn't over yet, Reilly,' one of them said as they left the kitchen.

I struggled to my feet and wiped the floor down quickly before dashing away. I managed to get into my line without the nun noticing that I was late. I'd heard the expression 'Saved by the bell', and now it had come true for me. Usually, I cursed the bells. This one had been a blessing.

The following day I found a moment to visit Loretta in the old peoples' section – as well as the orphanage, the nuns ran a nursing home for the old and infirm in a separate building. Loretta was laying out the body of a woman who had just died. Combing her hair, she told me that she was making her look nice for her coffin. I thought it was creepy, but it really didn't seem to bother her. In fact, it looked like she was quite enjoying the job.

'Don't worry about the dead. They can't hurt ye. It's the living I'm more worried about,' she said.

It was so nice to see her that I stayed to chat for a while, despite the risks. Loretta told me that she'd been in serious trouble a few weeks earlier. She'd taken a really bad beating from the nuns and showed me the scars on her back, which were a quarter of an inch wide and very long. They were vicious, and I felt really sorry for her. When they'd finished with her, she said, they'd carried her by the arms and legs and thrown her into an ice-cold bath. She said it very matter-of-factly, but I couldn't help expressing my anger. 'Don't ye worry about me,' she reassured me. 'I can take it, and I won't let them bastards break me.' Her brave words brought a bittersweet smile to my lips.

I watched her combing the dead woman's hair, curling it around her fingers to make it look pretty, and realised that I wouldn't be able to tell her about what Sister Thomas's pets had done to me. I didn't want her to get into any more trouble with the nuns, and knowing how much she cared about me, she'd probably have stormed off immediately to find every one of them, not stopping until she'd nearly killed them. Then she'd be punished again, beaten severely, and I didn't want that. Anyway, I couldn't always have her fighting my battles. It was time to start defending myself.

'Did ye get the sweet I put in yer mouth the other night?' she said. 'It was a bit late, and ye were all asleep. I didn't want to wake ye or leave it where Sister Thomas would find it.'

Finally, my curiosity was satisfied. 'Oh that was ye! I didn't know what the hell it was when I woke up. It scared the living daylights out of me!'

I told her the slug story and we laughed.

'Are ye all right, Frances? Ye seem to be miles away,' she said.

'I'm fine. I just really needed to see ye. I miss our talks.'

Suddenly, the dead woman's chest rose up and she gave a long, loud burp. I yelped and fled the room, terrified that she'd come back to life, and by the time Loretta had caught up with me, I was deathly pale and could barely speak. Meanwhile she was in fits of laughter.

'It's normal,' she said, going on to explain that dead people often release gas and that can make the body move, especially before rigor mortis has set in properly.

I refused to go back into the room, but I did see the funny side of it.

'At least us Reillys were born with a bloody good sense of humour,' she said, tears of laughter welling up in her eyes.

We hugged and I made my way back to the dormitory.

Seeing Loretta had cheered me up, even if it had frightened the wits out of me, and I couldn't wait to tell my friends about the dead woman. It was going to be better than any made-up ghost story. That night, after lights out, I related my grisly tale. No one blamed me for running out on a burping dead woman, and some of them were really spooked by the idea, which of course triggered a round of ghost stories.

For the next few days I was continually on the lookout for Gertrude, Agnes and the others. Then I started to think that they might have decided to leave me alone, perhaps because they were worried about what Loretta would do to them. But they were just biding their time. One morning, when I was alone in the main hall doing an errand for one of the nuns, they pounced on me again. This time there was no bell to stop them, and they were out to finish what they'd started.

The attack was brutal, but it was to be the last. I fought back with a savagery and strength that shocked even me, biting, kicking and scratching frenziedly. Perhaps if I hadn't struggled so hard, the whole thing might have been over sooner and they wouldn't have abused me so cruelly. But I had taken enough – from Tom and Barry Murphy, from the nuns and from the nuns' pets – and I simply refused to take any more, so I fought back, no matter what.

It took a while for them to pin me down, and several times I managed to fight them off and to break free, but each time they caught me again and dragged me back to the gym mats. It was a horrific attack and seemed to go on forever. They kept trying to pull up my skirt and touch me under my knickers with rough, fumbling fingers, and they kicked and punched and slapped me until I thought I was going to pass out. But I still refused to give in and kept fighting back. I couldn't show any weakness. If I gave up the fight, they'd go on picking on me forever. Finally, I got my head free and sunk my teeth into someone's arm, biting down until she screamed and released her grip. I kicked and thumped my way free of the others and ran across the hall towards my locker.

After the last attack I'd stolen a sharp knife from the kitchen and hidden it in my locker, hoping to move it to the dormitory when I got the chance. Now I reached inside the locker and pulled it out. Turning on the girls, I forced one of them to the floor and held the knife to her throat.

'I'll kill ye!' I screamed, pressing the blade into her skin. 'Ye hear me? Leave me alone, or I'll kill ye!'

The others backed off, shrieking hysterically. Just then a nun came through the door.

I got the blame, of course, and took the punishment, but I was a changed person. Something in me had snapped, and those four girls were now scared of me. They sensed that I'd been close to using the knife. If the nun hadn't walked in, one of them could have died.

After that, they kept their distance. The incident was never spoken of again, but all the other girls were aware that something major had happened. Suddenly, the seniors were wary of me, and everyone sensed a change in me. On the surface I appeared much the same, but something inside had been transformed. I refused to be victimised any more.

CHAPTER 21

Stowaways

I had no idea Loretta was planning an escape. She didn't warn me or say goodbye. She just vanished.

I was stunned when we were called into the hall and it was announced that she'd run away. I simply could not believe it. It was inconceivable that she'd go without taking Sinéad and me, or at least telling us where she was going.

Evidently the nuns felt the same way. Sister Thomas, particularly, was convinced that I must know something, but Loretta had second-guessed them and told me nothing so that they couldn't beat it out of me. They beat me all the same, as she must have known they would, breaking cane after cane on my head, arms and legs. Sister Thomas was determined not to stop until I confessed. It was one of the worst punishments I endured in all my years at the convent.

Later we heard that Loretta had made it to England with the help of a lad who did the bread deliveries to the convent. He'd fancied her for a long time, and although she didn't feel the same way about him, she saw him as her ticket out of there, so she'd given him the impression that she was interested. He'd told her that his name was Jack the Knife, which she'd found amusing. He carried a large flick knife but was weedy-looking and nothing like the type of gangster the name suggested.

Six months after she'd gone I was still angry with her, still raw with the pain of her betrayal. How could she have abandoned us? How could she have left us unprotected in this hell? She'd known how bad it would be for me when she left. She knew that I'd be beaten within a couple of inches of death. That's what really hurt me – that she knew and she left, anyway. She could at least have trusted me not to tell, however much I was beaten.

I didn't want to be angry with her, but I couldn't help it. I imagined her having a great time somewhere, enjoying the good life without even thinking about Sinéad and me. Sinéad still had her older sister. But for me, life was worse than ever. Without Loretta I suddenly found myself being picked on by the bullies who would have left me alone if she'd still been around. Then there were girls who had a grudge against Loretta and were now taking it out on me. And all this at a time when some of the girls had started to leave me alone. I'd been in several bad fights since she'd left. Other girls had suddenly become more of a problem than the nuns were, and their attacks were of an increasingly sexual nature, which horrified me. They'd learnt how to be vicious and spiteful from the nuns, and now they were even better at it than their role models.

I'd had enough. The only thing for it was to escape and make our own way to England, I kept telling Sinéad. But there didn't seem to be much chance of breaking out for now because we were locked in a room for getting into a fight and answering back to the nuns who'd discovered us scrapping. Sister Francis was furious with us. It wasn't the first time we'd answered her back, and she'd clearly had enough. We weren't allowed to speak to anyone. Our slop was passed in to us on a tray, and there was nothing to do except talk about getting on the boat to England and trying to find Loretta and our mammy.

For two nights we slept on the floor without blankets. On the third day the slop came in on a tray again, but there was a vital break with routine.

'She hasn't locked the door!' I whispered to Sinéad.

'Let's go, sure,' Sinéad said, without hesitating. 'Anything's better than sitting around waiting to be beaten.'

We sneaked out of the room and made our

way towards the back gate. There was no one around. The place seemed eerily deserted. All too easily, we found the key hanging from a hook on the wall. We unlocked the gate and stepped out onto the Ormeau Road. But something didn't feel right. Now Loretta had gone, I had a funny feeling that the nuns had decided to solve the rest of the Reilly problem by deliberately smoothing the path to our escape. It was unthinkable that they didn't know they'd left the door unlocked and had left the key to the gate in such an obvious place. It was all too easy, and that made me uneasy. I was waiting for something to go wrong.

'We'll need money if we're going to get anywhere,' Sinéad said, looking meaningfully at two large wooden collection boxes outside the chapel next to the convent. They stood on heavy plinths at either side of the door, each locked with a padlock.

'We can't take them, don't be stupid. We'd go to Hell. And even if it weren't a sin, we'd never be able to carry them. Look at the size of them!' I said.

Sinéad gave me a desperate look. 'We have to do something. It won't be a sin if we promise to pay it back as soon as we can. Anyway, they're not attached to the stands. They'll just come off if we lift them.'

'You don't know that for sure, do you?' I felt nervous that we were even discussing the possibility of stealing from the Church. The more we talked about it, though, the more it felt like we were going to go through with it.

'We'll have to pay every penny back,' I said. Sinéad nodded. 'OK, then, let's do it. As quick as we can.'

We looked to make sure nobody was watching.

'It's all clear,' Sinéad said. 'Let's grab them now!'

She ran over to one of the boxes, and I went to grab the other one, but neither box detached from its stand. Sinéad just lifted the whole thing and started running with it. With no time to think about it, I did the same and ran after her. Our hearts pounding and the adrenaline pumping, we made it to the park.

We crawled through some bushes into a concealed clearing, dragging the collection boxes behind us. Panting, we sat down to catch our breath. I hoped that we hadn't been seen. I knew that if the police turned up now, I'd be too puffed out to make a run for it. They'd be able to take me back without a fight, and I really didn't want that to happen.

'We need to find something to break the padlocks off,' Sinéad said.

Nothing came to mind, so I suggested leaving the collection boxes in the clearing while we had a quick search around the park. We covered them with leaves and branches to camouflage them, and confident that no one would find them, we crawled out through the bushes.

As we searched the park for something to prise them open with, Sinéad went into a fit of nervous laughter. With tears rolling down her cheeks, she pointed her finger at me and tried to say something, but I couldn't make out what it was.

'Your face was a real picture as you ran after me lugging that box,' she finally managed to say.

I couldn't help seeing the funny side of it, and we collapsed into giggles at the thought of how strange we must have appeared.

We weren't having much luck in the park, so we wandered through the gates and up the road.

'There wasn't any point in taking them if we can't get into them,' I said, beginning to feel frustrated.

'We could try turning them upside down and giving them a good shake,' suggested Sinéad.

On our way back we stopped outside a little fruit and vegetable shop. The shopkeeper was nowhere to be seen, and the fruit on display looked really good. We were seriously hungry, so when Sinéad said, 'Look out for the shopkeeper,' I knew exactly what she was going to do. I remembered someone telling me that if you steal because you're hungry then it's not a sin, and I tried to hold on to that thought. As I kept an eye out for the shopkeeper, Sinéad helped herself to the biggest piece of fruit on display and ran off towards the park. I casually followed her.

I caught up with her just inside the park gates, and soon we were crawling back to our hiding place in the bushes. We didn't have a clue what the yellow rugby-ball-shaped fruit was or what it would taste like. Sinéad had picked it simply because it looked big enough to fill us up. At least we weren't going to starve for a while.

'There's a lot more people around the park now, Sinéad. We'd better stay here for a while,' I said, although I didn't get the feeling that anyone had called the police yet.

We inspected the melon, wondering how we were going to eat it. 'Let's try banging it against the collection boxes and maybe it will break the skin.'

I brushed the branches and leaves away from one of the boxes.

'Right, then, are you ready for this?'

I held the melon as high as I could in the air, and Sinéad gave me a big grin. I banged the melon against the collection box, which only cracked the skin, so I banged it again. This time it split open and wet melon juice ran over my hands. I pulled the skin apart to reveal the fruit and seeds inside and began to scoop out the seeds with my fingers. It was a messy job, and I hoped it was all going to be worth it. The seeds fell to the ground in a sloppy mess, and I handed a large lump of melon to Sinéad. As we bit into it, the juice ran down our chins.

'This is lovely!' Sinéad said, and soon there was nothing left but skin.

I finished mine a few moments later. 'That feels better.' I rubbed my stomach.

Now we needed to try getting the money out of the boxes. It was going to be noisy, so Sinéad stood on lookout while I made the first attempt.

'OK, Frances, it's all clear.'

I shook the box vigorously and a few pennies fell out. I shook it some more; from the way it rattled, it sounded like there were only a few more coins inside.

'These boxes have been emptied lately. There's hardly any money in here,' I said. A few more pennies dropped to the ground.

Sinéad left her lookout post and stared at the pennies on the ground. 'That's not enough,' she said, like it was my fault.

Snatching the box away from me, she shook it hard. One more penny fell to the floor, and the rattling stopped. She threw the box to the ground in a fit of temper.

'There'd better be more in the other one,' she said. There was, but not much – some pennies, sixpences and a half-crown. 'It's not enough to get us on the boat,' she said, giving the box one last shake. It was definitely empty.

'We should have known there wasn't much in them,' I said, gathering up the money. 'If they'd been full, we'd never have been able to lift them and run with them.'

We spent the rest of the day in the park, making forays out of our hideout every time the coast looked clear. It felt great not to be locked in that room back at the convent. When it started getting dark, we headed off towards the docks without really knowing what we'd do when we got there. At least we were on the move, away from the nuns.

We'd heard from the other girls that the docks were a few miles away on the other side of Belfast, so we were going to have to walk through the town centre. It felt good to be walking freely. Most of the shops had already closed or were about to close, but the pubs were open and we could hear singing coming from inside them. We stopped a couple of times for a listen. The people sounded happy; they were obviously having a good time and we wanted to soak up some of the atmosphere.

The next time we stopped a man invited us inside. We followed him into a smoke-filled bar.

'Hello, girls, I'm Pat, would ye like a wee

drink?' he shouted over the noise of people talking and singing.

'We haven't got any money,' I shouted back at him.

We looked around us. Everyone was singing now, banging loudly on the tables and bar with their bottles or fists. We'd never seen anything quite like it before.

And it's no! Nay! Never!
No, nay, never, no more
Will I play the wild rover
No, never, no more.

Pat pointed towards some empty chairs and brought us over a glass of lemonade each. A warm, happy feeling flooded through us as we sat listening to the rest of the song. The people in the pub didn't seem to mind at all who we were or where we'd come from. The only thing they seemed interested in was having a good time. So we felt quite safe staying there for a while, to warm up a bit.

The bar was slowly filling up with men, and I noticed that we were the only females about. It made me feel slightly uncomfortable – and protective of Sinéad – but everyone seemed very friendly, so I thought we'd probably be all right.

'Can any of you wee girls sing a song?' asked a man standing at the bar, drinking a big glass of black liquid.

At that, Sinéad landed me in it. 'Frances can sing,' she said, quick as a flash. It always amused her to see my face glow bright red with embarrassment.

The men gathered around.

'Come on, then, give us a wee song,' one of them said.

I was mortified and looked over at Sinéad. She was laughing at how she'd managed to manipulate the situation her way.

'You just wait. I'll get you back,' I said, trying to think of a song.

Everyone was looking at me with anticipation. I took a deep breath and closed my eyes to shut out my surroundings. As I started to sing, the bar fell silent.

Oh Danny boy, the pipes, the pipes are calling. From glen to glen and down the mountainside.

I sang with as much feeling as I could muster. When the first verse was over, I risked opening my eyes to see if the men were enjoying it, and as I went into the chorus, I could clearly see by the expression on their faces that they were. I relaxed myself into the song and began to enjoy singing it. It wasn't cheerful like the songs they'd been singing earlier, but I definitely sensed that it was going down well, and by the time I'd reached the last chorus, a few of them had joined in with me.

But come ye back when summer's in the
  meadow,
Or when the valley's hushed and white with
  snow.
'Tis I'll be there in sunshine or in shadow,
Oh Danny boy, oh Danny boy, I love you so.

Soon everyone was singing along with me, and when I'd finished, they all clapped. Sinéad smiled proudly. I took a sip of my drink.

'More! Give us another one,' the men shouted. 'Sing us another one, that was grand,' said the bartender. I placed my glass on the table. I didn't want to disappoint them, but my mind was blank. I couldn't think of any other songs.

'"The Wild Colonial Boy," Sinéad whispered. Again, everyone joined in.

There was a wild colonial boy,
Jack Duggen was his name.
He was born and reared in Ireland.

We were having a great time but knew that we couldn't stay in the pub for long. We'd have to try to get to the docks soon, to see if there was a ferry going to England. We'd already seen a big sign for the docks with a picture of a boat on it, so we knew we didn't have far to go.

When the barman brought us over some more lemonade and a packet of KP nuts, we thanked him gratefully. Some of the men gave me money for my singing and told me to buy some sweets with it. I counted it up on the way to the docks.

'I don't think we'll have enough to get the boat, but at least we'll be able to eat.'

There were crowds of people queuing on the quay for the ferry to England, waiting to show their tickets to a man at the bottom of a long gangplank. We noticed that the couples with children were letting them walk on ahead – up the gangplank to the boat – while they stood in the queue.

'If we walk beside a man and woman, it might look like we're their kids,' Sinéad said. 'Then, when we get to the ticket man, we'll just run on ahead and onto the boat.'

It seemed like a good idea. I looked a lot younger than my age and Sinéad was only ten, so no one would guess we were alone.

'Let's find a mammy and daddy, then,' I said.

I spotted a couple standing at the end of the queue. They looked engrossed in conversation and perhaps wouldn't notice two girls walking along beside them. We squeezed in behind our temporary parents, and nobody paid us any attention. When we got to the ticket man, we simply carried on going. We didn't look back, not even for a second, and ran the last bit of the plank, trying to look like a pair of normal kids who belonged on the boat.

We'd done it. We were on a huge ferry going to England. We ran around the decks looking for somewhere to hide until the boat was on its way. I was sure that we'd be OK once we left the docks. Around and around we ran until I saw a toilet door.

'In here!' We locked ourselves in one of the cubicles. 'We'll stay here until it goes,' I said.

We were really excited and quite proud of ourselves for being so daring. The cubicle was small, and there wasn't really space for two people, but it was clean and warm. Sinéad sat on the toilet seat, and I leant against the door. We could hear people coming and going, so we kept really quiet.

After what seemed like a long time, we heard the boat's engines starting up. 'We're on our way,' I whispered excitedly.

It felt a bit claustrophobic to be stuck in our confined space, and we were dying to get out and stretch our legs, but we could still hear people talking and toilets flushing.

'Let's get out of here soon,' Sinéad said.

I gave in to her, even though my instincts told me we should stay where we were. I was worried that it would look suspicious that there weren't any adults travelling with us. Also, I was concerned that we'd have to lie about who we really were, if anyone asked. I was no good at lying. I'd go bright red, and then they'd know I wasn't telling the truth.

'Come on, then,' I said, when it sounded like everyone had gone. 'We'll go and find somewhere to sit. If anyone speaks to us just tell them that we're with our mammy, and she's gone to our cabin.'

'OK,' she said. She couldn't get out of the cubicle quickly enough.

As we wandered around, we could feel the vibrations of the engines beneath our feet. We entered a bar and I saw a few empty chairs. Taking Sinéad by the arm, I led her over to them. While we made ourselves comfortable, I became aware that people were staring at us.

'Who are you travelling with?' asked a fat lady wearing a headscarf who was sitting in the seat opposite us.

Before Sinéad could say anything to land us in trouble, I replied, 'We're with our mam, she's gone to see if she can get us a cabin.'

The woman gave us a worried look and seemed to know that I was lying, which made me feel uncomfortable.

'We'll be off soon,' said the man sitting next to Sinéad. He wasn't speaking to any-one in particular, but a few people nodded in agreement. That's when it dawned on me. The engines were running, but the boat wasn't moving. I started to panic. If only the boat would set off I felt sure we'd be safe then, and I couldn't foresee any trouble when we got off at Liverpool.

Just then I heard a man say, 'What are your names, then?'

I looked up in the direction of the voice. Two men in police uniform loomed over me. Suddenly, I felt sick. I looked away, hoping they would disappear.

'Could we please have your names?' one of them said.

I couldn't think for a moment or two. Everyone was looking at me. 'I'm Kathleen, and this is my sister Ann,' I said.

'Are you sure that's who you are? I think you're the Reilly sisters. Would you come with us and answer a few questions?'

With no choice but to go with them, we stood up, feeling embarrassed. They walked us off the boat and escorted us to a portable room on the quay.

'Now, girls, are you going to tell us who you really are? You fit the description of two sisters who ran away from Nazareth House Convent.'

Sinéad burst into tears. 'We can't go back there. We'll get beaten up again,' she sobbed.

The youngest police officer seemed concerned. 'Come on now, don't upset yourself. The nuns just want you brought back. They're probably worried about you. You've been gone all day,' he said kindly.

'We wouldn't have run away if it was a nice place to be,' I said, tears welling up in my eyes. 'They're really cruel, and they beat us. They don't care about us at all. They're always telling us that we'll go to Hell, that nobody wants us because we're Reillys! Can't you just let us get back on the boat? Please? We need to find our mammy in England.'

He glanced over at the older officer. Although he didn't say anything, we sensed that he believed what we were saying, but the older officer slowly shook his head from side to side.

'We can't let you get on the boat. We've to deliver you back to the nuns. But we will speak to them, if you want,' he said.

'That would just make things worse. You don't know what they're like!' I said despairingly. 'We'll get beaten even more, and they'll get away with it because they're nuns.'

I covered my face with my hands and howled. Sinéad was still crying in the seat next to me, and I wondered how much more suffering we could take before going mad. I thought about grabbing her and making a run for it through the door.

'Would you like a cup of tea?' the young officer asked, interrupting my thoughts.

'Yes, please,' I said, hoping to put off going back to the convent for as long as possible.

As we drank our tea, we told him about our

intolerable life in the convent. He reacted with shock, but the older one seemed unmoved and didn't make eye contact with us once. In the middle of a conversation he went off to phone the convent and let the nuns know that we'd be on our way back soon. The young officer excused himself and followed him.

I could hear him whispering about us. I heard him say that he and his wife couldn't have children and that they'd love to have us for a while.

His colleague told him not to get involved. 'This is the Catholic Church we're talking about. You don't want to take them on. They're above the law, they do what they like.'

I felt sure that he believed us as well now.

Not long afterwards we were led out from the docks and into a police car. No one said a word on the journey back. Sinéad and I just sobbed the whole way.

Back in the convent, we didn't have to wait long to suffer Sister Francis's fury. We were taken back to the room of our solitary confinement and beaten. The cane came down hard and fast, over and over again, until she was tired out. When she'd left, I tried to comfort Sinéad, but she was inconsolable.

'I hate those bitches!' she sobbed.

'So do I, but one day they'll get back what they've done to us. One day everyone's going to know what they're like. I'll make sure of it,' I said.

'Nobody will believe you,' she said dejectedly. 'We'll never be believed. We're the Reillys, remember.'

CHAPTER 22

Breaking Out

It was as if the nuns were playing cat and mouse with us because the next day our prison room was left unlocked again. Within an hour we were standing on a platform at Belfast Station.

'Let's go to Moira and see Siobhan Murphy!' Sinéad said.

At first I didn't reply. Even though I'd do anything for Sinéad, I had mixed feelings about going back to the farm. Part of me wanted to see Siobhan again – she was the nearest thing to a mother I'd ever known, the only person who'd given me a hug in my entire life. On the other hand, Tom and Barry were the last people on earth I wanted to see, but since Sinéad didn't know about Tom and Barry, and I didn't feel I could tell her, I didn't know what to say.

'Please, Frances!' Sinéad urged. 'We'll just go and say hello, stay for some tea and show her how much we've grown.'

'OK,' I said reluctantly. 'As long as we don't stay too long.'

'Well, it'll be better than just wandering

around,' Sinéad said.

She was right. The problem with getting out of the convent was finding somewhere to go afterwards. We'd tried our luck at the docks, but that hadn't worked, so what else were we going to do? Anyway, I liked the thought of seeing Siobhan one last time to say goodbye.

We worked out a story to tell her so that she wouldn't phone the nuns and report us. We'd tell her that we were out of the convent now and living with our mother in Belfast. We'd say that she'd let us come for a visit, but we only had a few hours before we took the train home. We discussed it at length so that we wouldn't contradict each other.

'Oh my God! I hope we're doing the right thing. Siobhan might not believe us,' I said. I always seemed to be the one to worry, especially when my little sister was involved. I felt responsible for her, more like a mother than a sister.

'Don't worry, sure, we'll be grand,' she said coolly. So, as usual, I gave in.

'Here comes the train now. We'll hide in the toilet,' I told her. The train came to a noisy stop, and people poured out onto the platform. We waited for a few moments to let them pass and stepped up into a carriage. Since we didn't have any money for the fare, we were just going to have to take our chances.

Just then a yelp came from under Sinéad's coat. On the way to the station she'd stolen a small boxer puppy from a pet shop. I knew the pup would be extra trouble for us, and I hadn't wanted her to take it, but I always found it hard not to go along with what my sister wanted.

'If we just take one, the man won't miss it,' she'd pleaded outside the shop. 'I'll really look after it, Frances, I promise.' So I'd kept the man talking while she made off with the cutest pup. She decided to call it Kim.

I pushed Sinéad along towards the toilet at the end of the carriage, and she sat on the toilet seat with Kim on her lap, stroking his head and trying to quieten him. It seemed to be working. He started to suck on her little finger.

'He looks hungry. We'll have to find him something to eat,' I said.

'He'll be dead on, sure, till we get to Siobhan's. She'll give us something for him.'

There was no view from the toilet, so every time we stopped at a station, I climbed up and looked out of the small ventilation window to see where we were. We were pulling out of Lisburn when I heard a man just outside the door asking to see tickets. We stayed very quiet and luckily so did Kim.

'Do you think we'll spend a long time in Purgatory for stealing Kim and telling lies to Siobhan?' I said.

'No, I just think that the nuns love to scare us with all that stuff. And anyway, if we get a conscience about it, we can always go to confession. It would make a change to have some proper sins to confess instead of having to make them up.'

We laughed at some of the sins we'd invented over the years, just so as to have something to say in the Friday confession.

We rushed through the crowds at the Moira Station ticket barrier and set out towards the Murphys' farm. It was nice walking along in the fresh air, and we laughed and talked as we went. But as the bungalow came into view, I suddenly felt very worried about seeing Tom and Barry again. Images of what had happened with them ran vividly through my mind. For a moment I didn't think I'd be able to go on. Meanwhile Sinéad had rushed on ahead.

'Wait, I'm not sure we're doing the right thing,' I called.

'Stop stressing, Frances. Sure, we'll not be there too long,' she assured me.

I took a deep breath and carried on, hoping that the men wouldn't be in. Suddenly, Siobhan was running towards us, her arms outstretched. She hadn't changed a bit in the year since we'd last seen her. Her apron was still covered in flour, and she looked hot from hours spent baking. I hugged her first. It was nice to feel her warm arms around me and to smell the familiar aroma of home baking. It was how she'd always smelt, a reminder of the great food I'd had whenever I'd come to stay.

'What are yous doing here? And do the nuns know where yous are?'

Listening with interest to our story about living in Belfast, she seemed really pleased to see us, if surprised. Suddenly, Kim started yelping, and his head appeared from under Sinéad's coat.

'Is that a wee dog you've got there?' Siobhan asked.

The Murphys were animal lovers, and it wasn't long before Siobhan was making a fuss of Kim. First she lined a cardboard box with an old jumper and put it on the floor. Then she placed a bowl of food and a bowl of milk into it. Sinéad put Kim in the box and tried to encourage him to eat, while Siobhan prepared some tea and sandwiches.

She asked us lots of questions about our mother. We gave her our well-rehearsed answers, and for the moment it looked as if she believed every word. I was relieved that we'd found her on her own. It was good to see her again and be in her warm kitchen, eating her delicious sandwiches and drinking a big mug of hot, sweet tea. I was surprised at how relaxed I felt now that my panic had subsided. I felt happy and imagined that this must be what life was like for normal people.

A few minutes later Barry and Tom walked in through the back door. I could hear them talking about the pigs as they took off their wellies. They looked shocked to see us at the kitchen table. As she explained why we were there, Siobhan poured them each a mug of tea and began cutting some bread.

Tom lit his pipe, and the smoke drifted across to me. The smell brought back many unpleasant memories, and I fixed my eyes on Siobhan to avoid looking in the direction of the men. I didn't want to make any eye contact. It would turn my stomach.

'Can I go outside and see the wee baby pigs?' Sinéad asked.

I jumped off the chair and dashed over to the back door. 'I'll come with ye,' I said, glad of the chance to get away from the men. We disappeared out through the back door.

The farm was just as I remembered it. There was the same terrible smell and awful squealing of the pigs. Hens walked freely around in the yard, pecking at the ground for scraps of food. It sounded to me like the pigs knew they were going to be turned into sausages and bacon, and I felt really sorry for them. They weren't loved like the dogs or the cats, and they were fed on slop and leftovers. I couldn't help but empathise because in many ways I knew how it felt to be treated like a pig. We looked over the sty wall. The huge mother lay in a heap while the baby pigs trampled one another in order to feed from her. We didn't linger.

Back at the bungalow, we walked past the living-room window to have a look at Edward's flowerbeds.

'Duck!' I said, pulling Sinéad down out of sight.

'What's going on?'

We huddled close together so that we couldn't be heard.

'They're going through our coat pockets. We'll have to get away from here now, before they call the nuns or police!'

'What do ye think they're looking for?' Sinéad whispered.

'I'm not sure, but I don't think they believe us about being with our ma. We'll go back in and get our stuff, but don't let on that we saw them searching our things. We'll just tell them that we have go now.'

We walked in the back door, trying to behave normally. The Murphys were also pretending.

'Did yous have a look at the wee pigs, then?' asked Tom.

We smiled and said that we had.

'We'll have to be off now, or we'll be late getting back,' I said, grabbing our coats while Sinéad retrieved Kim from the cardboard box.

'Could yous not stay a wee while longer, Frances?' asked Tom.

'No, we better get going. Sure, we'll be back soon for another visit.'

They watched us carefully as we put on our coats and made it obvious that they didn't want us to go anywhere for the moment. It felt awkward saying our goodbyes when all we really wanted to do was run for our lives.

Tom offered to walk with us to the station, but I was quick to refuse. 'Sure, don't bother yourself, we'll be fine. Anyway, we'll have to rush to catch the train.'

We walked casually away from the house, aware that we were being watched every step of the way. Once out of sight, we ran as fast as we could along a narrow lane until we came to a gate leading on to open fields. Climbing over the gate, we ran across the fields, stopping now and then to catch our breath. I carried Kim so that Sinéad could keep up. We had no idea where we were, but at least no one had seen us.

'I think we've done it,' I said, panting. 'We can stop running for a while, but we'll still have to be careful not to be seen.'

I sensed that I'd seen the farm for the last time and had mixed emotions about it. I'd never forget my time there because it had been such a big part of my childhood, and I wanted to keep the good memories with me always. But I knew that the bad ones would always haunt me, too. Now and then I felt tears welling up in my eyes, but I managed to hold them back. I didn't want to upset Sinéad and start her off crying, too. I needed to be strong for us both now that we were totally alone in the world.

Keeping close to the hedges, we walked around aimlessly until it started to get dark and cold. We needed to find an old barn to stay in, but since we couldn't see one, we decided to get ourselves back on a road. Soon we came to a residential building site. A few workmen were still hanging around, but it looked like they were getting ready to go home.

'We'll come back in a while, when they've gone,' I said.

The workers' van drove past about five minutes later. When it was out of sight, we turned back towards the site. Once there, we went round the back of one of the newly built houses and stood at the back door. The pane of glass at the top had just been fitted, and the putty was still fresh and soft. Sinéad poked her finger into it, making a pattern. I tried the door handle, but it was locked. We were now tired, hungry and very cold.

'We have to get in somehow. We can't stay out here all night,' I wailed. Then I had an idea. I picked up a broken brick and checked there was no one around. 'Ye'll have to move away a bit, I'm gonna have to break the glass,' I said.

Sinéad backed up a few feet, and I could hear her telling Kim not to worry as I lunged at the glass with the brick. The pane cracked but didn't break. More force was needed. That got me thinking that I was in danger of cutting myself, so I took my coat off and wrapped it around my hand, before making another lunge. Shards of glass rained down on both sides of the door. Seeing a key in the inside lock, I reached through the hole and turned it.

Glass crunched under our feet as we walked inside the house. I locked the door behind us and put the key in my pocket before looking around for something to cover the hole in the glass. Eventually, I poked my coat through it, which appeared to do the job.

While Sinéad dashed from one room to another, I walked around much more slowly, searching for the warmest place to spend the night. The house was quiet, and our voices echoed around the empty rooms. Between the living room and kitchen, I found a large cupboard containing some sort of a meter. It was just about big enough for us to lie down in and would be warm, provided we kept the door closed.

Sinéad took her coat off, folded it and put it the corner of one of the bedrooms. I placed Kim carefully on top, stroking him until he seemed to be settled. As we left, we closed the door behind us so that he wouldn't wander out onto the broken glass.

It was very dark inside our cupboard. We sat down on the wooden floor with our backs leaning up against the wall. There was nothing to do now but relax and wait for morning. We'd have to be out of the house early, before the workmen turned up. Plus, I said, I was convinced that the Murphys had called the nuns, and then the nuns would have called the police.

'We'll have to get as far away from here as we can as soon as it's light.'

But we couldn't make much of a plan, with no money to our name and little sense of where we were. There just wasn't anywhere to go to. Still, anything was better than being back in the convent.

We talked for hours before settling down for the night. I had too much on my mind to get much rest and the hard wooden floor didn't help. What's more, Sinéad kicked and fidgeted in her sleep, and Kim was making the strangest noises. I kept going to check on him but didn't want to bring him into the cupboard because he'd already weed all over the bedroom floor.

By daylight I was glad of the chance to get up and stretch my legs, even though I couldn't hold back the yawns. We made our way into Kim's room, stepping carefully over the small piles of dog poo scattered all over the floor. Sinéad gently picked him up and started stroking and talking to him.

'We'll have to find something to clean this mess up,' I said, as I didn't think it was fair to leave the house in a state. It wasn't long before I found a piece of plywood. 'This'll do. We'll scrape up the poo and throw it outside, then we'll have to get going.'

I'd just started cleaning up when I heard the sound of men's voices outside. 'Get back inside the cupboard!' I told Sinéad. I followed her in and shut the door, trembling with fear.

We could hear the voices clearly outside the back door now, discussing the broken glass. Grabbing Sinéad's arm, I could feel that she was shaking, too. Someone pushed open the back door, and we heard the crunch of broken glass. Holding my breath, my eyes tightly shut, I prayed over and again that no one would look in the cupboard.

The footsteps continued around the house. I wondered if we should try to make a run for it but felt paralysed. Then we heard noises on the other side of the cupboard door, and for a moment it felt as if my heart had stopped beating. The door opened to reveal two policemen.

'Come on now, out you come,' one of them said.

'Oh God, Frances, we can't go back!'

Sinéad whispered.

'Come on now, out!' the policeman barked angrily. There was nothing to do but give ourselves up. In the police car outside, we were asked to confirm who we were. This time we didn't see any point in denying that we were the Reilly sisters.

Back at the convent, the policemen took statements from us, asking us stern questions about why we'd broken into the house, while the Reverend Mother looked on. We didn't dare complain about the nuns. These policemen weren't anything like the policemen at the docks, and we didn't think they'd give us much sympathy.

We could tell from the Reverend Mother's expression that the cane wasn't going to be enough this time. So far the nuns hadn't succeeded in breaking our will, but I knew now that they wouldn't stop trying. I was very frightened for myself – and hoped that I could get through whatever punishment I'd have to take – but I was even more afraid for Sinéad. In an attempt to make things easier for her, I told the police that everything had been my idea. I said that I'd made her go with me, because I didn't want to leave her behind. Sinéad gave me a smile when no one was looking, which I took to be her way of saying thanks. Eventually, the questioning finished, and the policemen went off to talk privately with the Reverend Mother.

We were locked in a room for the rest of the day, giving us plenty of time to worry about the punishment to come. Eventually, night came, but we were far too anxious and cold to sleep. We just cuddled up to each other on a bench and got what rest we could. It was a long night. When we weren't talking or crying, we were trying to prepare mentally for the beating that lay ahead. Little did we know what surprises the next day held in store for us.

CHAPTER 23

The Remand Home

When morning came, instead of being punished, we were taken up to the dormitory and told to put on some new clothes. We were obviously going somewhere, but we had no idea where. Sister Francis came in to inspect us. She handed us each a new ribbon and told us to tidy up our hair. I wondered what on earth was going on. After two dramatic escape attempts, this was very unexpected. Why weren't we being beaten black and blue?

'That will do. Now come with me.'

We followed her through the convent to the main entrance. I felt scared and confused. We weren't being taken out for a nice day, so what was this all about? As we approached the entrance doors, a woman walked towards us. Sister Francis stepped forward and shook her hand.

'Miss Reed, I hope you haven't been waiting too long,' she said. 'Here are Frances and Sinéad Reilly.'

'Hello, girls, we'll have to be getting a move on,' Miss Reed said.

'Where are we going?' I asked.

She didn't reply. Sister Francis told me not to ask questions and to be on my best behaviour.

'Yes, Sister. Sorry, Sister,' I said, lowering my head, embarrassed that I'd been put in my place in front of a stranger.

Parked just outside the convent gate was an old red car. Miss Reed opened the back door and told us to get in. Soon we were driving down the Ormeau Road.

'Do you think she's taking us to our mammy's?' Sinéad whispered.

'I don't know. I don't think so,' I whispered back, not wanting to get her hopes up. I was trying to prepare for every eventuality, even if that meant making a run for it.

As we drove through Belfast town centre, I gazed in wonder at the different buildings and shops. People were walking freely about their business, and I wished that Sinéad and I were free to go wherever we wanted. The car came to a stop outside a large building, and Miss Reed asked us to get out.

'Here we are now,' she said, pointing to a pair of big doors.

She led us to a row of chairs lining a corridor. We sat down. A woman and a boy were sitting at the end of the row talking to a man in a smart dark suit. I couldn't make out what they were saying, but the boy appeared to be getting upset and was starting to cry. I strained to catch the drift of their conversation because it might give me some clue as to where we were and why, but their words were muffled by the sound of the boy sobbing.

The woman was trying to get the boy to dry his tears when she noticed me staring at them. I looked away and focused my attention on Miss Reed. In her brown coat, brown hat and brown shoes, she looked rather plain and ordinary, like one of the nuns dressed in normal clothes.

Another man in a suit appeared in the corridor. Miss Reed stood up, and they said hello. They walked away, talking softly so that we couldn't overhear them. Every now and then Miss Reed pointed to us, and the man glanced over, nodding his head slowly. I didn't like the feel of what was going on.

'We have to try to get away,' I said nervously. 'When Miss Reed comes back, we'll tell her that we need to go to the toilet. Maybe there's a window that we can get out of.'

'OK,' Sinéad said. 'What is this place, anyway?'

'I don't know, but I don't like it.'

Miss Reed came back to sit with us, and the man walked off. 'I need the toilet, miss,' Sinéad said, wriggling about on her chair.

'Me too, miss. I need to go as well.'

Miss Reed took us to the ladies'. 'I'll wait

here for you,' she said, standing outside.

Once inside the cubicle, I climbed up to the window and opened it, only to find that there were bars on the other side.

'We've had it Sinéad. We're stuck here,' I said. 'Oh well, I suppose we'll find out soon enough what's going on.'

Miss Reed banged on the door. 'Come along, girls.' She had two bottles of orange juice in her hand and offered one to each of us. 'We could be here for a while, so I thought you might need some refreshments,' she said kindly.

We weren't sure how to react. We weren't used to people being nice to us, and we didn't really trust it.

'Thank you,' we said.

The juice tasted really nice, and for a moment we forgot what was happening and just sat back and enjoyed it.

She explained that we would be going into a room where some very nice people would ask us some questions. Then she began to talk about the Poor Sisters of Nazareth, saying how wonderful she thought they were and how they must be completely selfless and dedicated to look after so many children in need. This was not what we needed to be hearing now. She has obviously not spent her childhood with them, I thought.

To be fair, she'd probably only made short visits to the convent, and the nuns would have put on a caring act. However, it showed in her face that she totally believed what she was saying, so we kept quiet. We didn't want her to pass anything on to the nuns and land us in more trouble.

'Sometimes when you're young,' she said, 'you don't realize that adults are just trying to help you. But have you really thought about where you would be now if the Sisters of Nazareth hadn't taken you in and cared for you?'

Her words sent awful shivers through me, and Sinéad didn't look too comfortable, either. Miss Reed clearly wasn't about to change her view on just how wonderful the nuns were.

'We will be going in soon,' she continued. 'You may be asked some questions, but don't worry. Just answer clearly, and don't let the nuns down. Show everyone what a good job they've done with you.'

Sinéad and I exchanged glances, wondering what planet this woman had come from. If the nuns had been so wonderful, then why did she think we kept running away?

The man in the suit returned and said that we could go in now. Miss Reed walked us into a strange-looking room with wooden panelling on the walls and large wooden benches. It reminded me of some sort of chapel or place of worship. She told us to sit down. Two men and a woman came in through another door, and she told us to stand up. The three people sat down at a high bench, facing the rest of the room.

'Sit down,' she said.

As we sat down, I really expected prayers to be said because when a priest enters a chapel everyone has to stand up in the same respectful way, but I couldn't imagine why we would have come to this place to pray. It didn't make any sense.

The men and woman in front of us began shuffling through a pile of papers. Every now and then they whispered to one another and looked in our direction. Eventually, one of the men gently asked me if the nuns were good to us. Miss Reed nudged me. I stood up.

'Yes, sir,' I said.

Miss Reed gave me a proud smile.

The man turned to Miss Reed and said that he'd a telegram from Mrs Reilly, who had wired to say that she had mental health problems and was unable to have her daughters living with her. He held the telegram up.

'Yes,' Miss Reed said, 'I am aware of it.'

It took a few moments for this new development to sink in. Tears welled up in my eyes as I stared at the piece of paper in the man's hand. Could it really be from our mother? Was it true that she still didn't want us? If so, there would never be any point in trying to find her. I was devastated. Nobody wanted us. We were totally alone.

Beside me, I could hear Sinéad quietly sobbing. Noticing how upset we were, the men and woman asked Miss Reed if she would please approach the bench, where they talked in whispers for a while, giving us time to dry our eyes and get ourselves together.

I could hear snatches of their conversation. The woman was saying that we were obviously running away so often because we missed our mother. One of the men said that the situation had to change because the nuns couldn't put up with us absconding from the convent every time their backs were turned, and something was said about the house that we'd broken into.

A song called 'Nobody's Child' began to run through my head. Loretta had taught it to me, and all the girls in the convent knew it. It was one of my favourite songs, probably because I could relate to it completely. Even though it made me feel sad, I'd often find myself quietly singing it, and Loretta had sometimes asked me to sing it for her. Thinking about Loretta reminded me of how much I missed her. I felt so lonely and unsupported.

Worried that I might be missing something important, I forced my attention back to the whisperings. One of the men said something about remand, but I wasn't sure what it meant. Then Miss Reed came back and sat with us. The men and woman stood up to leave the room, and Miss Reed nudged us and told us to stand up. We did as we were told.

It seemed to me that we had behaved very well. We'd done everything that Miss Reed had asked of us and given her no reason to complain to the nuns. It was obvious that she didn't know we'd tried to get out of the toilet window, which was just as well. I still didn't know what was happening and assumed that now we'd be going straight back to the convent.

She walked us back to her car. Before she started the engine, she glanced at her watch and said, 'It's past lunchtime. Are you girls hungry?'

'Yes,' Sinéad said.

I didn't answer because I felt sick with worry about what the nuns would have planned for us when we got back. Food didn't come into it, especially not convent food. I would rather miss lunch altogether.

'Then we'll stop off at a café and get you some lunch,' she said, starting up the car.

Our eyes lit up at the thought of going to a café.

'Just wait till the other girls hear about this,' I said, my appetite returning.

We drove away from the town and stopped at a quiet café just outside Belfast. There were only three other customers eating there. Miss Reed showed us to a table, picking the one furthest away from the other customers.

'This will do nicely,' she said, pulling out a chair.

We sat down and got comfortable. I thought that perhaps Miss Reed wasn't as bad as the nuns, but I still couldn't trust her because she was definitely a friend of theirs.

A young man with a lovely smile came over and handed Miss Reed a menu. 'Let me know when yous are ready to order,' he said in a welcoming voice. He looked at me and his smile broadened. 'Cheer up, the food in here is quite good,' he joked.

I couldn't tell if he was flirting with me or just felt sorry for me. Either way, it made me blush, and I could feel my face getting hot. I lowered my head, hoping that no one would notice.

By the time I'd raised it again, the boy had gone off to talk to someone at another table. After a bit of a discussion we all settled on cod, chips and beans. Miss Reed waved the boy back over to us. He wrote down our order on his pad.

'Would ye and yer daughters like a drink with that?' he asked. This time it was Miss Reed's turn to blush. Sinéad and I grinned.

'We'll have a pot of tea for one and two Coca Colas. Thank you,' she said.

He walked off to get the order, looking

back to give me another smile. I smiled at him politely. The food was very good, and by the time we'd finished, there was nothing left on our plates.

As we drove away from the café, Miss Reed informed us that we wouldn't be returning to Nazareth House. Instead, she said, we were going to St Joseph's Training School in Middletown, near the border at Monaghan.

'It's a remand home for difficult children,' she explained. 'The magistrates at court this morning thought it would be the best thing for both of you, under the circumstances.'

I was sure I could detect a strange tone in her voice as she spoke now, and I realised that the meal had been meant to soften us up.

'It's quite a long journey, girls,' Miss Read said. 'So sit back and enjoy it.'

Speechless, Sinéad and I stared at each other. We had no idea of what to make of our situation. I thought that it was good, in a way, that we weren't going back to Nazareth House, because it got us out of our punishment, but I wondered what my friends would think when we didn't return. I knew that the nuns wouldn't tell them anything. Would I see any of them again? Nothing seemed clear. All I knew was that everything was about to change for my sister and me, for better or for worse.

It wasn't long before Sinéad was asleep. I dozed off a few times but not for long, as I kept waking up to see if we'd arrived at our new home yet. The journey took ages and the further we went, the more I began to worry about what lay ahead. Would we fit in with the other girls, and how 'difficult' were they really?

At one point Miss Reed turned around and saw how stressed and fidgety I'd become. 'It's not so bad at St Joseph's, Frances,' she said. 'I'm there a lot, and I know the nuns and girls very well. I'm sure you'll both fit in.'

It was easy for her to say, I thought. She wasn't being told to live in the place. I also remembered what she'd said earlier about the nuns at Nazareth House, and she couldn't have been more wrong about them.

'And there are some lovely walks,' she went on. 'The countryside around here is beautiful.'

I was not convinced.

'Here we are,' she said as we pulled up to a pair of iron gates. A man appeared and opened them; he and Miss Reed smiled and waved at each other. She explained that he kept the grounds looking nice and did all the odd jobs. There wasn't a job that he couldn't do, apparently. I thought he looked friendly. I woke Sinéad up to tell her that we'd arrived. She looked better for having slept a bit.

As we approached a set of redbrick buildings, we passed some large colourful flowerbeds, a row of rhododendron bushes and a wide expanse of well-kept, bright-green lawn.

'That's the nuns' part of the convent and the chapel,' Miss Reed said as we drove past the first building.

We stopped outside a second building, which was about twenty-five metres further on, and got out of the car. Miss Reed led us through an archway. Here, she explained, was where the girls who smoked were allowed to have their nightly cigarette at ten to eight, as long as they'd behaved themselves. I found it hard to believe that the nuns actually let the girls smoke, but I kept quiet.

There were two girls working on the staircase as we entered the building. One was polishing the wooden banisters and the other was scrubbing the stairs, but my most memorable first impression of St Joseph's was the distinctive smell of Jeyes Fluid. It was everywhere.

A group of girls stopped to say hello to Miss Reed and have a good look at the new arrivals. It felt very strange being new. At Nazareth House we'd always been the ones to show the new girls around.

'Where's the Reverend Mother?' Miss Reed asked.

'In her office,' said the girl scrubbing the stairs.

Miss Reed apologised for having to walk over her hard work, and we kept to the edge of the stairs all the way up to the top of the building, where Miss Reed knocked on a large wooden door.

'Enter,' said a voice.

Another convent, another Mother Superior. My stomach turned over as Miss Reed opened the door.

'Come on, girls,' Miss Reed coaxed.

The Mother Superior stood up and shook Miss Reed's hand. Staring hard at us over the top of her glasses, she said, 'So you are the Reilly sisters, sent to us from Nazareth House in Belfast.'

'Yes, Mother,' we chorused.

She studied us for a moment, wearing an expression that made me feel like we were a couple of murderers or thieves.

'Goodbye, girls,' said Miss Reed, turning to go. 'I'll leave you in the good hands of Mother Petronella. I'm sure I'll be seeing you the next time I visit.'

We said goodbye and she left.

Towering over us, Mother Petronella said, 'I've heard all about both of you from the Mother Superior at Nazareth House, and I am not impressed. Your nonsense will not be tolerated here. Is that clear?'

'Yes, Mother.'

'Every girl is here because nowhere else can cope with her and the trouble she's caused. We have a way of dealing with troublemakers like you. Do you understand?'

'Yes, Mother.' My knees began to shake.

Marching us out of her office, Mother Petronella called out to a nearby girl. 'Sadie,' she boomed. 'I want you to show these girls around and let them know how we run things at St Joseph's. Oh, and get them some suitable clothing. Their clothes will have to be sent back to Nazareth House.'

'Yes, Mother,' the girl said.

Sadie seemed friendly. She asked us a lot of questions about ourselves as she showed us around and introduced us to some of the other girls. Filling us in on the St Joseph's routine and giving us information about every girl we met, she told us quite a few stories about how the nuns treated the girls.

'They're just frustrated old women,' she said, 'who get their kicks taking their unhappiness out on us.'

I liked her honesty. St Joseph's sounded pretty similar to Nazareth House, except for the cigarette smoking and the fact that we had to go on a long walk every day accompanied by nuns. Plus, there was a netball team. Apparently, the team got to play against other schools and quite often won the local league cup. According to Sadie, the other schools hated the convent girls, and it wasn't uncommon for fights to break out between them.

'They think we're scum because we're in a remand home,' said Sadie. 'But not everyone gets the same break in life. Some are born with a silver spoon, and others with a load of shit.'

'Yeh, we know what you mean,' I said warmly.

Sinéad nodded in agreement. It felt good to make a friend so quickly. It would definitely help us to settle in. A little later we were given new clothes and allocated beds in a dormitory.

And so our new life started, hardly varying from the old one. When the bell went, we lined up. All the prayers and prayer times were the same. The food was just as disgusting. The place stank of Jeyes Fluid, and the nuns were weird, bitter and cruel.

There was a crucial difference, however. The girls at St Joseph's weren't abandoned orphans – they were rebels who didn't fit in anywhere else and were 'naughty' by definition. This made for quite a different atmosphere to the one at Nazareth House. There was far less respect for the nuns here, although the friction between the girls was often worse. As yet, I didn't know who and who not to trust, which put me in a position of weakness. But in time, and with Sadie's help, I'd find out.

CHAPTER 24

Rebelling

I didn't think that anywhere could be as bad as Nazareth House, but the regime at St Joseph's was every bit as harsh and took just as much of a toll on me, both mentally and physically. Although I didn't have Sister Thomas on my case every single day and I wasn't being picked on just for being a Reilly, I received countless punishments and beatings during my time at St Joseph's, and some of the other girls were completely terrifying. They hadn't been imprisoned in a remand home because they were orphans or because their families were having difficulties; they were there for committing crimes and acts of violence – anything from shoplifting to GBH – or because their parents couldn't cope with their antisocial behaviour. At the very least, they were disobedient and rebellious, but some of them were aggressive to the point of being disturbed.

I was constantly looking over my shoulder at St Joseph's. Anything could happen. I'd be walking down a corridor and suddenly a girl would jump out of the shadows and attack me, for no reason. I'd wake up in the middle of the night with someone hovering over me. Even the smallest disagreement could develop into a shouting match or a fight. Bullying was rife. Violence was an everyday fact of life. For the first few weeks I was scared almost all of the time. It was hell. I could never relax. And even though Sister Thomas wasn't physically near me, she haunted my waking hours and gave me nightmares.

Going for a walk every day was torture, lined up in long crocodile formation with two nuns at the head of the line and another two at the back. I hated trudging across fields in the rain, snow and hail, not knowing who was behind me or what they might do. Netball practice was vicious. If another girl bore you the slightest grudge, you'd get a ball in the face or several sharp kicks when the nun on duty wasn't looking. Even your most meagre possessions were stolen or broken by other girls.

Surrounded by hard, unruly teenagers, I quickly toughened up. I had to. To survive at St Joseph's, you had to rebel along with the others, and anyway, it was impossible not to get sucked in by the defiant atmosphere. As the months passed, I stopped caring about the nuns and their stupid rules. I was disrespectful and answered them back, even when I knew that to do so would result in a

340

vicious punishment. It was partly my age – I was fast approaching adolescence – and I think that in many ways I was taking out my anger towards the Nazareth House nuns on the nuns at St Joseph's, who were from a similar order and just as cruel and oppressive. Plus, you got respect from the other remand-home girls if you were seen to be answering the nuns back. Gradually, I began to be accepted by some of them.

Unfortunately, Sinéad and I drifted apart when she started hanging around with a gang of girls who were trouble. They thrived on aggression, and I hated to see my sister turning into a bully. I tried to talk to her about it several times, but she didn't want to know — she was enjoying her newfound popularity and power too much. On two occasions her friends beat me up and she went along with it, just to prove her loyalty to the gang. After that I began to ignore her. I didn't like the person she'd become.

I spent the next few years with just one thing on my mind: escape. I desperately longed to be free and tried every trick in the book to get away. Sometimes, as we rounded a corner on our daily walk, I'd duck under a hedge with another girl and run off when no one was looking. Or we'd find an excuse to go to the laundry at the back of the convent, where there was a stretch of wall out of sight of the nuns. I must have climbed over that bit of the wall fifty times.

There was never a shortage of people who wanted to go with me, but unfortunately, we kept getting caught and being brought back. One of the problems was that there were several head counts during the day, so if you went then, you'd soon be missed. The nuns would raise the alarm, and the police would be after you in no time. They even had people at the border watching out. So it was much better to go at night, when you wouldn't be missed until the morning, but it was also much harder to escape from the dormitory than to slip away in between bells during the day.

All I thought about was getting out and no longer being beaten. My dreams for the outside world didn't go a lot further than that, because I had almost no concept of what life could be like without the constant threat of bullying nuns and girls. At times I got very depressed and a black cloud would hang over me for days on end. But then I'd come up with another escape plan and be filled with hope again. I spent almost every waking minute trying to devise a new route out, sizing up windows and doors and observing the nuns' routines. I just wouldn't give up. I was desperate. The only thing I could focus on was getting beyond the walls. And the more escape attempts I made, the more I was accepted by the other girls.

I was up for trying anything. So when a girl called Marion suggested that we put the nuns out of action by lacing their evening cocoa with laxatives, I jumped at the idea.

'If we manage to smuggle some in, it'll have the nuns on the toilet for ages,' she said, her face beaming with joy.

'Let's do it, sure!' I said breathlessly.

Not long after that she persuaded one of her visitors to bring in three bars of laxative chocolate. I hid them under my pillow until the time came to make cocoa for the nuns on duty that evening.

At St Joseph's none of the other girls tried to talk you out of taking risks. However much they fought or argued with you on a day-to-day basis, they would always be willing to help you escape. So this time we'd arranged for a whole load of girls to occupy all the toilets in our building so that when the nuns on duty started feeling the effects of the laxatives, they would have to go to another building to use the toilet.

It worked like a dream. The sight of the duty nuns clutching the banisters for support with their stomachs audibly rumbling and gurgling was hysterically funny. I couldn't help laughing, even though I was nervous about climbing the wall and getting away, and watching them try to get into the girls' toilets was hilarious. Every cubicle they knocked at was occupied, and every girl gave the same excuse: 'Sorry, Sister, I'm really constipated, Sister.'

'If you girls are playing games, you'll be punished! I'm not finding this very funny.'

'We're not playing games, Sister, honestly, Sister.'

The duty nuns had no choice but to leave the building in search of empty toilets – and the moment they were gone, so were we. A couple of girls gave us a leg up, and soon we were over the wall and running across the field on the other side.

Marion and I ran over many empty fields until eventually we came to an old derelict house. The garden was overgrown, the windows were broken, and it looked like no one had lived there for ages. We decided that it might make a good hiding place until things had calmed down and the police had given up their search.

We walked through a broken gate and down a path to the front door. I knocked on the door just in case there was someone inside – a tramp, perhaps, using it for shelter.

'Hello, is anyone here?' I called out. I knocked again. 'Hello?'

'Come on now, Frances, who'd be living in this dump?' Marion laughed. 'Just look at the place. There's been no one here for years.'

'Well, don't blame me if some scary old man jumps out on ye, then,' I warned her. I didn't like it when people made fun of me for being cautious. It was in my nature to be careful.

Marion tried the door and it opened with a creak. The house was a real dump inside, with dust and cobwebs everywhere, and rubbish strewn all over the old furniture. There was a horrible stale stench that made me want to run back outside and take my chances in the fields. The atmosphere was really spooky, too.

'It's disgusting,' I said. There wasn't anywhere to sit down without getting filthy. 'Let's get out of here, Marion, and just keep on the move. This place gives me the creeps.'

'Wait,' she said.

I followed her up the stairs into a room containing a long wooden table and chairs. She began dusting down the table with an old curtain. Suddenly, a huge spider ran across its surface. We screamed as it crawled down onto the floor and disappeared under a ragged bit of carpet, and then we collapsed into a fit of relieved giggles. Finally, the table was clear, and we climbed up to sit on top of it.

We sat very close together and talked in whispers for hours, barely able to see one another through the darkness. I couldn't believe we were out. As night wore on, the temperature dropped dramatically, and I was glad that we'd managed to find shelter.

There was no possibility of sleep, but at least we weren't out in the fields.

Just before dawn we were disturbed by noises outside. Someone was walking about. We sat in silence, hanging on to each other's arms, our teeth chattering with fear and cold. Torchlight flashed through the windows.

'Oh my God, I hope that's not the police, Marion. Let's make a run for it now!'

'Whoever it is doesn't know we're here yet. Let's just sit quietly and they might go away,' Marion whispered.

The front door creaked, and we heard footsteps in the house. Now they were making their way up the stairs. A torch beam shone through the door.

'Come on now, let's be getting you back.'

Behind the glare of the torch I could just about make out a policeman's uniform. I gritted my teeth and swore that next time I'd get away for good.

But we always got caught, mostly because we didn't have anywhere, or anyone, to go to. Still, I didn't stop hoping and planning. It was the only way to survive. As time went on, I became more disobedient. I wasn't scared of the nuns any more, and I was so used to being beaten that I could get through most of my punishments without crying, however painful they were, and the more beatings you got, the more respect the other girls gave you.

One time, a whole group of us rebelled against the new Mother Superior. Mother De Richie had summoned everyone to the refectory, where she was pacing the stage with a cane in her hand, wearing a very stern expression.

Surveying us with disgust, she said, 'Some of you girls probably found it very amusing to steal bottles of wine from the sacristy, but I do not find it amusing and I will not stand for it! I want the girls responsible to come forward now.'

There was silence. Most of the girls knew nothing abut the missing wine and searched each other's faces for signs of guilt. I pretended to do the same, even though I was the culprit, along with two other girls. A few weeks before, while I was cleaning the sacristy, where the altar wine was kept in a cupboard, I'd found the keys to the cupboard lying around. Half an hour later I was passing bottles of wine out of the window to Kathleen and Mary, and we drank it during recreation. I exchanged glances with Kathleen and Mary and could almost hear them willing me not to say anything.

'Come forward now if you're responsible for stealing the wine from God's house!' Mother De Richie boomed.

A shudder went through me, but I stayed perfectly still.

'All right, then, I will leave you for a while to think about the sin that has been committed against Our Lord. He will be angry with the thieves if they don't repent, and I'm sure they'll burn in Hell. When I return, I hope the girls involved will be ready to tell the truth. If they don't own up, all privileges will be suspended and holidays cancelled.'

We began whispering the moment she swept out of the refectory. No one seemed bothered about the wine being stolen, but some girls were annoyed that they hadn't got to drink any of it.

'Whoever took it, good luck to them,' Sadie said. 'I'd have done the same if I had the chance.'

Everyone nodded.

'Those nuns are all hypocrites, anyway,' Rosemary said angrily. 'They steal all the best food, while we live on slop. It's not like any of us get cocoa before bed, is it? Or proper meat or fruit. They steal it all! And now they have the cheek to say that the altar wine is God's wine, as if He's going to be popping into the sacristy for a quick drink every now and then.'

'Yeh!' Sadie said. 'It's not bloody fair!'

'Sure, don't they treat us like skivvies and beat the hell out of us?' Rosemary went on heatedly, waving a fist.

'Yeh, they treat us like animals,' Sadie said.

'Yeh, and the pigs get better slop,' I added,

thinking back to the Murphys' farm.

'I wish we could do something about it,' Mary said dejectedly, rubbing her stomach. 'I'd do anything for a decent meal right now.'

'We should make a stand and demand decent food and better treatment,' Bernadette said.

The hall fell silent. Yes, we should, I thought. We should make a stand. It turned out that quite a few of the others were thinking the same thing.

'We should do it right now!' Kathleen said. 'Let's barricade ourselves in here until they give us what we want. It's about time they listened to us.'

'Let's make a list,' Sadie shouted.

A ripple of excitement went through the refectory.

But although everyone would have liked to have been a part of the rebellion, most girls were worried about losing their holidays. Others, like my closest friend, Patsy, were due to get out soon and couldn't afford to jeopardise their release dates. So it was decided that the girls who weren't going to get involved, for whatever reason, should be first in line to leave the refectory when we were given permission to go. Once they'd gone, the rest of us could shut the door behind them and barricade ourselves in.

Mother DeRichie came back, and we

stood to attention.

'Is anyone going to come forward and own up?'

No one moved.

'All right, I'm giving you until tomorrow evening, and if I don't get the truth by then, no one will be going home for the holidays. Now get to your dormitories.'

We lined up and started to file out through the refectory door. As arranged, Rosemary was behind the last girl who needed to leave and wasted no time in slamming the door after her, leaving about a dozen of us in the refectory.

'What's going on in there? Open this door at once!' Mother De Richie shouted.

'Quick!' Rosemary said, straining to keep the door shut.

I dragged a table across the room to stack up against it, and Sinéad pushed over a heavy trolley. As she lined the trolley up with the doorway, Sinéad's eyes met mine and she smiled. In that moment I forgave her everything, and my resentment towards her melted away. She was my sister, after all, and I'd always felt very protective of her, maternal even. I scanned the refectory and noted that most of the girls in her crowd were absent.

By now tables, chairs and trolleys were stacked up neatly against the door. There was no way anyone could get in – or out, so it was too late for a change of heart. I could hardly believe we were doing this. It had all happened so quickly.

We could hear another nun, Sister Mary, shouting on the other side of the door. 'You had all better be out of there by the time I've counted to ten!'

Kathleen started singing 'We Shall Not Be Moved', and the rest of us joined in. In for a penny, in for a pound, I thought, and handed out some serving spoons to bang on the tables in time to the song. It was tremendously exciting to take control for once. This felt like something that would be talked about for years to come. Our spirits rose ever higher, and soon we were blasting out the chorus at the tops of our voices.

We shall not, we shall not be moved.
We shall not, we shall not be moved
Just like a tree that's standing by the water,
We shall not be moved.

Outside the door, everything had gone quiet. Just as we were wondering what the nuns were up to, someone knocked on the kitchen hatch. We all jumped up.

'It's only me, open up.' It didn't sound like one of the nuns.

Margaret opened the hatch a fraction. 'It's Nula. She's got us a pencil and some paper,' she said.

We ran over to the hatch. 'Where are the nuns?' Sinéad asked.

'They're in the office talking about you lot,' Nula said. 'You're doing great, though. The singing was fantastic; we were all laughing up in the dormitories, but the nuns looked really mad. Anyway, I'd better go before I get caught.' She dashed off.

'We should get some food from the kitchen while the nuns are busy,' Marion said. 'Who's small enough to go in through the hatch?'

'Frances, ye're the smallest,' Sinéad said. She'd always been good at volunteering me for stuff.

I climbed through the hatch and rummaged around the kitchen cupboards for food. I'd managed to pass through some bread, milk and a box of the nuns' biscuits when I heard voices on the stairs and dived back through again. Removing one of my shoelaces, I wrapped it tightly around the hatch door handles.

'Ye've done great, Frances. This box of biscuits is nearly full,' Mary said, stuffing a chocolate biscuit into her mouth. We sat down to some milk and a biscuit each, aware that our rations might have to last a long while.

Mother De Richie banged on the door again.

'Are you girls ready to come out?'

We kept quiet.

'If that's the way you want it, then I can wait much longer than you can,' she said.

We still said nothing. We hadn't even started on our list of demands. When she'd gone, we began discussing what should go on it. Rosemary took charge of the writing, and everyone had something to say.

'We want another slice of bread at teatime. One isn't enough.'

'And a bit more butter.'

'Yeah, there's hardly enough for one slice.'

'Properly cooked food, instead of the undercooked slop we get served up.'

'And extra blankets.'

'And proper meat.'

Rosemary wrote everything down as fast as she could. Then I asked her if she could write a note at the end saying that I owned up to taking the altar wine. I didn't want everyone to get punished because of me. Getting home for the holidays was the only thing that kept some of the girls going. I didn't mention Kathleen and Mary's part in it, though. I thought it was up to them if they wanted to say anything.

'Did ye really take it?' Sinéad asked, looking really surprised. She was usually the one that got up to things like that. I was supposed to be the more sensible one.

'Mother De Richie is going to kill ye when we get out of here,' Rosemary said.

I wanted to enjoy the moment, so I changed the subject. 'Anyway, how are we doing with the list?' I said.

'It's just about done, unless anyone can think of anything else.' Kathleen started to read it out. 'Another slice of bread at tea-time, more butter...'

We started laughing.

'That's great. Why don't we put it through the hatch now?' Sinéad said. She listened at the hatch doors, untied the shoelace, and Marion shoved the note through.

Early the next morning, twelve hours after we'd shut ourselves in, no one had had much sleep, but we were feeling great. We were just starting a game of I-Spy when Mother De Richie banged on the door.

'This has gone on long enough now! You'd better come out, or things are going to be a lot worse for you when you do.'

'We're not coming out until our demands are met,' Kathleen shouted. 'There's a list through the hatch.'

With baited breath, we listened to foot-steps going through the kitchen to the hatch and then back out again.

I giggled nervously. 'Oh my God, I wonder what they'll do now.'

A few moments later Mother De Richie gave us her response: 'I will not be giving in to your list of demands. I can wait as long as it takes for you to come out. You can't stay in there forever, and you're not going anywhere. So I'll just wait until you get very tired or very hungry.' There was a smugness to her voice that I didn't like one bit. It seemed that our demands weren't going to be taken seriously.

Shortly afterwards nature took its course and the inevitable happened. During the night we'd used a bucket for a toilet, but now someone said that they needed more than a wee. It turned out that most of us needed more than a wee. Not having thought this far ahead, we were at a loss as to what to do. Suddenly, the atmosphere changed.

Need soon turned into desperation, and then some girls began to get stomach cramps. No one wanted to give in, but time was running out. We decided to wait until everyone had gone to the hall for breakfast before trying to sneak people out to the toilet, but although we dismantled the barricade as quietly as we could, the nuns barged in the moment we turned the door handle. The rebellion was over.

We'd had our moment of glory and now there was a price to pay. But even though I was beaten practically into oblivion later in the day, I still thought it had been worth it.

CHAPTER 25

The Top Window

The night before my best friend, Patsy, was released she gave me her address in Derry.

'If ye ever get away, Frances, try and make your way to Derry and find me. I'll help you out and so will my friends, I promise,' she said.

It was obvious that she meant it, and I hugged her. I already had another idea for an escape. This time, whoever came with me would have to be as small as I was. We'd also need the help of everyone in the dormitory, although that wouldn't be a problem because whenever anyone ran away, everyone would be rooting for them to succeed, no matter who they were. No one wanted the nuns and police to win.

That night, instead of telling stories, I talked about my new plan. I intended to climb through the window in the washroom next to the dormitory, which was the only window without bars. It was tiny, but I was sure that I'd be able to force myself through the gap. The only other person who might fit was Mary Steel. I wouldn't have picked

Mary if I'd been going any other way. We weren't enemies, but we weren't exactly friends either. But Mary wanted to go even before she'd heard the whole plan, and she began to get really excited.

I explained that after lights out, when there were no nuns about, we'd take the sheets off our beds and tie them tightly together. They would have to be strong enough to take our weight and long enough to reach the laundry roof. Once we were safely on the roof, the sheets would be pulled back in and the beds made again. Mary's and my beds would have to look as if we were asleep in them; that way, the nuns wouldn't know that we'd gone until the bell went for morning prayers. By the time the police were informed, we'd be miles away from the convent.

We whispered about the plan late into the evening, and the more we discussed it, the more we liked it. It hadn't been tried before, and one of its main advantages was that we'd be going at night. We decided to go the following evening. I tried to sleep so that I was rested for the next day, but I found it hard to get settled now that freedom was a possibility again. I probably should have been concerned for my safety because the window was four floors up, but it didn't even enter my head. Instead, my brain whirred with the hope of being free at last.

The next day dragged along slowly, but

finally, it was bedtime. Everyone was excited because if the plan worked, they'd know that they'd all played a part in it. Also, they were amused by the thought of the nuns puzzling over how it had been done.

We yawned and pretended to be tired as Sister Mary said, 'Lights out. Now straight to sleep, you lot.'

'Goodnight, Sister,' we said.

After a few minutes, when we were sure the coast was clear, we jumped out of bed.

'Quiet, everyone! We're never going to get away with this if we're not as quiet as mice,' I whispered.

Mary and I got dressed while the others crept around taking the sheets off their beds and tying them together with tight knots. Soon the girls were in a sort of tug-of-war across the dormitory, testing the rope they'd made for strength.

We all moved off to the washroom and Mary opened the window using a window pole. A couple of girls climbed up on the sinks, and a third girl climbed up on their shoulders. The rope of sheets was passed up, and they soon had it secured. After giving it a few good tugs, we agreed that it was strong enough to hold us, and we threw it out of the window. As it fell, I experienced a rush of adrenaline. Was I finally going to get away for good this time?

Suddenly, Mary was treating me like her

best friend, but I didn't mind too much. Once we'd got out, we'd have to rely on each other totally. We climbed up onto the sink, and the others helped us to get into a position where we could begin to squeeze through the tiny gap. I went first. I struggled for a while, hanging half out and half in, but I wasn't going to give up.

'Ye can do it, Frances,' someone whispered.

Grabbing on to the sheets, I gripped them tightly and pulled myself through the window, scraping my face on the way. It really stung, but I was outside now, hanging on to the sheets. Looking down to see how far I had to go, I noticed that the rope didn't reach all the way to the laundry roof. There was nothing for it but to jump. First I lowered myself to the bottom, one hand at a time, and then, taking a deep breath, I let go. I came down hard, but I was OK.

Looking up, I saw Mary's legs dangling out of the window. Relieved that she'd already done the hardest bit, I willed her to go on. I decided not to tell her about the drop at the end of the sheets until she was near the bottom, but then she got stuck, and I heard her telling the others that she couldn't go any further. I began to think that I might be going over the wall on my own.

'You can do it, Mary,' I found myself saying over and over again.

Then she was out of the window, hanging on to the sheets. The other girls waved at me as she edged her way down the rope.

'Good, she's done it,' I said, waving back.

As she neared the end of the sheets, I thought that now would be a good time to tell her about the jump, before she noticed it and freaked out. 'Mary! Ye'll have to jump soon. It's not as bad as it looks.'

She looked down. 'It's too far, Frances! I'll break my legs!'

'Ye'll be OK. I managed it.'

'I can't!'

'Well, ye can't go back up, can ye? Mary, trust me. Just let yerself drop and we can get out of here. Everyone's looking at ye. Come on now, just jump.'

It was a leap of faith. She let go and landed with a thud on the roof.

'Are ye OK?' I asked.

'Yeah, I think so,' she said, getting to her feet.

The sheets disappeared quickly up the wall and in through the window. I pictured the others untying them and making the beds up, and I wondered if they'd remember to make it look as though Mary and I were still in bed. Of course they would, I reassured myself. They weren't about to let us get caught over something as crucial as that.

Our ordeal wasn't over yet, though. Next we had to get off the laundry roof and scale down some drainpipes. I went first, sliding slowly down the sloping roof until my foot reached the guttering. Using it to support my weight, I carefully shifted onto my front. Then I reached down and grabbed hold of a large square piece of iron on the top of the drainpipe. Keeping a tight grip on it, I swung down and clung on to the drainpipe, ready to make my descent.

Now Mary was edging her way down towards me. Gripping the drainpipe with my thighs, I guided her feet on to the guttering and talked her through turning her body around. Then I began to climb down the pipe, which was rusty in places and slimy in others, so it was hard to keep a grip. At one point it occurred to me that I must be totally nuts to be doing this, but finally, I got to the bottom. My arms and legs were scratched, and I was shaking with fear, but at least I'd reached the ground.

'Oh my God!' said Mary, and I looked up to see what was going on. Her legs had slipped away from the pipe and she was dangling precariously.

'Ye're doing great,' I said. 'Ye haven't far to go now.'

She regained her grip and made it down. We waited for a moment to catch our breath and make sure that there weren't any nuns around. Outside the laundry room, we found a large wicker basket and carried it over to the wall to use as a step. Soon we were over the wall and sprinting through the field on the other side.

I ran faster than I'd ever run before. Mary kept pace with me, and we didn't speak for a while. Eventually, we came out onto a road. For about twenty minutes there was no sign of traffic. Then we heard a car engine. I looked back into the bright glare of head-lights, certain that it was a police car, but it wasn't. Without thinking, I stuck out my thumb. The car moved past us and then came to a stop. Mary gave me a nervous look as we approached the car window.

The window rolled open, and a man asked, 'Where are ye going, girls?'

'Derry,' I said.

'I can't take ye all the way, but I can take ye as far as Antrim. Jump in.'

We could hardly believe our luck. Now we could relax a bit. The car pulled off, carry-ing us far away from the remand home. The driver seemed glad of the company and asked us what we were doing so far away from home, obviously assuming that we came from Derry. I spun a tale about how we'd travelled down in a car, with a couple of boys we knew. I said that we'd just come along for a day out, but after an argument the boys had driven off without us. He seemed to believe me and said we should be careful about who we picked as friends. I agreed and said that we would in future.

The journey to Antrim was about sixty miles, and the further we went, the more relaxed we became. We chatted to the driver most of the way, and the time seemed to pass really quickly. He told us that if he'd had the time, he'd have taken us all the way to Derry, but someone was expecting him.

'Sure, we'll be fine,' I said, 'and we're really grateful to get as far as Antrim.'

He dropped us off on the road to Derry, and we said goodbye and thanked him. It was cold standing on the side of the road, so we decided to walk to keep ourselves warm. We walked and ran for miles. Cars and trucks went past, but none of them stopped. We kept looking at the road signs to see how far we'd gone.

It was almost dawn before we got another lift. By now we had no idea where we were. A truck driver pulled over and said he was going as far as Newtownstewart. We climbed into the warm truck and thanked him for stopping. He didn't talk much, which pleased us because we where getting tired and appreciated the rest. It was getting light now, and we were worried that he might notice our remand-home clothes, but he didn't say anything. I liked sitting high up in the truck, looking down at everything along the road. When we arrived at Newtown-stewart, he said we had about thirty miles left to Derry. We jumped out, said goodbye, thanked him and waved him off.

We were pleased to have come this far but were aware of how careful we still had to be. The morning bell would have rung by now, and the nuns would know that we'd gone, so we needed to be on the lookout for the police. Tired, hungry and thirsty, we got paranoid about every car we heard and ducked in and out of people's gardens. The milkman had been, so we helped ourselves to a couple of bottles from the doorsteps.

After thumbing for about an hour, a lorry pulled over, and the driver said he could take us all the way to Derry. He asked a lot of questions, and we gave a lot of answers, hoping to satisfy his curiosity. I thought about what would be happening at St Joseph's. The nuns would be wondering how we could possibly have got out. They prided themselves that runaway girls were always caught, so right now they'd be going mental. I couldn't help the smug smile that broke out on my face. It was nice to get one over on the nuns, especially after the way they'd treated us. When we got to Derry, the man asked us where we were going. Mary said the Cragan Estate.

'Sure, I'll drop ye off there,' he said.

As we walked through the Cragan Estate, we passed groups of children on their way to school. We didn't know which uniform

Patsy's would be, so every now and then we stopped someone to ask if they knew her. Eventually, a girl said that she did. I asked if she could pass on a message, explaining that we were friends of Patsy and that we'd come a long way to see her. She told her friends that she'd catch them up and then turned back to me.

'Were ye in that remand home with Patsy?' she whispered, covering her mouth as if afraid that someone would lip-read her words.

I instinctively liked her and trusted her enough to tell her the truth, so I admitted that we needed to see Patsy soon, before the police spotted us.

'Come with me,' she said, leading us to a children's park that was set back from the road. 'Stay here till I get back with Patsy, and don't worry, I'll not be telling anyone else ye're here.' She told us her name was Marie and ran off.

'Do ye think we can trust her?' Mary asked.

'I think she's all right. Anyway, we don't have a choice if we want to find Patsy,' I said. 'Everything's gone OK up till now, so let's stay positive.'

We waited in the park for about an hour and a half and were just starting to worry when Marie arrived back with Patsy.

'I thought I was never going to see ye

again, Frances!' Patsy said, hugging me. 'I can't believe ye've done it. Ye're here!'

She wanted to know all about how we'd escaped, so we sat on a bench and went through our story. Patsy couldn't believe what she was hearing, and Marie listened open-mouthed. When we'd finished, she asked Patsy if we were for real. Patsy gave a bit of a laugh and told her that I definitely was. I thanked her for going to find Patsy.

'That's OK. Now we get to bunk off school for the day,' she said, in a very matter-of-fact way.

Patsy and Marie went off to the shop and returned with sweets and crisps for all of us. Then we hung around the park for a while, talking and laughing. I was free, happier than I'd ever been. I kept thinking about how the nuns' faces would have looked when they realised that we'd gone. I imagined them patting my padded bed as they tried to wake me in the morning.

'We'll get ye some different clothes at dinnertime,' Patsy said.

In the meantime we didn't mind hanging around the park. It was so much better than being at the remand home. And, good as her word, Patsy came back at around one with Marie, carrying some bags of clothes. She'd asked all her friends to sneak whatever they could out of their bedrooms, without their mums noticing.

'There should be something in here that will fit yous,' she said. We took the clothes out of the bags. They were really nice, much nicer than anything I'd ever worn before. I slipped a pair of jeans on under my dress. They fitted perfectly, and Patsy said they looked great. Mary found a pair of trousers that she really liked, and Patsy and Marie stood guard as we put on jumpers. Patsy handed me a little denim jacket, and Mary picked out a blue anorak. In our new outfits we no longer looked like runaways, just like any other girls of our age.

Patsy fixed my long, black hair into a loose plait to give me a different look and said that we could walk around with her and her mates after school to figure out where to hide out. I was sure that the police wouldn't be able to find me now. My new look gave me a confidence that I'd never felt before.

When school was over, we met up with some more of Patsy's friends and went to a café for chips, which tasted great. The conversation turned to where we could hide out. Everyone seemed much more concerned about us than about getting into trouble themselves. I appreciated that they were putting themselves out for us and listened carefully to what they had to say. They were all really nice, genuine people.

We needed somewhere warm and safe to spend the night. After a lot of debate it was decided that the best solution would be to hide in the local Catholic church. If we managed to conceal ourselves while the priest locked up for the night, we'd be able to come out and sleep on the benches after he'd gone. Patsy's friends would take it in turns to bunk off school and bring us food every morning – whatever they could pinch from their homes. It sounded like a good plan, until we could come up with a better one. We didn't want to be walking around in the cold all night, and Patsy and her friends had done more than enough to help already.

The conversation turned to one of Patsy's friends, whom they'd nicknamed Ozzy. Apparently, he'd escaped from Borstal about two years before and so far hadn't been caught. He stayed in a different place each night. They hadn't seen him for a few days, but they would try to find him the following day.

'He's a good bloke, and he'll help if he can. He knows Bernadette Devlin, the MP,' Patsy said. 'She helped him out a few times and now they're really good friends.'

A few hours later Mary and I were hiding behind a pillar in the church, listening to the priest shuffle about in the sacristy. We didn't have long to wait before he left. The lights went out, the door banged shut, and the key turned in the lock. It felt strange and spooky to be there alone at night. We lay down on some benches and fell asleep, exhausted.

We woke early, feeling stiff and uncomfortable, with no idea of what time it was or when the priest was going to turn up again. We had a good look around for the best place to hide, which turned out to be under the altar. There was plenty of space, and the altar cloth would conceal us. So we crawled under the cloth, and some time later we heard the church door being unlocked. We stayed still and kept quiet, listening to the sound of footsteps. I guessed that there must be quite a few people in the church.

I stifled a laugh when Mary pulled a cold bag of chips from her anorak pocket and started eating them.

'I'm starving,' she whispered.

It was such a strange and funny sight that I had to cover my mouth with my hand to stop myself laughing. She handed me a chip, and I decided that I might as well join her in some breakfast.

The organ started up, and a few moments later we saw the priest's feet poking under the altar cloth. Mass had begun. We stayed as quiet as we could but carried on eating the cold chips. At one point I wanted to sneeze and had to pinch my nose, which of course set us off again. It took all our energy not to roll around laughing. We were utterly relieved when Mass finished and the priest returned to the sacristy.

'We'll have to sneak out soon – when everyone's gone – and sit on one of the benches,' I said. I was starting to feel claustrophobic.

We heard our names being whispered. Peeping out from under the cloth, we were pleased to see one of Patsy's friends. We crawled out from under the altar, went outside and set upon the sandwiches that she'd brought with her.

We soon got into a rhythm. During the day we hung out with Patsy and her friends; by night we hid in the church. It was so exhilarating to be free at last, far away from the bells and the nuns and the constant threat of violence. It felt amazing to do what we liked and go where we wanted. Then one night Patsy took us to meet Ozzy. I was looking forward to meeting him because she'd talked about him a lot and with great fondness. He was sitting on the steps leading up to a big council block.

'This is Ozzy,' she said, going over to give him a hug.

He looked like he'd lived on the streets all his life, but I still thought he had a charm about him. We joined him on the steps. I was freezing, but he didn't seem to notice the cold. As he spoke, it became clear that he'd been ducking and diving for a long time and obviously got a buzz from it. I couldn't imagine him ever being the kind of person who would live conventionally, working nine to five to pay his bills.

But Patsy was right, he was a nice person, and he seemed genuinely to care about our predicament. He offered to phone Bernadette Devlin to see if she could help us in any way. I wasn't sure what she'd be able to do but thought it was worth a try. He went to phone her while we waited on the step.

He came back with a smile on his face. 'I've got yous a lift to see her at her house in Cookstown,' he said. 'It should be here any moment.'

I had no idea how far Cookstown was, but there was no time to think about it. A car beeped nearby. 'That will be yer lift now. Don't worry, she's great and she'll help ye.'

Ozzy and Patsy walked us to the car, and the driver told us to get in. We waved to Patsy, not knowing when we'd see her again. It was a long drive, lasting well over an hour, but at least the car was warm.

When we arrived at Bernadette Devlin's house, she was standing at the door waiting for us. We got out of the car, feeling a bit unsure of why we were there. She was very welcoming, shaking us by the hand and asking us to come in, but as we entered the house, I caught a glimpse of some nuns and a priest through the living-room door. Anger shot through me when I realised she'd betrayed us. I turned to make a run for it.

'Wait,' she said. 'Come on through to the

kitchen and we'll talk.'

I didn't move, even when she reassured me that the nuns would remain in the living room. She said that, as an MP, she had to respect the law and inform St Joseph's that we were coming to her house, but she promised that we wouldn't be disturbed and that we could have a good talk about our grievances.

I fought my instincts to flee and followed her through to the kitchen. Over tea and biscuits, Mary and I described what it was like in the convent, why we'd run away and why we couldn't go back. We talked for a long time, but all the while I was aware of the nuns in the living room and couldn't help feeling uncomfortable. They were probably devising our next punishment with relish.

Bernadette Devlin seemed really nice, but she told us that she could only help us if we went back with the nuns. Obviously, we didn't like the sound of that.

'Ye don't know what they're like!' I said. 'We're not going to get away with running away and talking to ye about them. They'll go mad on us!'

'Please don't send us back, or it will all have been for nothing!' Mary blurted out.

We were terrified, but it seemed inevitable that we were going back to the convent.

'If yous want me to help ye, then yous will

have to trust me,' Bernadette said. 'I will talk to the nuns before ye go back, and I don't think that they'll be punishing yous this time. Come on, girls, you can use my bathroom to clean up your faces and tidy your hair.'

I was brushing my hair with a round wooden brush when she came in to tell us that she'd spoken with the nuns and it was time to go. Not wanting to meet her eye, I stared sadly at the hairbrush in my hand.

'You can keep that, if ye want. Take it with ye,' she said.

I couldn't believe it. This was going to raise my status back at St Joseph's. We were allowed a few basic possessions, like clothes and photos, but no one there could say that her hairbrush used to belong to Bernadette Devlin, MP.

A few months later, Sister Mary came to find me in the sacristy. I was on my knees next to a bucket of Jeyes Fluid and water.

'Reilly!' she barked. 'Go to the dormitory and get your things together. You are leaving us today.'

I put down my scrubbing brush and stood up. 'What do ye mean?' I stammered. 'Where am I going?'

'You are going to work for a good Catholic family in Portadown, and I hope they work you hard, Reilly. Good riddance to you, that's what I say. You won't be missed at St Joseph's, that's for sure. A car will be picking you up at three.'

My mouth fell open. 'I'm getting out? Today?'

'I've already told you that, Reilly. Now get yourself to the dormitory, sort your possessions out and report to the Mother Superior.'

'Yes, Sister!'

As I turned to run out of the sacristy, I knocked over the bucket of Jeyes Fluid and water. Sister Mary shouted at me to come back and clear up the mess, but I just went on running as if I hadn't heard her.

I rushed to find Sinéad. She was in the laundry with a couple of her mates.

'I'll come and visit ye as often as I can,' I promised.

'When ye do, don't forget to bring me stuff,' she said.

'As much as I can carry,' I said, hugging her.

At three o'clock that afternoon, dizzy with fear and excitement, I walked out of the main convent building and into a waiting car, carrying nothing but an extra set of clothes, a nightdress, a comb and a toothbrush in a case supplied by the nuns. Bernadette Devlin's hairbrush had been stolen a while back, so I had nothing of my own, apart from the emotional scars left by a childhood of abuse. As the car pulled away, I looked back and saw Sinéad standing on the steps, waving goodbye. I waved back and went on waving until she was out of sight. I had no idea what lay ahead of me as the car passed through the gates, but one thing was clear: at last I was free.

EPILOGUE

Sinéad left the remand home two years after I did. By then I was back in Omagh. She came to find me and moved to Omagh, too. A few years later I moved to Antrim, and she followed me again. I love her, but we never became really close again. The only thing we ever talked about was the convent; it was so hard to move on from it. A few years later she had to move away, and we lost touch. I've not seen her now for about thirty years.

I met Loretta again when I was twenty-three. She was living in London with my mother and two younger brothers. My first question to her was, 'Why did you leave without telling us?' She said nothing, just gave me a look as if to say 'just did, so what?' I visited her again several times after she moved out of my mother's. We got on well, and I was always pleased to see her, but all we really had in common was the convent and my mother. Both were painful subjects for us. She still could not write, and the scars on her back were still clearly visible. The visits triggered painful memories, and over the years we saw less of each

376

other. Then, after about ten years, the visits stopped altogether.

I almost wish that I hadn't met my mother again: she was a huge disappointment to me. I'd hoped and imagined her to be something like Siobhan at the farm, the only mother figure I'd ever had, so I was disgusted to find her in a drunken state when I arrived at her house at eleven o'clock in the morning. The house was a mess. I asked her why she'd put us in the convent. 'I didn't want yous girls growing up and stealing my blokes,' she said with a harsh laugh. I took a good look at her and thought to myself, I'll never be like you. I visited her again several times, searching for a more satisfactory explanation and for some glimmer of remorse. Eventually, I realised there was none.

I finally met Marie, my eldest sister, when I was twenty-five. She was a wonderful woman, but seriously scarred by her childhood, just like the rest of us.

I retained my enthusiasm for singing and spent many years working as a professional singer in pubs and clubs throughout southeast England, though I have not sung professionally since my youngest child left home, about thirteen years ago.

I learnt how to read and write with my children, using simple ABC books and watching children's television. Soon I was picking up adult books, skipping over the words I didn't understand. A very patient shopkeeper taught me about money. He'd wait until all his other customers had left the shop before saying, 'Show me what ye've got, sure, and I'll tell ye what ye can buy.'

After leaving the remand home, my interest in the supernatural deepened. I continued to have premonitions and also found that I can sometimes pick up on people's thoughts. Normally I have no control over what I pick up, and often it seems to happen when I am feeling low. My friends tell me I have a gift, but I have never thought of it like that.

I didn't see any of the girls I had grown up with until a few years ago, when we met at a Nazareth House reunion in Belfast. It felt strange – a group of women asking each other, 'What was your number, then?' Later we had a bit to drink and started singing the songs that we had sung as children. I remembered the words of all the songs that got us through the bad times. When I told them that I was taking the nuns to court, they were very sympathetic, but only one of them, Ann Marie, felt able to support me. She had already contacted the police and had asked to make a statement, but she backed out because she felt that without support from other victims she would not be believed. I knew how she felt. We have kept in touch and I visit her regularly in Belfast.

I never saw Francy again, the boy who saved me from drowning, but I've never forgotten him. I would not be here to tell my story if it wasn't for his bravery. Thank you, Francy.

Shortly after I started taking legal action against the Nuns, I felt unable to cope with my depression and went to see my GP. She suggested that I have some counselling and set up an appointment for me with a counsellor, Merril Mathews.

Merril was a great counsellor, and the sessions with her began to put the events of my childhood into perspective. During our sessions I relived my experiences in the convent. Then I went home and wrote about them, while they were fresh in my mind. It was around this time that I wrote some of the hardest chapters of the book. Counselling proved to be the best thing that I have done to help myself. It wasn't only her counselling skills that helped me. She was caring and warm; a genuinely wonderful person who I know shared my pain at our sessions. I considered myself very fortunate to be placed in such good hands. Merril and I still keep in touch on the phone, and I have a lot of respect and love for her.

Putting my thoughts down on paper was very painful, but in conjunction with the counselling, it helped me understand what had happened to me. Also, and most importantly, it helped me realise that it was not my fault. Very slowly, I felt that I was gaining control over my memories. Now, when I think about my childhood, it's still painful, but I no longer feel the devastation that I felt when I first started writing.

Finally, after nine long years, my legal action against the Poor Sisters of Nazareth has been settled. It has been a long and difficult struggle, but one during which I have gradually gained in strength and confidence. I know I still have some way to go, but at last I feel that my life is heading in the right direction. I have been asked by so many people why, after so many years, it was so important to me to pursue this case. Why put myself through the pain? My answer to that was simple enough, I had no choice: my life had fallen apart and if I was to move forward I had to confront the demons of my past. An important part of the healing process for me has been transferring my memories to paper.

It is my hope that publishing my story will not only help but will lead to a better understanding of the long-term damage that abuse can do. When I came into contact with other girls from Nazareth House, during the writing of this book, I saw that all of them were victims who have been damaged to some extent. Meeting them again, I realised that for too long we have suffered in silence. It is time for our story to be told.

The publishers hope that this book has given you enjoyable reading. Large Print Books are especially designed to be as easy to see and hold as possible. If you wish a complete list of our books please ask at your local library or write directly to:

Magna Large Print Books
Magna House, Long Preston,
Skipton, North Yorkshire.
BD23 4ND